P9-APP-104

WITHDRAWN

WITHDRAWN

LIFE ON THE OUTSIDE

Anthropology, Culture and Society

Series Editors:
Dr Richard A. Wilson, University of Sussex
Professor Thomas Hylland Eriksen, University of Oslo

LIFE ON THE OUTSIDE

The Tamil Diaspora and Long-Distance Nationalism

Øivind Fuglerud

Pluto  Press

LONDON • STERLING, VIRGINIA

First published 1999 by Pluto Press
345 Archway Road, London N6 5AA
and 22883 Quicksilver Drive,
Sterling, VA20166–2012, USA

Copyright © Øivind Fuglerud

The right of Øivind Fuglerud to be identified as the author
of this work has been asserted by him in accordance with the Copyright,
Designs and Patents Act 1988.

British Library Cataloguing in Publication Data
A catalogue record for this book is available from
the British Library

ISBN 0 7453 1438 4 hbk

Library of Congress Cataloging in Publication Data
Fuglerud, Øivind
    Life on the outside: the Tamil diaspora and long distance
nationalism/Øivind Fuglerud.
        p.   cm. —(Anthropology, culture and society)
    ISBN 0–7453–1438–4 (hbk)
    1. Tamil (Indic people)—Relocation. 2. Tamil (Indic people)
—Migrations. 3. Tamil (Indic people)—Government policy—Sri Lanka.
4. Forced migration—Sri Lanka. 5. Sri Lanka—Race Relations.
6. Sri Lanka—Politics and government. I. Title. II. Series.
DS489.25.T3F84   1999
305.89'4811—dc21   98–42632
                                                              CIP

Designed and produced for Pluto Press by
Chase Production Services, Chadlington, OX7 3LN
Typeset from disk by Stanford DTP Services, Northampton
Printed in the EC by Athenaeum Press, Gateshead

CONTENTS

1 INTRODUCTION

What does it mean, at the end of the twentieth century, to speak like Aimé Césaire of a 'native land'? What processes rather than essences are involved in present experiences of cultural identity?

J. Clifford, *The Predicament of Culture*: 275

At a press conference in Colombo in December 1995, the Sri Lankan president, Chandrika Kumaratunga, declared that out of a pre-war population of 950,000 in the Northern Province of Sri Lanka 400,000 people had now settled outside the country. In order to understand the implications of this statement, one needs to know at least two things. The first one is that since the late 1970s Sri Lanka has been involved in a civil war. The island's main categories of people are the Sinhalese, who make up 74 per cent of the population, and several Tamil-speaking groups, and the war is being played out between representatives of these communities. The second one is that, while members of the Tamil minority are also settled elsewhere in Sri Lanka, the Northern Province referred to by the president is in fact *the* Tamil-dominated province of the island. The statement, therefore, indicates the degree to which this particular minority has been subjected to displacement from its home areas.

Unfortunately, the main advantage of the president's estimate is that it is official. Like most figures on refugees provided by governments, this is too low. Not only do more realistic calculations suggest a total closer to 700,000 Tamil refugees,[1] that is one-third of Sri Lanka's entire pre-war Tamil population, but with respect to the effects of the war one must take into account that another third of the members of the same minority have been internally displaced since the war started. These are the disturbing facts.

Nowadays, when concepts like 'diaspora' and 'transnationality' are finally attracting interest in departments of anthropology, the Tamils

1

from Sri Lanka are certainly a case to consider. The people displaced, mainly from the Northern Province, can now be found on every continent. While the largest settlements are located in Canada, England, Germany and Switzerland, there are Tamil communities in most countries of the world from Japan, Botswana and Lithuania to Malaysia, Panama and Finland. The choice of the main field site in this study, the Scandinavian country of Norway, where about 7000 people of Tamil origin live, may therefore be less idiosyncratic than might appear at first sight. My argument is that among the first generation of Tamils from Sri Lanka, wherever they live, one may expect to find some of the same processes at work. Norway is as good a place as any to look for them.

In fact, in some respects, a country like Norway may be better than many for such a study as it is a relatively new member in the league of refugee-receiving countries and it is still struggling to develop a public perspective in which facts and events may be arranged in a meaningful order. The reason is that what it means to be an immigrant in a Western country might be perceived more clearly in the case of Norway than it would be in the case of Canada or England. Norway is still a country where most people can remember when and under what circumstances they first met a person who was not born here – especially one of different creed or colour. While there have been small groups of migrant workers living in Norway since the late 1960s, the dilemma brought about by international migration has only been faced by the population at large through the presence of asylum seekers since the mid-1980s. This book is an attempt to place the interaction between Tamil refugees and Norway within a wider setting of social processes.

In my opinion this kind of academic exercise has been neglected for too long by anthropologists. I can only agree with Turner (1994) when he says that, with respect to the field of multiculturalism, 'most of us have been sitting around like so many disconsolate intellectual wallflowers waiting to be asked to impart our higher wisdom and more than a little resentful that the invitations never come' (p. 406). While international refugee research is dominated by law, migration research has tended in general to be very specialised and 'applied', mainly in the sense of being adapted to the needs of national governments. In Norway one can find numerous studies on 'this group in the labour market' or 'that group and the welfare system' – mostly undertaken by sociologists with their questionnaires in good order. Efforts to achieve a 'thick description', however, are few and far between. The prevalent view among anthropologists has, in Rosaldo's apt words, been that 'if it's moving it isn't cultural' (1989: 209).

For someone who believes that anthropology may still yield some insights, this situation is unsatisfactory. I should make it clear, however, that my goal here is not to promote studies of ethnic 'boundary maintenance'. On the contrary, I find this analytical perspective, in spite of its Norwegian tradition (Barth 1969), not entirely suitable for my purpose. Through my involvement with the refugees in question I have become convinced that if we focused solely on inter-ethnic patterns of interaction we would find that the motives and intentionality, and therefore also the rationality, of neither parties can be understood within a local setting. At least two questions would need to be discussed if we chose to adopt such a perspective: the first one concerns the importance to the interaction of images of the other derived from outside the interactive field itself. If it were possible, one cannot in our society presume an interactive basis in individual autonomy and empathic understanding alone. The origin of such images, the structuring and distribution of information, would need to be included in the analysis.

The second question concerns the extent to which such a focus would capture what is most significant to the parties in their day-to-day lives. As an opening statement I will offer the opinion that for most Tamils in Norway it would not. Harsh as it may sound I venture the claim that maintaining relationships to Norwegian people is not a major concern. There is no doubt in my mind that the situation inside *Eelam*,[2] and people's connections to their fellow countrymen around the globe, are of far greater importance in their exiled existence. For this reason I am also hesitant to emphasise too strongly the refugee aspect in the present work. We have recently seen a tendency among researchers to treat 'refugees' as a *cultural* category, maintaining the explicit or implicit understanding that one can deal with people in their capacity as refugees without taking into account their cultural background and the political circumstances of their flight. This seems a misguided approach to me. As feminist anthropologists have argued with respect to women (Moore 1994: 17), refugees are 'universal in their particularity', and we must take note of both the universal and the particular in our studies.

I should also make it clear that the present work is not, or at least not primarily, a study of 'integration' or of 'ethnic discrimination'. I am more interested in what goes on behind, or inside, the ethnic boundaries; that is, the way in which a society transforms itself when such a large section of it is thrown into exile. With regard to South Asians in general, and Asian Indians in particular, much valuable work has been done on this question already (e.g. Clarke, Peach and Vertovec 1990, van der Veer 1995). While recognising the importance of these contributions, the focus in this book is slightly different, partly because these works seem to place more emphasis on the local adjustment of migrants than is warranted in the present case. This, no doubt, is due to the fact that a major theme in the research on Indians outside India has been the situation of the indentured workers and their descendants, that is, the consequences of migratory movements which took place around the turn of the century when the means of communication and the possibilities of onward migration were radically different from those of today. Compared to present-day Sri Lankan Tamils the situation of the Indian migrant workers was characterised more by geographical displacement than by diasporic processes in the strict sense, that is, the maintenance of group consciousness defined by a continued relationship with an original homeland within a population dispersed between several different locations (Safran 1991). Moreover, the migration from other countries of South Asia affected the societies from which migrants moved only to a limited extent. The migration of Tamils, on the other hand, is intrinsically linked to a radical transformation of Tamil society as such. The future of Eelam depends on the Tamil diaspora as much as the future of the diaspora, in a certain sense, depends on the fate of Eelam.

With respect to the individual migrants and refugees I do not mean by this remark simply that their relationship to home is one of *heimatweh*, of 'let peace come and I will go', and that this is a deciding factor in their lives, but rather that it is the troubled relationship between here and there which needs to be focused on. One may, perhaps, argue that the relationship between a migrant population and their society of origin can, basically, only be described in one of two ways. One possibility is that individuals remain part of social relationships at home: the slots they used to fill are, so to speak, left open; they are informed of everyday events, consulted in matters of importance, and the exile situation remains an extension of the primary social field until, one day, they are able to go back. Excellent studies have been made of such migratory patterns. The other possibility is that migrants leave in a more fundamental sense; that, while cherishing their memories and struggling to cultivate their ties, the door nevertheless slowly closes until, finally, there is no way back. *If* these are the options, this work, the way I see it, is about a group of people in the latter situation. It is not the case that they don't take an interest – most Tamils are literally consumed by events at home – but there are factors which make active participation difficult.

Most Tamils living in Norway would, however, not agree to such a view. To most of them the experience of exile is too new, their feelings towards events in Sri Lanka too mixed and their hopes of going home with dignity too pressing to formulate the worries of tomorrow in such words. This study, it should be observed, is about a process which is still going on – one could even say that it has only just begun. Present Tamil migration from Sri Lanka only reached sizeable proportions after the so-called 'Colombo riots' in 1983 where, in the space of a few days, probably more than 2000 Tamils where killed by the Sinhalese mob. In the following years the Sri Lankan situation developed into a very complex civil war with shifting alliances, but where the Sinhalese army fighting for a unitary state and Tamil guerrillas fighting for a separate Tamil homeland have been one set of ingredients.

In order to avoid any misunderstanding, however, I must emphasise that little will be said here about the inter-ethnic conflict in Sri Lanka as such. In the last ten to fifteen years a number of studies dealing with this issue have been published and I refer interested readers to these (e.g. Tambiah 1986, Wilson 1988, Kapferer 1988, Manogaran and Pfaffenberger 1994). Leaving the tragic development of Sinhala state chauvinism as playing only a minor part in this particular story, in dealing with Sri Lanka my focus will be on Tamil nationalism and Tamil intra-ethnic disputes. This is not because these are more important in understanding the Sri Lankan situation in general but because, in my opinion, they are more important in understanding the particular situation of the Tamil refugees. During the last hundred years or so Sri Lanka (Ceylon) has been transformed from a society where caste was the overriding principle of differentiation into one where ethnic nationalism, that is, the claim for territory by groups who define themselves in ethnic terms, has replaced it. On the Tamil side the breakdown of caste society has entailed not only a closure towards what is outside and different but also the unleashing of internal conflicts in order to achieve this closure. Within the larger fluctuations of power, opposing groups of Tamil militants have taken turns to hunt each other down. At every turn one recurrent consequence has been civilians and deserted guerrilla soldiers fleeing the war-torn areas of the north and east; to Colombo, to India, to the West – and to Norway. This process of flight and its vicissitudes is one of the subjects of this work.

The migration of Tamil refugees to Europe is, however, part of a much larger picture. As an object of study, refugees may best be pictured as located in the midst of three concentric circles. When we enter the innermost area of their life-worlds we discover that we are already standing within the wider circumference of the second and third; to be at the centre of any of them is to be at the centre of all three. The second circle, so to speak, is the nature of migration as such and the challenges that go with it. Migration not only concerns the movement of individuals through space but, as defined through legal and other means of control, is also a mediating concept in the relationship between 'the West and the Rest'. During the last ten to fifteen years questions related to migrants of different categories have become, without exaggeration, among the most difficult and most debated political issues in Europe. During this time laws have been made, constitutions have been changed and ministers have had to go because of questions concerning who shall and who shall not be able to enter and remain within their borders. While in the 1960s and early 1970s migrant workers were, if not welcomed, at least accepted because of a general need for labour, the 1980s and 1990s has been a period when population movements have forced Europe's old skeletons – nationalism, racism and ethnic violence – out of the closets. As a general trend one may observe that restrictions on entry have become tighter and right-wing anti-migrant political forces have become stronger. Economic migration to Europe is, generally speaking, no longer legally possible and the focus of public attention has turned to the 'asylum seekers', people arriving at national borders claiming refugee status and asking for protection.

No doubt, the troubling effect of migration on Europe partly has to do with numbers. The practical problems related to an increase in the number of asylum seekers in Western Europe from 67,400 in 1983 to more than ten times that number in 1992 should not be overlooked and the monetary cost of handling and settling the 2.9 million asylum applications which were registered in the same period has been enormous.[3] However, the fact that most of the so-called 'new refugees' (Martin 1988) during this period have come from non-Western countries has undoubtedly contributed to the heat of the question. The rising number of asylum seekers has been perceived by many as an 'implosion' of the Third World into the First and horror scenarios of European cultures being swamped by dark-skinned foreigners seeking material wealth have been exploited by news agencies and clever politicians. The Tamil refugee has been a central figure in this discourse.

It may just be that the actual crafting of legal and administrative procedures related to refugees and displaced people must be left to diplomats and to our legal colleagues. This, however, does not mean that anthropologists should not enter the debate. The process of what is now called 'globalisation', in which refugee migration is one central element, has both moral and conceptual implications for our discipline. This work is grounded in a belief that the anthropologist is needed not only as an observer but also as a participant and a provider of perspectives in dealing with one of today's most burning issues – the reshuffling of people. 'Refugee', in Roger Zetter's words, is 'one of the most powerful labels currently in the repertoire of humanitarian concern, national and international public policy and social differentiation' (1988). It is a fact that many refugees have their origin in areas where anthropologists conduct their studies. If it is the case that the world, as they say, is becoming smaller, that countries where anthropologists live and work must find ways of dealing with complex processes encompassing both our field areas and our own societies, we should have something to say about these matters. In fact, it has been argued (Steen 1993) that refugees are a condensed expression of the present world condition, its 'symptom', and reflect the fundamental flux, fluidity, partiality and fragmentation of our time. If this is true it may just be that the more general questions contained in the study of refugees and displacement is what future anthropology is going to be about.

At present, however, I think that to many anthropologists a focus on refugees still brings a feeling of uneasiness. As so often pointed out in recent years' discussions, the anthropologist's authority used to lie in the fact that he or she was the one who had *been there*. His or her traditional role, as scientist and cultural critic, rested upon a monopoly of transcultural understanding which is now broken. The latter half of the twentieth century has been a period characterised by displacement: of artefacts, of people, of traditions and of national boundaries. As for myself, I admit to being puzzled and intrigued when I now see Norwegian citizens performing *pujas* in Oslo's East end where my grandfather, as he used to tell me, felt a stranger when he arrived here from Sweden seventy years ago. Old differences have been replaced by new distinctions. Together with a globalisation of capital, an accelerating process of what Robertson (1987) calls 'global compression' has taken place. This does not mean that cultural differences are erased, in fact quite the opposite may be true. Robertson's point seems to be that while we see in the world today an increasing concern with tradition, indigenisation, ethnicity and nationalism, these formulations and expressions of unique identities rest on ideas which are globally produced and shared. Moreover, worldwide trade links, information systems and migration networks not only convey information about such ideas, but are also themselves instrumental in the formulation of identities. If you wish to locate the driving force behind Sikh separatism in Punjab it might be necessary to go to Canada. The Tamil diaspora's most important source of cultural authenticity is the video.

There is no need to rehearse here the general crisis of ethnographic representation that this situation has brought forth and which has found its main outlet in discussions on 'post-modernism'. On the other hand, we cannot go on as if nothing has changed. We must, it seems to me, take Clifford (1988) seriously when he states that 'ethnography today will have to start from the inescapable fact that Westerners are no longer the only ones going places in the modern world'. We must get used to the fact that what are perceived as *primordia* in the construction of people's local identities – be it religion, language, kinship or regional origin – have become spread over vast and irregular spaces (Appadurai 1990). Without offering any comprehensive theoretical answer to the questions that this fact brings forth, this book is an effort to examine some of them and deal with them analytically.

The question must be asked, however, what is this 'exotic' which today is being brought together by the drift of capital and manpower. As pointed out by Gupta and Ferguson (1992), the 'cultural critique' of the post-modernist position takes difference as a starting point, not as an end product (e.g. Marcus and Fisher 1986). In spite of their sensitivity to the fact that this difference is now among us, there is a tendency to regard cultural variability as an effect of pre-existing entities. What is at stake in their critical project is mainly our *representation* of the other, not as such the unity of 'us' and the otherness of the 'other' which make the opposition possible in the first place. Therefore, in a sense, they have continued the traditional anthropological discourse which through its rationale of translating cultural difference has helped produce and maintain it.

I personally agree with Friedman (1994) that the collapse of the order within which the anthropologist could pass himself off as a master of otherness is a symptom of disorder in power relations and not the emergence of a new truth. As we all know, the present era is not the first one to have witnessed large-scale movements of people. The system of indentured labour already mentioned brought approximately 1.5 million Asian Indians to other European colonies (Clark, Peach and Vertovec 1990). Between 1840 and 1930 an average of 416,000 people a year emigrated to the United States.[4] What is needed, I argue with Gupta and Ferguson, are therefore studies of the *production* of difference within common, shared and connected spaces; in other words, a move away from seeing cultural difference as the correlate of a world of 'peoples' whose separate histories are waiting to be bridged by the anthropologist and towards seeing it 'as a product of a shared historical process that differentiates the world as it connects it' (p. 16). In this perspective power should not concern the anthropologist only when 'writing culture'; the distinctiveness of his subject(s) is always already constituted through relations of power before the moment of representation occurs. This question of a politics of identity constitutes the third circle pertaining to Eelam and its refugees.

In the present work I see the management and manipulation of 'national' references as fundamental in producing difference. Here the contexts where such management takes place constitute what Hannerz would call 'strategically selected field sites', where '... the confrontations, the interpenetrations and the flowthrough are occurring between clusters of meaning and ways of managing meaning; in short, the places where diversity gets, in some way and to some degree, organised' (1989). It is also here, in the structuring of these contexts, that we must seek the change in subjective experience and political significance of migration from that of the nineteenth century to that of the late twentieth. As pointed out by Anderson (1992), last century's migration eventually resulted in a reintegration of personal sentiment with a public and civic ideology founded on the concept of territorial unity. To what extent the same will take place in the future is more uncertain. The combined effects of political marginalisation in countries of settlement and closeness to the *land van herkomst* in terms of communication contribute to what Anderson terms 'long-distance nationalism'. The present study may be seen as an effort to document one such case.

NATIONALISM AND INTERCONNECTIONS

I felt a need to put the word 'national' in inverted commas above since the two nations of importance here, Eelam and Norway, are radically different. Because this will be dealt with later, mainly by implication, an explanation of this difference should be given here.

It is reasonable to ask, perhaps, if the harsh realities of Sri Lankan society may be compared at all to the seductive tranquillity of Norway's welfare state. In Tamil Sri Lanka we are confronted with the effects of what has been termed 'New Nationalism' (Kaldor 1993). What Kaldor describes as the 'Wild West atmosphere of Knin or Ngorno Karabakh peopled by young men in home-made uniforms, desperate refugees and neophyte politicians' also applies very well to Eelam. In contrast to earlier versions which were unifying and centralising, this nationalism, she argues, is decentralising and 'fragmentative'. This, I would say, is putting it rather nicely. In Tamil Sri Lanka we have a situation where life periodically corresponds to Hobbes's famous picture of it in the state of nature: 'solitary, poor, nasty, brutish, and short'.

What, then, is the nation? Answering this question of Renan with Anderson (1983) and Gellner (1983), we may first observe that the nation is a phenomenon born of modernity. For all nations, it is the arbitrariness of the sign, the separating of language from reality, which ruptures the mediaeval ontology of temporal fulfilment and enables the establishment of an imagined community in a 'transverse cross-time, marked ... by temporal coincidence, and measured by clock and calendar' (Anderson 1983: 24). In this perspective the national sentiment is not something original rising from the depths of time but rather something contingent, erasing earlier differences, making individuals replaceable within the economic machinery. Herder's *Volk*, the 'Gemeinschaft' of primordial loyalties, is in Gellner's view a construction resulting from the needs of a historically specific 'Gesellschaft':

[N]ationalism as a phenomenon, not as a doctrine presented by nationalists, is inherent in a certain set of social conditions; and those conditions, it so happens, are the conditions of our time (p. 125)

This imaginary character of the modern is the *common* element between nations. To my mind, one thing that separates the nation states of Western Europe from an emerging nation like Eelam is the ability to fulfil the obligation of having already forgotten ('doit avoir oublier') of which Renan spoke.[5] As pointed out by Bhabha (1990), it is through the syntax of forgetting – *of remembering to forget* – that the problematical identification of a national people becomes visible. Forgetting the French origin in violence, in the anti-Huguenot pogroms of 'la Saint-Barthélemy' in the sixteenth century or the extermination of Albigensians in 'les Massacres du Midi au XIIIe siècle' is not a question of personal or historical memory but of the construction of a discourse where the national totalisation can be sought. This remembering to forget, which presupposes the ability of forgetting to remember, is not possible in Sri Lanka where the massacres are a daily affair. This gives the nation a different character.

This is because being obliged to forget and being able to fulfil this obligation become the basis for remembering the nation, for peopling it anew, but also for contemplating its boundaries and thereby imagining the possible existence of contending units of identification. This is the central paradox we encounter: what is characteristic of the well-established nation state is *not* that its guaranteed territorial finality secures a national totalisation. On the contrary, its subjects can *no longer* be contained in the national discourse of teleological progress. The representation of the nation through its borders interrupts the self-generating dissemination of national production and carries with it the potential of diverging narratives. The border itself, in other words, helps to transfer the threat of difference from outside in. What this amounts to, in Bhabha's words, is a 'splitting of the national subject', a splitting which takes place *within* the national borders and *in* the subject.

The fundamental ambivalence of the nation state is the result of a double movement where incorporation into the body politic is attempted through a social fragmentation which, it is true, always remains unfulfilled. This, I think, is what Foucault (1988) has in mind when, talking about the main characteristic of modern political rationality, he points to the fact that the integration of individuals in a totality now results from a constant correlation between an increasing individualisation and the reinforcement of this very totality, and that modern political rationality, therefore, 'is permitted by the antinomy of law and order' (p. 163). This rationality, the legal ordering of the *rechtstat*, produces in a sense its own difference – a difference the aim of which, according to Bhabha, is to re-articulate the sum knowledge from the perspective of the 'other' that resists totalisation (1990: 312).

This is a study of refugees, not of nationalism. However, the point is crucial, not only because without borders there would be, in a legal sense, no refugees but also because the nature of the nation is a significant condition for exile identity production. Allow me, therefore, to approach this matter from a somewhat different angle.

Kaldor's differentiation between 'old' and 'new' nationalism corresponds in large measure to what Smith (1991) alternately depicts as Western, territorial, rational, lateral and civic versus Eastern, ethnic, organic, vertical and genealogical nationalism. As a starting point it is important to see that common to both versions are certain basic assumptions of what constitutes a nation as opposed to other collective cultural identities, such as a relationship to a historic territory, a minimum of common historical memories, a shared public culture, etc. It is in mixture and emphasis that the two are different. In 'Eastern' nationalism the inherent 'will of the people' is the decisive ingredient and, even where not actually mobilised for political action, the ethnic collective provides the *rationale* for nationalist aspiration. In 'Western' nationalism, on the other hand, the ideal of active participation of all citizens on a territorial and civic basis is a dominant strand of thought. Territorialism here is mainly conceived as a political commitment to a particular spatial location among other territorial nations, something which gives the abstract belonging through legal citizenship strong moral overtones, becoming in formal terms the main device for inclusion and exclusion, irrespective of individual origin. In the shaping of these different varieties of nationalism the role of the state has been and still is important. According to Smith the latter version was created through the agency of the new bureaucratic state dominated by a lateral *ethnie*, that is, by an upper stratum with a predominantly intellectual-ist relationship to national symbols. This state was gradually able to incorporate, more or less successfully, lower classes and outlying areas within the territory. In the former version, on the other hand, there is an opposite process of sorts at work. Here the march towards the nation passes through vernacular mobilisation, something which often implies a purification of the *Volk* through a narrow redefinition of historical morality and ethnic past.

We are now approaching the central point of the argument. I do not wish to comment on the historical truth of Smith's argument. In a synchronic perspective, however, we can see that nations are in fact different. Under new nationalism the 'splitting of the national subject' takes the form of actual, potential or symbolic ethnic cleansing. If this is a concept which has arisen out of the conflicts in former Yugoslavia, the phenomenon as such is certainly much older – Sri Lanka is one example of this. Under old nationalism, on the other hand, I would argue that this splitting takes the form of a fundamental ambiguity in the relationship between the state and outlying groups of subjects. This is because under this form the nation is what provides the state with its legitimacy; it serves the state rather than the other way around. The state is there to protect national identity which still has its core of ethnic sentiments. At the same time this state is an actor among other states. To be able to act with legitimacy in this context the state must show that its citizens are both differentiated from citizens of other states and internally undifferentiated. The world of 'nation states', therefore, requires a degree of homogenisation which is sought through an individualisation undercutting the very nation which the state is expected to protect. While the new nationalism with its reversal of former state formation processes has become one of the most common forms of refugee-producing violence, the Catch-22 situation of established nation states has serious consequences for new groups, like refugees, in their effort to establish a foothold within their borders.

For the record I would like to say that in my view, the reproduction of different nationalistic frameworks should not be seen as a matter of 'culture'. Neither is it a question of inherent 'ethnicity'. Wherever we use the term 'ethnic' we should keep in mind that this concept is what should be explained and not be doing the explaining. In the same way, differentiating between old and new nationalism is analytically useful but is not in itself an *explanation* of anything.

What we would have to do, were it our objective, would be to seek an explanation for different forms of nationalism in shared historical processes of a high order. Of relevance to our present discussion would be the incorporation in Sri Lankan consciousness of bits and pieces of nationalist ideology produced in Europe. On the Sinhalese side the period characterised by 'national awakening' saw the growth of racial theories founded by linguistic and ethnological studies in Europe. One of the most effective propagandists of such theories was Max Müller, who for more than half a century dedicated his work to the identification of 'the cradle of our race' (Müller 1888: 121). Müller argued in the 1860s that he had been able to 'class the idioms spoken in Iceland and Ceylon as cognate dialects of the Aryan family of languages' (in Gunawardena 1979: 36). About the same time Caldwell (see Chapter 9) established that there was 'no direct affinity' between the Sinhala and Tamil language groups. In other words, the Sinhalese were Aryans, the Tamils were not. De Alwis's essay from 1866 on the growth of the Sinhala language is one of many examples showing how these theories were received in Ceylon, preparing the ground for the later development of inter-ethnic antagonism:

Though the complexion of the Sinhalese presents different shades, the 'copper colour' is that which prevails over the rest, and this it would seem is the colour of the Aryan race, so much honoured by Manu ... when he declared it an offence to pass over even the shadow of the copper-coloured man. (De Alwis 1866)

Racism is still alive and well among large sections of the Sinhalese population.[6] Today, however, this 'ideoscape' (Appadurai 1990, 1991) of imported theories is overtaken by the 'finanscape' of international economics. The main thing here is not so much a reinforcement of centre–periphery relationships but more what Friedman (1994) has described as the effects of a decentralising of capital. With respect to Sri Lanka it is worth noting that the refugee crisis and the whole ethnic debacle developed during the rule of the United National Party with its implementation of the IMF-sponsored liberal economy between 1977 and 1994 (Gunasinghe 1984). In this sense, at least, Sri Lanka is a truly modern country: while capital goes in, refugees go out.

This is for the record, however. What I will try to do in this book is to approach these interconnecting processes at a much lower level and see how they affect and are affected by one group of displaced people. What we find when we study the case of refugees is that the exile situation is like a room of mirrors. Life on the outside is inseparable from events at home. These events, on the other hand, are not independent of the exile population and their Western refuge. Not only is the European-bred concept of 'the nation' of fundamental importance to liberation movements like the Tamil, but the struggles themselves are also often largely funded by the exiles. Refugee existence, therefore, is like a prism where representations of the other are present in all refractions.

The recent anthropological questioning of 'culture' as a totalising concept becomes acute when the issue is refugees. This has implications when it comes to writing on these matters. Based on a particular understanding of society, as a geographically situated whole into which individuals are born and become part of through a process of socialisation, most anthropological monographs have until recently tended to adopt a particular mode of presentation. Starting from the outer limits of geography – region, country or continent – the author gradually closes in on a group of people by working his or her way 'inwards': spatial location, mode of production, social structure, household organisation, etc. This unpacking normally concludes with the author discussing one or two native concepts in which the essence of the culturally constituted person, or the inner dynamic of society as a whole, is articulated. Writing a monograph in this conventional sense on the topic of refugees becomes impossible because no easy correspondence between people and place can be assumed. Not only that, but this lack of 'setting' is the subject's main characterising trait; so when writing about refugees we have to look for other ways of organising the material.

In an attempt to address the question of complexity in social life, with reference to Bali, Barth (1989) argues that the characteristic social form is not a result of any 'all-embracing and compelling logical consistency' of a cultural nature but is rather the result of social processes where:

People participate in multiple more or less discrepant, universes of discourse; they construct different partial and simultaneous worlds in which they move; their cultural construction of reality springs not from one source and is not of one piece. (1989: 130)

While I find Barth's approach to be a stimulating starting point for my own enquiries, I should say that I do not feel confident that he would approve of the direction in which it brings me. For one thing, my understanding of 'discourse' may be different from his. While he uses the term interchangeably with what he calls 'streams of cultural traditions' (p. 130), my understanding of discourse is informed by Foucault (1972) and Ricoeur (1981a, 1981b, 1992). That is, I see discourses as linguistically mediated configurations of meaning, systematically constructing and reconstructing the objects which they speak of.

Seen against our traditional understanding of 'culture', the concept of 'discourse' has two characteristics which should be emphasised. The first is that it helps overcome the timelessness which has been part and parcel of our anthropological concept of culture (Abu-Lughod 1990). Discourse is something which by nature is always changing and any outline given should openly admit only to be a freezing of history at a particular moment in time. The second is that it questions the distinction, built into the culture concept, between a realm of ideas and material realities. Discourses are never totally coherent, they are not closed universes of meaning, but always *strive* toward totalisation by aligning themselves with aspects of reality – demarcations, regulations, institutions, practices – which also legitimate non-linguistic means of control. They are, in other words, intrinsically linked with the exercise of power.

It seems reasonable, therefore, to take the political nature of refugee identity as a starting point for the present discussion. It is a simple fact that if it were not for politics, in one form or the other, most Tamil refugees would not be refugees at all. It should be stressed, however, that the political nature of exile identity is itself a very complex and controversial matter. The characterisation of the Tamil-speaking people in Sri Lanka as a 'community' is encumbered with problems and, therefore, the designation and description of a Tamil 'refugee community' is also difficult. In this respect the present case differs from that of certain other diasporas which have recently been described, for instance, the Nevisian case as depicted by Olwig (1993, 1997). I find her point about 'cultural sites' (1997: 35) a useful reminder when she says that if we take the trouble of doing fieldwork within the translocal networks of relations existing between mobile people we may be able to detect socio-cultural contexts 'sustained by institutions which tie them to homelands in much more concrete ways than through the imagined worlds erected by the creative resources of fantasy'. In the Tamil case, however, there are in Sri Lanka and within the diaspora deep conflicts over the nature and legitimacy of precisely such 'cultural sites'. As a consequence of this we must look for modes of presentation which allow interconnections between different levels of complexity to be taken into consideration.

The outline of the study is as follows: in Chapters 2 and 3 I present a very brief description of Tamil society and history. In Chapter 4 the history of Tamil migration to Norway is traced and shows that there are both continuities and differences between the old and the new migration. In Chapters 5 to 7 I concentrate on certain aspects of Tamil life in Norway, in particular their fragile internal relationships and their effort to find a common ground from which to manage their shared interests. In Chapters 8 to 10 I discuss two 'cultural models' in the Jaffna Tamil universe which I coin the 'traditional' and the 'revolutionary', both of which are defined in terms of their relationship to history. These models both originate in the Tamil cultural tradition but carry different conceptualisations of what it means to be Tamil. The particular reason to locate this discussion here, at the end of the study, is to emphasise that the most pressing concern of Tamil refugees is not how to achieve 'integration' but how to remain in touch with their Sri Lankan Tamil origin. Located on the outside of their primary social field by an act of their own choice, and cut off from the process of violent social change taking place in their country of origin, refugees must construe the meaning of their own migration by confronting, and drawing upon, representations of the migrant and the West available within the two models of Tamil society.

Finally, turning to the question of data, it should be said that the basis of the present study is not the standard one-year anthropological fieldwork. It is a rather more prolonged relationship with the issues of nationalism and human rights in Sri Lanka and with representatives of the Tamil community, during which time I have, in different capacities, been as much a participant as an observer. I completed my first fieldwork assignment in Sri Lanka in 1984, having worked on the ideological background to the ethnic conflict (Fuglerud 1986). In need of a job I started working for the Norwegian Red Cross Society, organising the reception of refugees, only to find that the majority of asylum seekers coming to Norway in the mid-1980s were Tamils from Sri Lanka. Many of my contacts with the Tamil community in Norway date from this early period, a fact that I consider important. This means, among other things, that they have become known to me, some of them as close friends, not in my capacity as an anthropologist, or at least not *only* in this capacity. The knowledge I have about their lives has come in bits and pieces, freely offered the way it normally is between people who become acquainted. It also means that, in the case of some of them, I have been able to follow a process of exile adjustment over quite a number of years. Whatever we teach our first-year students, there *are* processes which do not follow the calendar and which take more than one year to reach their end.

Since my first fieldwork in 1984 I have had the opportunity of renewing my acquaintance with Sri Lanka on several occasions. In 1988 I started working as a regional adviser for Asia to the Norwegian immigration service. With the exception of three years on leave to work on this project, I held this job until 1997. During these years I visited Sri Lanka several times a year, meeting regularly with representatives of research institutions, NGOs, diplomatic circles and fellow colleagues from the international brotherhood of immigration. On several occasions I conducted interviews with internally displaced in Colombo, in Puttalam and in Jaffna. I had the opportunity of going twice to Jaffna on an official basis in 1988 and 1989, both times when the area was under Indian occupation and off limits to civilian visitors. These frequent visits have no fieldwork status but they have definitely allowed me to obtain information which, for many, would be difficult to come by.

The most important factor in being employed by the Norwegian immigration service to the present work is not, however, that I had the possibility of keeping track of what was going on in Sri Lanka. As will become apparent, the present study can partly be regarded as a response to Gupta and Ferguson's (1992: 17) pertinent question: why have so few anthropologists had anything to say about immigration law considered as a politics of space and otherness?

For the record I have not completely avoided more conventional fieldwork however. From August 1992 until June 1993 I conducted fieldwork among Tamil refugees in Norway, mainly in the Oslo region but with excursions to Finnmark, the northernmost administrative region in Norway, where many Tamils work in fish-processing factories (Fuglerud 1994). This fieldwork was mainly done on a basis of participant observation but included several series of structured interviews with selected categories of people, in particular unaccompanied minor asylum seekers. This fieldwork was supplemented in 1994 with a series of interviews with 'long stayers', Tamils who arrived in Norway as migrant workers before 1975. Information on the situation in Sri Lanka was complemented by data collected on a visit to Jaffna in 1995.

There is no doubt that to some readers the case of an anthropologist not only working for his country's immigration authorities but going on to write a monograph on his former 'clients' will seem ethically questionable. There might not be much I can do about that, except to say that all anthropologists who are doing their work properly will sooner or later find themselves in possession of information which is potentially harmful to someone and must make a conscious decision not to misuse this information. This I have done. To my informants I have never made a secret of my professional background. In spite of this I have never been met with anything but friendliness, generosity and interest. While I have no doubt that some people may have kept their distance due to my background, the fact is that during (and after) fieldwork my own knowledge of immigration rules represented a scarce resource to many Tamil migrants and allowed them to explain and discuss their often intricate legal difficulties. Looking back, I have no doubt that my background as an immigration officer made fieldwork easier, not more difficult. Another matter is that when I started as an adviser to the immigration service I had a strong belief in the necessity, and the possibility, for governments to assess refugee claims in order to provide protection to those who need it most. Today I seriously doubt both the possibility of establishing legitimate legal criteria within this field and the ability of government bodies to implement such criteria. Together with some of my other writings (in particular, Fuglerud 1997) I offer this study as an explanation for my doubts.

2 HISTORY AND NATIONALISM

Pfaffenberger (1994) has stated that when he interviewed untouchable labourers in Jaffna in the 1970s they referred to local members of the landowning Vellala caste as 'Tamils'. Neither they nor the Vellalas, it turned out, considered the labourers themselves to be Tamil but carriers of an emblematic connection to a specific part of South India. Being 'Tamil', Pfaffenberger found, was tantamount to being 'Vellala'; ethnic identity, if it may be called so, was closely linked to conceptions of caste. Today, I suggest, neither untouchables nor landowners in Jaffna would limit the application of ethnic labels in this way. To get a grasp on this transformation we must start with a listing of groups as they were perceived until a few years ago.

There have been four main categories of Tamil-speaking people in Sri Lanka. In the central part of the country we find what is normally termed the 'Indian Tamils', or 'Tea Tamils', descendants of Tamil plantation workers brought to Sri Lanka (Ceylon) from South India by British planters in the nineteenth century. Today they comprise about 7 per cent of the country's population. Although not directly involved in the civil war, the situation of the Indian Tamil population since independence has been an important part of Sri Lanka's 'national question' more broadly defined (e.g. Hollup 1994). On the east coast of Sri Lanka there are two groups of Tamil-speaking people living side by side. The Sri Lankan Moors represent another 7 per cent of the population and trace their origin to visiting Muslim traders from centuries back. Until recently about 75,000 of these could also be found in the Northern Province, but in 1990 these were forcefully evicted by the armed Tamil militant group known as the Liberation Tigers of Tamil Eelam (LTTE). Despite their language the Muslims generally do not identify with the ethnic community of Tamils and are today struggling to carve out their own destiny in a precarious position between the two major ethnic groups. On the east coast we also find

20

one part of the country's 'Sri Lanka-Tamil' population, merged in official registers with the Tamils of the Northern Province. As a whole this group makes up 11 per cent of the population. The common categorisation makes sense in that by all measures Tamil people in the east and north now look upon themselves as belonging to the same group to a *larger* degree than what used to be the case (Wilson 1994). At the same time there are regional differences between the two which are still accorded meaning by the people involved. In particular the east coast population has a different composition of castes which, together with a greater availability of land, has mitigated the effects of caste ideology (McGilvray 1973, Jayapalan 1991). Furthermore, due to poor communications, the east coast has been more shielded against orthodox religious influences from India and has retained popular forms of Hinduism and cultural folk traditions which are now extinct in the north. These differences do have importance in the present-day political situation because while the east is regarded as 'backwards' and 'uncivilised' by many urbanised Tamils of the north, east-coasters often find it difficult to accept what they perceive as a northern, high-caste arrogance.

A majority of the Sri Lanka-Tamil population live in the country's Northern Province. The Sri Lanka-Tamils as a group are proud of their connections to India, but until a decade ago used this name – or more often '*Ceylon*-Tamil' – partly to distinguish themselves from the Indian Tamils, partly to underline the fact that their local origin give them an unquestionable right to have a say in the country's affairs. Today a more common label would be '*Eelam*-Tamil'. Jaffna, which is of central importance to this study, is the northernmost administrative district in Sri Lanka, comprising the Jaffna peninsula and a small strip of the mainland. Except for military forces this district is today an exclusively Tamil area. Jaffna is also the name of the main town within this district, the cultural centre of the Sri Lanka-Tamils and before the war a low-built city of about 130,000 inhabitants with a collection of beautiful buildings from the Portuguese, Dutch and British periods of colonisation. The Jaffna region constitutes a unique geographical unit in the so-called 'dry zone' of Sri Lanka. The peninsula is an arid limestone-coral formation and has little or no surface water except during the monsoon, but an abundant well water supply makes agriculture possible. The area has a distinct socio-economic pattern not found in other parts of the country. Population density used to be extremely high by Sri Lankan standards (Selvanayagam 1966). This carrying capacity stemmed from an intensive agriculture in the form of market gardening practised by the Tamil peasants, with tobacco, onions and chillis being the most important cash crops.

Tamil Sri Lanka is part of the South Indian, Hindu–Dravidian cultural region where the basic social structure of society has been that of caste organisation. Indeed, according to Pfaffenberger, far from being a marginal area in relation to the Indian mainland, Jaffna is 'an extremely conservative and very South Indian region which to this day preserves ... the very heart of the South Indian cultural design' (1982: 28). In general, villages in the northern part of the peninsula and on the islands off the coast seem to be composed of a broader spectrum of castes, while one-caste villages are only found on the mainland. The hardships imposed upon the people of low standing by those of high standing have been the ones familiar in Indian villages; traditionally, untouchable women were forbidden to cover their breasts, wear gold earrings, go through Brahman–officiated life cycle rites or live in concrete homes. Untouchable men were forbidden to wear shirts, cut their hair, use umbrellas or ride bicycles. All untouchables were forbidden to buy land, cremate their dead, enter temples, teashops and high-caste homes, walk on pavements used by high castes or marry without permission (Pfaffenberger 1982). The Thirumbar caste, washing clothes for the unclean castes, were forbidden to show themselves in daylight.

While I have no intention of framing this study specifically in Dumontian terms, it may be useful to relate certain aspects of the situation in pre-war Jaffna to Dumont's (1980) well-known analysis of Indian society. In Dumont's understanding the opposition between pure and impure is the fundamental principle ordering caste society into differentiated groups which are hierarchically structured. Power has no place in this opposition, it enters only at a certain level in the hierarchy. Power pertains to a secular politico-economic sphere being encompassed by the religious domain which is governed by the opposition between the pure and the impure.

Broadly speaking, the situation in Jaffna may be said to have conformed to this picture. While most Jaffna Vellalas will recognise that Brahmins rank higher on a scale of ritual purity, at least in the specific sense of being required for the performance of certain religious functions, they seem little troubled by this fact. Brahmins in Jaffna are not only few in number, they also have little influence in the day-to-

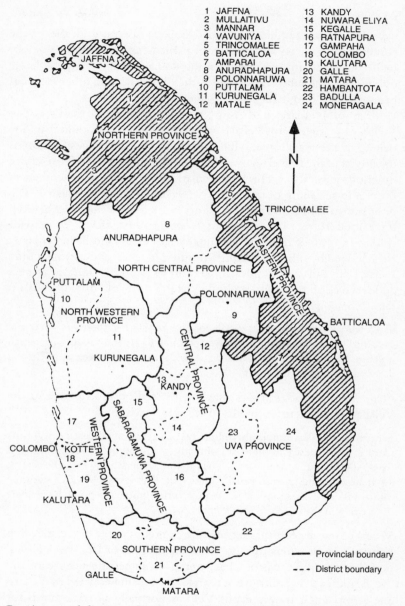

1 JAFFNA
2 MULLAITIVU
3 MANNAR
4 VAVUNIYA
5 TRINCOMALEE
6 BATTICALOA
7 AMPARAI
8 ANURADHAPURA
9 POLONNARUWA
10 PUTTALAM
11 KURUNEGALA
12 MATALE

13 KANDY
14 NUWARA ELIYA
15 KEGALLE
16 RATNAPURA
17 GAMPAHA
18 COLOMBO
19 KALUTARA
20 GALLE
21 MATARA
22 HAMBANTOTA
23 BADULLA
24 MONERAGALA

JAFFNA

NORTHERN PROVINCE

N

TRINCOMALEE

ANURADHAPURA

NORTH CENTRAL PROVINCE

EASTERN PROVINCE

POLONNARUWA

PUTTALAM

NORTH WESTERN
PROVINCE

BATTICALOA

KURUNEGALA

CENTRAL PROVINCE

KANDY

SABARAGAMUWA PROVINCE

COLOMBO

KOTTE

WESTERN PROVINCE

UVA PROVINCE

KALUTARA

GALLE

SOUTHERN PROVINCE

MATARA

—— Provincial boundary

- - - District boundary

Provinces and districts of Sri Lanka, 1981. The shaded area indicates the envisaged Tamil state (Eelam).

day affairs of society and are accorded limited respect outside the temple context. Politics, on all levels from parliamentary debates to village bickering, has until recently been the domain of the energetic land-owning Vellalas who constituted in the region what in other areas has been called a 'dominant caste' (Raheja 1988).

More problematic with respect to Dumont is the status of the Vellala caste itself. Most Vellalas will without hesitation admit that they belong to the *sudra varna*, which, according to sastric classification, is the lowest of the four categories of castes, determined to perform service functions in society.[1] This is particularly interesting since members of the Karaiyar fishing caste implicitly (David 1977, also Tanaka 1991), or as lately more explicitly (Sivaram 1992; see also Chapter 9 below), trace their roots to the superior *kshatriya varna*, that is to warrior origin. In spite of this, Vellalas judge themselves, and have generally been judged by others, as taking a position in terms of purity next only to the Brahmins and to possess the right to claim the honour, respect and services of most non-Brahmin castes. In the 'old days' a Vellala is said to have lived

like a feudal lord with all his vassals round him. He had therefore slaves and vassals to serve him on all occasions, and these slaves and vassals represented different castes who served him in such capacity whenever the occasion demanded. (quoted in Hocart 1950: 7)

Pfaffenberger (1982) argues that this exalted position is due to the Vellalas' investment in rituals; rituals which while they

benefit the whole community indirectly, ... are actually focused on Vellalar patrons, and produce in them, it is thought, a condition so auspicious that it makes their impurity irrelevant ... The mystical, generative power of Vellalars, a potency stemming from ritually induced order, invests Vellalars with the right – indeed the responsibility – to possess that which it reproduces, namely the stock and the crops. (p. 58)

Whether one accepts this explanation or prefers to see the relationship between landownership and ritual in reverse order, the Vellalas' position as temple patrons has been a characteristic feature of the social landscape in Jaffna. Most temples are privately owned by Vellalas and even when they are not Vellalas normally provide funds for construction, repair, salaries, etc. As the son of one wealthy landowner expressed it to me: 'We pay, the Brahmins pray.' The Vellalas, in other words, have tended to regard Brahmins as salaried specialists who should stick to their job and otherwise leave business to them.

One danger of focusing caste within a narrow purity/impurity perspective may be the possibility of overlooking aspects of diversity in the arrangement of society. The form of social interaction most often analysed by anthropologists in India has been the unequal interaction between landowners and their service castes, where differences in ritual purity coexist with the kind of economic arrangement termed 'jajmani-system' in the anthropological literature (Wiser 1936). This kind of arrangement was also found in Jaffna, but it was not the *only* form of social interaction between castes. In an article, which due to the war has only become more important since its time of writing, David (1977, also 1973a) has pointed out that in Jaffna two contrasting modes of inter-caste interaction could be found, each guided by different 'normative schemata' encoded in symbols. These are what he terms the *bound mode*, guided by the hierarchical aristocratic schema, and the *unbound mode*, guided by the non-hierarchical mercantile schema. These two modes correspond to local categorisations of interaction. The bound mode of relationships (*kattupatu totarpu*), which are found between the dominant landowning caste and their serving castes, largely corresponds to *jajmani* relationships as described from India. They are multicontextual, asymmetrical relationships which exist due to the relative social categories with which individuals are identified at birth and are characterised by what David calls 'hierarchical amity': diffuse, enduring, hierarchical solidarity. Between artisan castes and fishing castes on the one hand and the other castes on the other hand, non-bound relationships (*ishtamana totarpu*) prevail. They are mainly unicontextual relationships established for trading purposes, where each exchange is symmetrical of nature. As opposed to bound mode relationships, the unbound ones are voluntary, of no set duration and not restricted to certain kinds of people. According to David they are guided by a normative schema emphasising instrumentality, that is, non-diffuse, non-enduring, non-hierarchical relationships.

In the context of my own study David's paper is interesting for several reasons. If one accepts his argumentation, and I see no reason not to do so, his analysis is of considerable theoretical importance in documenting how diversity may be reconciled with unity. David's argument is not directed against Dumont. What he is saying, in effect, is that while the opposition purity/impurity orders relationships between castes as and when these are seen in relation to the divine order, this need not be the case on a lower level. In the day-to-day interaction taking place, so to speak, outside the presence of God, these relationships may be guided by symbols which are not primarily religious but are derived from more immediate concerns. Even more important to my own material, the documented coexistence of two contrasting systems of symbols, or 'normative schemata', may be seen as a 'discursive opening', a faltering in the totalising rhetoric of caste, providing a capacity for incorporating change. In pre-war Jaffna, which is David's concern, the unification of diversity could be found in the different castes' hierarchical relationship to the religious domain. As I will try to show at a later stage, this is not the case in exile. Here, outside the temple perimeter, bound mode behaviour comes to express diversity and conflict, and a common ground may only be found by redefining interaction in terms of unbound relationships.

THE GROWTH OF TAMIL NATIONALISM

When the Portuguese arrived in Ceylon in the sixteenth century, they found three kingdoms on the island: a Hindu state in the Jaffna peninsula, a Sinhalese kingdom in Kandy and a second Sinhalese kingdom on the west coast. The Portuguese opened an era of 330 years of colonial rule in the country. In the context of my concern in this study, however, the most conspicuous aspect of colonial administration in Tamil Ceylon (Sri Lanka) is what it did not do: it did not fundamentally change the structure of society.

This may seem a misjudged claim in face of the deep religious impact made by Christianity. Jesuit missionaries had founded, under Portuguese protection, Christian communities among Tamil fishermen in South India. Through these the new religion spread rapidly in the Ceylon coastal areas, a process which was reinforced after the Portuguese annexation of Jaffna in 1619. During their relatively brief rule, lasting until 1658 when they were expulsed by the Dutch, Catholicism penetrated deep into Jaffna-Tamil society, a fact testified to by 10 to 12 per cent of the Tamil population who have remained Catholics until this day. Dutch Protestantism and the Anglican Church arriving later could not possibly compare to this influence.

However, there were factors limiting the degree of change brought about by religious conversion. One such factor was that Catholicism adapted to the social structure of the area and organised services on a caste community basis. The Portuguese and the Dutch also established civil administrations which not only reproduced but also entrenched and made status categories from the kingship era more rigid. The earlier territorial division was retained, each district now being headed by European officers in control of revenue collection and police functions (Arasaratnam 1994). Under these officers were a large group of Tamil functionaries recruited among the Vellala landowners, their individual positions corresponding to their origin within the internal hierarchy of this caste. In particular, the leading functionaries, the *Mudaliyars*, strengthened their power during this period as their former customary positions were now underpinned by official appointment papers. The exception to the powers of the *Mudaliyars* were the Karaiyar fishing caste who, throughout the Portuguese and Dutch periods largely managed to retain their autonomy. Partly due to large-scale conversion to Catholicism, their independence from Vellala dominance was protected by the Portuguese. Later, they were sometimes used to counteract the Dutch administration's own powerful functionaries.

Both the Portuguese and the Dutch nations were mercantile powers, their imperialist interests focusing primarily on dominating the coastal areas in order to extract revenues from international trade. In 1796 the British took over the administration of Ceylon and, with the conquest of Kandy in 1815, became the first European power to unify the island under one rule. A *katchcheri*, the office of a Government Agent from the Colonial Civil Service, now became the focus of regional power in Jaffna. Although the British administration continued the former practice of appointing *Mudaliyars* to administer on district and village levels, with the tighter and more uniform rule of this administration new ways of exerting influence became increasingly important to the landowning caste. To this must be added that from the latter part of the nineteenth century the northernmost district saw an increase in population pushing land prices to phenomenal heights. In 1921 the Jaffna peninsula had the highest density per cultivated square mile in the whole island.

Landownership was concentrated in the hands of Vellalas, but even within this community land holdings became progressively reduced in size to the point of becoming uneconomical. Furthermore, in

Jaffna there was no industrialisation or viable urbanisation which could absorb the excess population from villages. What there was, however, was an excellent school system developed by the various missionary institutions providing education in English. The Catholics were no longer alone in the field and American Methodists were now particularly active. As early as 1822 there were 42 schools in the peninsula manned by Americans fluent in Tamil (Russel 1982). As Arasaratnam puts it: 'In the course of the 19th century, every village in the Jaffna peninsula, regardless of their size, became the venue of a mission school' (1994: 47). Thus developed the Tamils' dedication to learning which persists until this day. Education substituted for industrialisation in a modernising colonial economy, helping to 'mop up' excess manpower left over from an intensified agricultural production geared towards export. To English-educated youths there were job openings in the southern part of the country, both within the private mercantile and plantation sectors and within government administration.

From such a description one may be led to assume that the unified administration of the British led to a more radical transformation of society than that of its predecessors, breaking down traditional barriers between castes and regions. Like Christianity, the ideology of education claims to represent universal values, focusing on individual qualities rather than on social origin. The Vellalas of Jaffna were not so easily beaten, however, and the spread of education came to be a political controversy in the Tamil areas. Although in principle it *was* possible for an individual from any caste to traverse the long road from a Jaffna village to the Colombo elite, social control and Vellala conservatism saw to it that in colonial times this did not become a frequent journey. Neither did the new economic opportunities in the south much transform the Jaffna scene; new incomes were largely spent on reinforcing a village lifestyle. Arasaratnam states (1994: 51) that the social life of the Jaffna peninsula in 1900 was not fundamentally different from what it was in 1600 and the social fabric showed a tremendous ability to 'stretch' in order to cope with changing situations.

Nevertheless, ethnic violence in Sri Lanka is connected to a mounting pressure on this hierarchical social structure, to the transformation of vertical, caste-based loyalties into unified state ideologies where horizontal bonds predominate. On an all-state level ethnic animosity is clearly linked to the period starting in 1931 when the Donoughmore Constitution with its territorial representation based on universal suffrage was enacted under British administration. Before then, local Ceylonese participation in the administrative political process was limited to a small group of mixed origin who knew, or knew about, each other. In a letter from 1908 to the British Colonial Office, demanding participation by elected representatives in Parliament, James Peiris refers to an already existing electorate in the capital. This was:

... a highly intelligent one, composed of members of the Government Service, professional men, graduates, landed proprietors and merchants of all races, who [could] be safely entrusted with the task of electing their representatives in Council. (in Roberts 1977)

The existence of this group, which may be called the 'national elite' (Roberts 1977), was also recognised by the British administration. In a letter to the Colonial Office where he comments on the demand for reforms, Governor McCallum stresses that these are put forward by a minority from Jaffna and the west coast, constituting 'a small and peculiar class of the native population, alien in training, education, civilisation, and interest to the bulk of the people' and without 'any close and authoritative knowledge of the rural population which form the bulk of the rest' (in Roberts 1977). Within this group religious and linguistic background was of minor importance, as is shown by the election of the Tamil gentleman, Sir Ponnambalam Ramanathan, as the first representative for the all-island Educated Ceylonese seat by a mixed electorate in 1912. Singer (1964) has described this ruling elite as broadly *Ceylonese* – as opposed to Sinhalese or Sri Lanka-Tamil – high-caste, urbanised and Western-educated. Outside the towns Ceylon was still a country dominated by village life, where people's knowledge of and interest in what went on in Colombo was minimal. The implementation of universal franchise in 1931 changed this and over the next thirty years transformed Westernised politicians into spokesmen for ethnically defined interests (Fuglerud 1986).

On the Tamil side we see that the demand for mechanisms of regional control grows in strength with the increasing 'integration' of the state from the late 1920s. I use the word integration in inverted commas, because what we see are two parallel processes. On the one hand, there *was* an accelerating process of integration in the sense of increased political participation by individuals, of equality as citizens within the framework of the law. On the other hand, this integration, due to the lack of safeguards for the minority communities, carried within it the seeds of disintegration on the basis of ethnicity. The two processes are in fact very closely connected. On the Sinhalese side parties and politicians managed, by way of propagating a populist religious ideology, to draw support from the enlarged electorate. The price they had to pay was never to waver in the defence of majority interests. On the Tamil side the situation was more complex. Because of their minority status and their lack of a unifying ideology, the political process took the form of interaction between separate groups and a state centre which they could not control. It is important to realise that what are the best interests of the Tamil community in Sri Lanka has always been a disputed question, closely interlinked with the issue of caste. The Tamil Vellala elite resented the intruding efforts of the state trying to interfere in their local caste practices. For example, the Vellalas saw it as their natural right to dominate the educational institutions. While some castes, such as the Parayars, were excluded from education altogether, non-Vellalas who were admitted to school used to sit on the floor or on chairs a few inches lower than the Vellalas. When the non-Vellala castes, with support from the colonial administration and local government representatives in the late 1920s, initiated an 'equal seating campaign' in Jaffna, it caused a public uproar among the Vellalas, resulting in several schools being burnt to the ground. S.W.R.D. Bandaranaike, then Minister for Local Administration, observed in 1939 that 'the caste problem is much more acute in Jaffna than in any other district'. In one of his books he cites an example where two members of a village committee who belonged to a non-Vellala caste had not been given chairs to sit on during a committee meeting (in Russel 1982). The democratisation inherent in the Donoughmore Constitution meant an intervention into the internal Tamil hierarchy which put the Vellala elite in a difficult position. On the one hand, the benefit of political participation was difficult to deny, on the other, such participation would endanger their own privileged position. After the implementation of the Donoughmore Constitution, and after independence in 1948, the Vellala elite continued to protect their own interests in the face of an ongoing national democratisation. Several measures proposed were strongly resisted by the Tamil elite on the basis of a defensive group-oriented conservatism, as when a large fraction protested against the 1945 provision for free education, disturbed at the prospect of English education being opened to poor low-caste Tamils. Even more controversy was created by the question of political representation. From the early 1920s onwards we see that 'equal rights' was a principle argued by the British against strong opposition from the Tamil elite. The commission preparing the Donoughmore Constitution, for example, noted in their report that universal suffrage would be the only way to prevent 'placing an oligarchy in power without any guarantee that the interests of the remainder of the people would be consulted by those in authority'. They especially remarked upon 'the 80,000 persons of low caste among the Tamil community' which had caused them 'most anxiety'. The conservative fraction of the Vellala elite, on the other hand, argued that the giving of the vote to non-Vellala castes and women was not only a mistake, leading to 'mob rule', but also that the principle of equal say was 'an anathema to the Hindu way of life' (in Russel 1982: 16).With respect to Tamil politics, I therefore agree with Pfaffenberger when he says that:

> From all appearances, Jaffna represents the classic case of a traditional society, riven by hierarchical distinctions of caste and set apart from other regions on grounds of unique ethnicity, in conflict with the external imposition of political modernity. (Pfaffenberger 1994: 145)

This view, it should be emphasised, in no way ascribes to the Tamil community the responsibility for the unfortunate turn which history has taken in Sri Lanka. There is no doubt that the main responsibility for the political catastrophe which Sri Lanka is must be put on the shoulders of opportunistic and short-sighted political leaders on the Sinhalese side. What it means, however, is that Sri Lanka's problem is one of democracy. Solutions must be sought on the level of political models where minority interests must be safeguarded.

BOYS AND SOLDIERS

There are three questions which, without exception, are stressed by Tamils in judging the intention of the Sinhalese community toward themselves, all decided by means of a Sinhalese majority vote. One is the 'Sinhala Only' policy of 1956 where Sinhalese was made the country's single official language, the second is the colonisation policy where landless Sinhalese peasants and slum-dwellers have been settled within what Tamils regard as their own 'homeland', and the third is

the so-called 'standardisation' of examination scores for admission to
the universities which was implemented in the early 1970s and which
meant that Tamil students would need a higher score than Sinhalese
to be admitted. The heated debates about the first two questions led
to the first ethnic riot in 1958 which broke out when a group of Tamil
demonstrators were attacked by Sinhalese colonists at Polonnaruwa
and from there spread throughout the country.

During the 1970s the Sinhalese–Tamil relations got out of control.
The procedure of 'standardisation' created a situation where many Tamil
youths who had legitimate expectations of attending university were
not able to do so. Tamil youths of 'good family' had come to regard
university education, and a subsequent position in the civil service, as
their traditional prerogative, and when this changed there seemed to
many few possibilities of a meaningful civilian career. It is symptomatic
that the militant organisation which called itself the 'Tamil New
Tigers' and which in 1976 changed its name to the Liberation Tigers
of Tamil Eelam (LTTE) was established in 1972 by members of the
Tamil Manavar Peravai – the Tamil Students' Union (Hellman-
Rajanayagam 1986, also Taraki 1991).

The Tamil United (Liberation) Front (TULF) was a democratic party
with non-violent traditions. Although it still drew support from the
well-established Tamil community, the party lost initiative in the face
of an increasing ethnic antagonism. Even its adoption of the goal of
an independent Tamil nation in 1976 must, in the light of history, be
said not to have strengthened its own position but to have provided
legitimacy for organisations which were willing to fight for this goal
by other means. In the mid-1970s Tamil militants began targeting police
officers in armed operations and robbing banks to fund their activity.
During the 1974 World Tamil Conference in Jaffna a protest was staged
against the government, resulting in eight people being killed by the
police. In 1977 anti-Tamil riots broke out in several parts of the
country, taking 128 lives and opening the way for secession which
was now perceived by Tamils as a precondition for physical security.
The murder of four police officers in Valvettithurai in 1978 drove the
government to proscribe the Liberation Tigers and similar groups
through a bill which in 1979 was converted into the notorious
Prevention of Terrorism Act (PTA). This bill made possible arrests
for prolonged periods without warrants and the admissibility of
confessions made under duress as evidence. Emergency was declared

in Jaffna and hand-picked army units were despatched with orders to solve the problem by any means. These measures, and the brutal way in which they were implemented, boosted the popularity of the militants and from this period stems their pet name, 'the boys'.

The developments of the late 1970s continued into the early 1980s as an ongoing worsening of the law and order situation in the Tamil areas. Among the events which have remained in Tamil memory, and which gave a measure of legitimacy to the militants' activity, is the burning down of the Jaffna library in 1981, one of the area's cultural treasures. The fire is rumoured to have been instigated by high-ranking Sinhalese politicians. The real watershed came in 1983, however, when in July anti-Tamil riots broke out in Colombo and spread from there throughout the areas of mixed population. This human and political tragedy has been described in detail by a number of writers (Dissanayaka 1983, Piyadasa 1984, Meyer 1984, Tambiah 1986, Spencer 1990, Hole *et al* 1990) and I will only give a brief summary of it here.

The immediate cause of the ensuing events was the attack on an army convoy on 23 July by a group of militants at Tinneveli in Jaffna, resulting in the death of 13 soldiers. In Jaffna the army went on the rampage the next day killing 41 civilians. In Colombo the violence started in the early morning of 25 July with groups of Sinhalese systematically burning Tamil shops and private houses, often killing their proprietors and residents. In less than a week probably between two and three thousand Tamils were killed (Spencer 1990: 12) in the most brutal manner, many doused with petrol and set on fire while still alive. Fifty-three Tamil militants were also massacred in Welikade prison. Many thousands were rendered homeless.

One aspect of the situation was that much of the violent activity was systematic. In most of the literature referred to above the possible existence of a link between street-level organisers and the ruling United National Party is indicated, a link which, admittedly, has never been conclusively documented. A distinct possibility is that the happenings of 1983 were a result of both political instigation by particularly chauvinist members of the government *and* a general fear among large parts of the Sinhalese population, creating a combination of single-stranded factors opening for moments of encompassing horror. Spencer (1990) has pointed out that in detailed stories of killings from 1983 crowds seem to have believed that those they were attacking were not 'ordinary Tamil' but 'Tigers'. In the weeks before the riots fear of the LTTE had been built up in the Sinhala press and rumours had been spread that they were planning to attack the Temple of the Tooth in Kandy, poison water supplies and that they were travelling south from Jaffna hanging on the underside of trains etc.; these rumours expressing partly developed but usually unacknowledged collective fears which 'in their rapid development and dissemination ... seem to represent a kind of instant mythologizing in which terrifying new experiences were reinterpreted in terms of more familiar cultural structures' (Spencer 1990: 15). These structures were the revitalised Buddhist narratives where the Tamil appears as a representation of evil (Fuglerud 1986).

After 1983 we enter a period in Tamil history where any comment becomes controversial to the people who lived through it. There are no 'facts' after this point, only an ongoing controversy of what really happened and who did what and why. I will venture just a few comments.

From the late 1970s there were, and to some extent still are, a large number of Tamil militant groups with confusing abbreviations of long names existing side by side: LTTE, EROS, EPRLF, PLOTE, TELO, TELA, TNA, TLF, TMP, TELE, ENLF, ENDLF, etc. The dynamics between these groups, of which I will make no attempt to provide a detailed genesis, is of major importance to young Tamils who have been raised in the climate of violence sustained by them. Here I wish to make three points:

To the outside observer, and I here stress this position, there were no major differences between these groups in terms of political ideology. They all started out claiming to be socialist, they all wanted to free Tamil Eelam from Sinhalese suppression and they all proved completely ruthless with respect to the means they employed. In interviews, former participants themselves seldom claim ideological reasons for having joined one particular group among the large number of organisations. In general the 'choice' among diversity is referred back to coincidence, to the fact that one particular group was active in their region or to personal connections with people who were already members.[2] This, however, is not to say that there *are* no differences between the organisations. Rather than ideological choices, the groups constitute what may be called frameworks of interpretation, embodied in violent trajectories of events. To some extent, these different frameworks reflect alternative positions on strategy and tactics (Hellmann-Rajanayagam 1986) but, more important, they represent micro traditions of legitimacy linked to specific dates, persons and actions. For example, while killing political opponents has been done by all groups, whether killing a specific person in one particular situation was correct or not may be a question over which organisations clash. Similarly, while most organisations have at some point co-operated with the government, the decision about when to do so has been a source of bitter conflicts. As pointed out by Staub (1994: xiv), perpetrators make many small and not so small decisions as they progress along the road of destruction. They elect leaders adopt and reject ideas, make plans, and engage in harmful and violent acts. Their circumstances and characteristics move them in certain directions from which it may be difficult to turn back. This is one aspect of living on the edge: your actions tend to stick with you and there is little room for remorse. To guerrillas in exile ascription of responsibility for strategic decisions and tactical operations by others is important in the construction of identity; in Sri Lanka it may be a question of life or death. For example, under Indian occupation many youths were conscripted at gun-point into their service in the name of the local organisations EPRLF and TNA. Whole classes of schoolchildren who had no wish to fight were abducted and forced into uniform. Nevertheless, many of these were executed by the LTTE when the Indians left.

The second point I wish to make is that differences between groups may be understood as a direct continuation of inter-caste and intra-caste conflicts, that is, as conflicts of factionalism and segmentation. In the period leading up to the civil war we find in the Tamil areas processes where inter-caste relationships increasingly are broken up by capitalism and state intrusion, but where bonds of *intra*-caste loyalty become more important in the competition over rights and resources. These are processes which are familiar from the Indian mainland (Dumont 1980, Barnett 1977). That there is a certain degree of correlation between caste origin and militant groups seems clear, e.g. PLOTE in the early 1980s had a relatively large following of Vellala members, LTTE's leadership came from the Karaiyar caste, EPRLF drew its main support from the Eastern Province, etc. It is also clear, however, that this correlation is not complete, either on a caste, region or village level. This creates an epistemological uncertainty where different understandings may be ascribed to events. National liberation and caste interests here stand as contending paradigms of interpretation and the *possible* importance of caste loyalties is a matter often brought up in order to credit, or more often discredit, actions performed by political rivals.

The third point I wish to emphasise is the important role played by India with regard to the militant groups. Through the late 1970s and the first part of the 1980s most of the important groups operated out of South India and there is little doubt today that India, through one of its intelligence agencies, supplied and trained at least five of these groups as part of a covert operation (Gunaratna 1993, Hole *et al* 1990). The way this training was conducted – separately for the different groups and with a strong element of competition between them – served to entrench in military training and technology differences which from the beginning may have been more or less incidental. This backing also made the groups largely independent of support from the people they were supposed to defend. One response from the government to this build-up was an increased Sinhalese colonisation in the east which, combined with an arming of the colonisers, prepared the ground for a frontier type of war in these areas.

The situation in the Tamil areas changed rather radically around 1986–87. The Liberation Tigers of Tamil Eelam (LTTE) remained alone as protectors of Tamil sovereignty and, from the point of view of the government, the problem of law and order developed into a fully-fledged military situation. From January 1987 a blockade of Jaffna was implemented and in May the so-called 'Operation Liberation' was initiated. The politics of starvation and the scale of attacks on the civilian population which followed represented a new development in Sri Lanka at the time. For the first time the air force used their 'barrel bombs', home-made napalm explosives made of barrels filled with petrol and rubber liquid which were thrown by hand out of helicopters and transport aeroplanes. According to one eyewitness 48 such bombs were dropped over Valvettithurai, a town with a few thousand inhabitants. In the Marriaman temple in Alvai, where people had been told over the radio to take cover, 35 people were killed by fire from the army. In Polikandy the army killed 20 people during a door-to-door search, most of them aged over 70.[3] When an Indian Red Cross ship approached the harbour in Kankesanthurai with supplies on 25 June, the crowds waiting are said to have fallen on their knees crying, 'India

– save us!' In July 1987 an agreement was signed between India and Sri Lanka to the effect that India took upon itself to disarm the local militant groups and impose a situation of law and security in the Tamil areas. By October 1987 the friendly relations between the Indian command and the LTTE had already broken down and the army had to do the job by force. For the soldiers, often knowing little or nothing about Jaffna (Sardeshpande 1992), it was a shadow hunt. The guerrillas did not wear uniforms and every Tamil was a possible enemy. To the population in the north-east the period was a mental shock. In 1987 war was no news to the war-ravaged people of the north, but to the Tamils India was still a symbol of the good powers of the world, an image strengthened throughout the preceding years of confrontation with their own government. The occupation was implemented with an almost mechanical brutality. The period of the so-called Indian Peace Keeping Force (IPKF) – or the 'Indian People-Killing Force' as it is often nicknamed by Tamils – from July 1987 to March 1990 was a time when, as one Jaffna resident said to me, 'The only thing you could do was to hold your breath and concentrate on how to survive.' Whether the Indian withdrawal brought any relief or not is a matter of contention, however.

3   SEMANTICS OF TERROR

'Look what they have done to my country', the stately grey-haired Government
Agent said to me as we were waiting at the checkpoint outside Jaffna Fort. It
was 1988 and I had flown in from Colombo. The Government Agent had
come to meet me together with the Jaffna Chief of Police. After soft drinks
and chattering inside the old Dutch fort in Jaffna they had taken me for a
walk around the embankments pointing out some of the landmarks which could
be seen. The Chief of Police in particular seemed to be happy that there was
someone in this world who would listen to his worries. I had asked him why
there was so much damage on the buildings and he explained how the Fort
in 1986, occupied by the Sinhalese army, had been surrounded by LTTE
forces who for weeks held the place under constant bombardment. He showed
me the small church where the roof had been blown away by shelling, and as
we walked through the rubble on the floor he told me he had only three months
left of his assignment in Jaffna before he could join his family in the south. *'I
hope I may live to see them'*, he said. What kept worrying him was that his
predecessor had been killed by the LTTE and he did not feel convinced they
would not do the same to him. The situation was different, he reasoned to
himself; now LTTE's enemies EPRLF were outside the Fort, supported by
the Indian forces, and the police were locked inside. *'We must ask permission
to go out'*, he explained. Still, it was the LTTE he feared. At this point
LTTE from its hiding places had ordered Jaffna shopkeepers and public officers
only to work half days in protest of the Indo-Lankan accord, and even with
the streets crowded by Indian soldiers who tried to pressure them to stay open,
everybody, including the Government Agent himself, obeyed. The Chief of
Police thought they might punish him for not taking action against the
EPRLF thugs who worked under the Indians. If they decided to do so he
was as good as dead.

38

Leaving the Chief of Police to his worries I left Jaffna Fort with the Government Agent. In front of us at the checkpoint just outside, three EPRLF youngsters, 15-16 years old, yelled and waved their guns while harassing an elderly poor man who had been dragging a hand-lorry behind him. The situation, which was what the Government Agent referred to by his statement, seemed to sum up the results of years of conflict; the victory of arms over civility, of anger over reason, of young impatience over the slow wisdom of seniority. 'The EPRLF boys are the worst', the Government Agent continued in a low voice while we were looking. 'At least the LTTE keep some discipline. They know what they are doing.' After staying in Jaffna for a short while, I left. When I returned about one year later the Government Agent was dead, shot by the LTTE.

At the experiential level there is no way a description of war, and the terror that goes with it, can do justice to the fact itself. Indeed, it has been forcefully argued by social scientists that violence and pain are the dimension of human existence which escapes analysis, the 'counterpoint' to culture, resisting culture's 'recuperative powers' (Daniel 1991: 8).

While I am in sympathy with Daniel's argument, there is reason to point out that if we accept it *in toto* we seem to face a predicament. Not only do most people in the world relate to territorial borders as significant facts in their lives, borders which in many if not most cases have been established through war or threats of war. Moreover, from the most casual glance at the world order there seems to be little doubt that the daily existence of organised groups is often profoundly influenced by visions, goals and aspirations – that is, by *cultural claims* – which in people's own understanding are linked to the actual or potential use of violence. So what to do?

One clue to how to proceed, I suggest, lies in the *excess* of violence we so often find in situations of armed conflict, its non-instrumental character; in the mutilations, decapitations, the killing of children and pregnant women; in what must crudely and cruelly be termed the *aesthetic* character of violence.[1] This aesthetic character serves to displace issues from real to symbolic grounds (Graziano 1992).

The relating of violent acts to cultural claims is made possible by two conditions. One is the referential fluidity of the human body. War's ability to ensure a binding result must be sought not so much in the losing part not being able to fight as in the dead or wounded body's ability to sustain the fiction of society. In this respect war is similar to sacrifice – the *sacer/facere*, the making sacred of the victim – the translating of the material fact of the body into the unsubstantiated fiction of culture. The other condition is the arranging of participants in violent contests into two – and never more than two – sides in order to engage in an activity which will make it possible to designate one winner and one loser. In this respect killing is here not a sacrifice but a competition, because by entering into war the parties not only seek to sustain their own fiction but agree to certify if not their own, at least the other side's issues. As Scarry (1985) puts it:

... in consenting to enter into war, the participants enter into a structure that is a self-cancelling duality. They enter into a formal duality, but one understood by all to be temporary and intolerable, a formal duality that, by the very force of its relentless insistence on doubleness, provides the means for eliminating and replacing itself by the condition of singularity ... (p. 87)

What soldiers do in war, and what is done to the civilian population, is to deconstruct the state as it normally manifests itself in their bodies. By accepting to kill, the soldier consents to perform an act which under normal circumstances would put him or her outside the moral space of the community. By killing civilians the soldier removes the taken for granted lawfulness and protection which allows civilian life to proceed. By so doing their bodies are laid open for symbolic possession by the winning side.

Scarry's point is important, in particular in relation to 'dirty wars' like the Sri Lankan one, because the social institutions legitimated by violence rest on a mytho-logic rejecting internal complexity and differentiation. While on the Sinhalese side a transformation from multiplicity to unity was accomplished before the war started, on the Tamil side this process is only now about to reach its conclusion. Focusing on this particular aspect of development, we may say that 'ethnic oppression', 'Sinhala aggression' or whichever way one wishes to designate the role played by their significant other has entered the Tamil life-world primarily as an instrument assisting the construction of a fictitious unity.

DRAWING BOUNDARIES

For 'separation' to be established what was formerly united must be dissolved. This is true for family structures and political loyalties, but also for space as a cognitive configuration. Separation demands a reordering of people in space and of space in people's minds. In this perspective the riots of 1977 and the events of July 1983 have a particular significance. They worked to destabilise the cultural construct of geography and made ethnic identity of relevance to location. While many acknowledge the assistance given by good-hearted Sinhalese, the Tamils I have spoken to about politics *never* fail to mention the summer of 1983. These events are normally described by people who were in the affected region at the time with an insistence which indicates that they are more than historical facts, they have become part of their own personal constitution.

Driving tens of thousands of Tamils into the Tamil heartland, the events of 1983 are, however, only the most conspicuous part of an ongoing process of drawing boundaries between communities. From Mannar in the west through Vavuniya and the Welioya area, down to Trincomalee and south past Batticaloa, a conceptual border zone has since been reproduced through continuous violence. In a destabilised topography a reordering of people and place is organised through symbolic performances of cruelty. Notice the ritual aspect of the following incident, taking place at the frontline checkpoint:

A witness described to Amnesty International the public execution of ten prisoners that took place near Thandikulam, north of Vavuniya, on the morning of 6 July 1992. A group of armed cadres brought ten prisoners, including two women, to the road junction at Paranathan. A large crowd of people who were travelling to Colombo from the north were gathered there, and forced to watch the proceedings. The prisoners had been accused of giving information to the army. They were taken down from the vehicle and told to stand on the sandbags which had been placed ready 'so that their blood would not stain the soil'. They were told to proclaim their guilt. When two of them said that they had confessed falsely because they had been beaten during interrogation, a member of the LTTE ordered the shooting to start. The ten were shot in the back. An LTTE member then cut off the head of one of the executed prisoners ... The head was put in a box and a woman traveller at the scene was told to take it to the sentry point at the Vavuniya army camp ... (AI, February 1993; Index: ASA 37/1/93)

This border zone is the land of massacres too many to recount or even to remember, where both parties erect landmarks of civilian destruction: Anuradhapura 1985: LTTE members attack the bus station – 150 Sinhalese civilians dead; Kituluttuwa 1987: the LTTE unload two buses and kill their passengers on the roadside – 126 Sinhalese civilians dead; Kattankudy 1990: the LTTE attack two mosques during Friday prayer – 103 Muslim civilians dead; Kokkadichcholai 1991: an army unit goes berserk in village – 150 Tamil civilians dead; Kallerawa 1995: the LTTE attack the village – 42 Sinhalese civilians dead; to mention but a few. If these incidents should give the impression that the army is more restrained than its adversary, this must be corrected. Amnesty International has reported that between June 1990 and September 1991 more than 3000 Tamil people 'disappeared' in the custody of government forces and verified extrajudicial executions in the same period amounting to hundreds.[2] By October 1990, some 3000 Tamils were estimated to have been killed or to have 'disappeared' in the Amparai district alone during the previous four months; in Batticaloa town over 1500 people were registered as 'disappeared' between June and December 1990.

Victims of extrajudicial execution have reportedly been shot, bayoneted, stabbed, hacked or beaten to death. Some were said by witnesses to have been burnt alive. Many people were apparently detained or killed because they had contact with the members of the LTTE, sometimes of the most minimal kind during the period the LTTE controlled the area. (AI Index: ASA 37/14/91: 17)

In her living quarters in Jaffna, a bombed-out house abandoned by its owner, a displaced woman told me the following about her background:

I am a mother of six. I come from the village XX 12 miles north of Batticaloa. My husband died many years ago. When we were young our village was a good place to live. No one there thought about government or politics. Even when all this trouble started no one in our village wanted to fight. When the people they call 'tigers' ruled [in Batticaloa] they came many times and wanted our boys to fight. We told them they should not go. Also our village leader told them they should not go. When the army came [to the area] we were glad. We thought they would protect us. Then soldiers came to our village. They said soldiers had been killed [by a bomb] and that our men had done it. When we said no, they took eight boys with them. One was my eldest son. They said they would come back.

Two days later they came early in the morning. They set fire to the houses near the road. All people woke up from the screaming. When our village leader tried to stop them they shot him. The woman living in the house next to us tried to run away into the fields with her two children. They also shot them. They told everybody to come out and stand together outside. My eldest daughter had hidden under the bed. I did not know. When they went in to search the house she screamed. They killed her with their knives [bayonets]. She was twelve. Later I heard that also four more people were killed that day. Since then my two other sons have gone to fight [with LTTE]. I don't know where they are. My eldest son I have never seen again. For five years now I have lived here with my second daughter.

Such actions must be interpreted as messages directed not primarily to the 'enemy' but to the population at large. The Sri Lankan civil war is enacted as a cultural metalanguage where the disembodiment of culture implies the simultaneous embodiment of terror. Dismembering the organism serves to sever the body from the body politic of the state, preparing the re-membering of the nation, the rendering whole through the affirmation of a new identity. What should be observed is the relationship between processes at different levels. While military actions may be parts of overall strategies, they often interact with local dynamics. One characteristic of the border zone is the mixed population of Sinhalese, Tamils and Muslims living close together in separate groups. Another characteristic is the fluid military situation where the Sri Lankan army and the guerrillas operate in the same areas, villages often being controlled by the Sri Lankan army during the day and the guerrillas during the night when soldiers return to barracks for their own safety. Karapola, Muthugala and Alanchipotana are three such villages off the Polonnaruwa–Batticaloa road. While Karapola and Muthugala are *purana* – 'old' – Tamil villages, Alanchipothana is a recent Muslim settlement established on the not so arable land in the area. As a result, farmers of Alanchipothana used to work the fields of Karapola and Muthugala as leaseholders until in mid-April 1992 the Tamil villagers decided no longer to lease their fields to Muslims. The Muslims alleged that the Tamil villagers could not have taken such drastic steps without the moral and financial backing of the LTTE and made this allegation clear to them. Shortly before midnight on 28 April 1992 a group of armed men and women in uniforms attacked the southern part of Alanchipothana, setting fire to houses and killing the inhabitants with bayonets. When they left 60 people were dead, 30 of them children below the age of twelve. The soldiers were heard shouting LTTE slogans while attacking. Some villagers claim, however, that they saw young men from the nearby Tamil villages among them, and at dawn Karapola and Muthugala were subsequently attacked by armed men from the civil defence squad of Alanchipothana. In these two villages 50 persons were left dead, again more than half of them children. Today remaining members of both communities live in separate refugee camps.[3]

Like in the urban landscape of Belfast discussed by Feldman (1991), the symbolic reproduction of the border zone has served in Sri Lanka to codify cognitive geography into a tripartite structure of 'sanctuary' – 'interface' – 'targeting community' along a mutual, interlocking inside/outside polarity; the Tamil and Sinhalese sanctuaries being Jaffna and Colombo respectively. While the border zone interface is by tacit agreement transformed into a scene of absurd theatrical violence, sanctuaries become idealised spaces, substantiating sacred values of political ethnicity. This structure is something more, or other, than simply the withdrawal from the explosive mixed areas in order to ensure civilian life; the creation of the sanctuary is not primarily a way to *avoid* violence, but to *channel* it, to impose form, to manage it through spatial devices.

When focusing on Tamil nationalism it is important to recognise the double character of the sanctuary. In terms of conceptual topography the sanctuary of the Jaffna peninsula constitutes the inner core of national geography; it is where the Ceylon-Tamil communities trace their origin in Sri Lanka and the refuge they seek in times of danger; it is a eulogised space. Like in South America, as described by Franco (1985), in Jaffna this sanctuary status rests upon the existence of sacred qualities pre-dating the armed conflict; on the location of Hindu temples and Catholic churches, of centres of traditional wisdom and contemporary education, all associated with the continuity of Tamil culture and traditional civilisation as such. As will be elaborated in later parts of this book, these sacred qualities are further associated with cultural notions of female purity, familial unity and biological reproduction, values contributing to an ideology of resistance. The *transformation* of this sacred quality of the sanctuary is of immense importance to the logic of war in Sri Lanka. In South America, Franco argues, the utopian values of the sanctuary are appropriated by the state in co-ordination with its destruction of physical sanctuaries and the imprisonment of its inhabitants. The signifiers of the sanctuary are expropriated and universalised into 'de-territorialized' sign systems (1985: 415).

A parallel process may be observed in Jaffna, but here local guerrilla authorities appropriate these values with the assistance of the violence of the other. While the sanctuary itself is maintained through the complementary space of the confrontational border zone, reserved for the ideological reproduction of community through violence, sanctuary signifiers are appropriated and 'de-localised' into national designata through regular transgressions of the performative prescriptions inherent in the sanctuary/interface structure. It has been argued by reliable observers of the Sri Lankan situation that during the Indian occupation the LTTE systematically staged military actions from sanctuary spaces – churches, hospitals, refugee camps, etc. – drawing fire against the civilian population (Hole *et al* 1990: 210 ff.). Without making a judgement on possible motives, it is a fact that the LTTE at least on two occasions have attracted massive retroactive violence against 'confessional space', thereby transforming the signified sanctuary into the defended territory in its entirety. The first of these occasions was in June 1990 when the LTTE broke the ceasefire by abducting and killing several hundred police officers in a co-ordinated action, leading to a prolonged massive bombing of Jaffna, including St Patrick's College, Manipay hospital and the refugee camp at St Anthony's church. The second occasion was in April 1995 when the LTTE broke again a negotiated ceasefire by surprise, leading to a combined land and air attack on Jaffna. Let me conclude this section with a brief description taken from the sober situation report written by the Government Agent of Jaffna, concerning the bombing of St Peter's church during this last operation. The report was smuggled out of Jaffna and subsequently sent on the Internet:

With Security operations from the early hours of 9th morning thousands of families from Chankanai, Sandiipay, Tellipalai and part of Uduvil started fleeing from their villages towards safer areas of Nallur and Jaffna, and makeshift arrangements were made to look after the needs of these families in places of religious worship, inclusive of St Peter's Church, Navaly ...

At 4.30 p.m. on 09.07.95 an aircraft bombed this church where hundreds of families have taken refuge under the existing calamity ... resulting in the death of a total of 117 and a number of 180 injured. On the fore-noon of 12th I personally inspected this disaster site and I am convinced that a few more bodies, limbs and pieces which were unclaimed and not collected has been cremated adjoining the church. A few human skulls remained unburned and stench from putrefying human flesh emanated from the debris ...

Families from locations considered unsafe started leaving their homes and villages and many of them who feared even the town areas of Nallur and Jaffna started migrating towards Thenmaradchy. In this process they left behind old and invalids who cannot be shifted ... and sometimes even the seriously injured as well. A total of 187,589 persons consisting of 41,686 families are displaced ...

(*Lankanet*, July 1995)

The news agency Reuters confirmed on 13 July 1995 that 13 of the people killed in the St Peter's incident were babies.

This last quote points to the breakdown of social infrastructure through forced movement. From the mid-1980s to the mid-1990s, out of the Tamil pre-war population of 2.1 million about one-third has permanently been internally displaced, often trekking from site to site according to the fluctuations of war. According to NGO workers I spoke to in Jaffna in 1988, during 'Operation Liberation' which started in May 1987, about 500,000 civilians were pushed up towards the northern coast, fleeing continuous shelling from the south. When the Indian army started its offensive in October of the same year, the shelling and troop movements started from the north, pushing the same civilians towards the southern coast. When the Sri Lankan army in 1990 took hold of the islands off the coast of Jaffna, transforming them into military encampments, most civilian houses were bulldozed and the inhabitants sent across to the mainland. Like those who can now watch the outline of their home islands from the Jaffna seashore, people in Sri Lanka are often displaced within a distance of kilometres from where they used to live their daily life.

I think that the wider ramifications of such experiences are worth considering. In Tamil Sri Lanka, as a caste society, social epistemology is anchored in a direct relationship between people and space, in the knowledge of who lives where and in prescriptive regulations on who may or may not move within segregated areas – regulations which cannot be upheld under refugee conditions. Schutz and Luckman (1973) argue that human life-worlds rest upon the illusion that their integrity remain unchallenged. Routine transmission of knowledge on which life-worlds are based is founded on social structure. When such frameworks are threatened, people will endeavour to reconstruct a sense of reality by borrowing from epistemological systems which can be made compatible with their immediate experiences. For populations in areas where communities are laid waste and families are broken up, one of the few systems of knowledge seen to be operating intact is the politico-military in which force is made equal to right (Nordstrom 1990). People inflicted by violence may come to absorb and accept knowledge constructs based on brute force. One systematic study on psycho-social problems in Jaffna, based on an examination of 294 camp refugees and 74 displaced individuals living in villages in the area, concludes that:

The study proves significantly that all the participants in the target groups are affected of one or more symptoms according to the war conflict and the present living conditions. More than 50% are suffering from sleeping, eating and memory disturbances and irritability and anger which indicate heavy psychological distress due to existential problems. More than 50% suffers psychosomatic manifestations and more than 50% have heavy depressions ... (Reppesgaard 1993)

Psychological disorders of this magnitude are more than individual problems. In particular it is well known that post-traumatic stress may create a sort of addiction to the thrill of violent situations, fuelling perpetuating spirals of bloodshed.[4]

Refugee existence is not the only mechanism to work in this way. As mentioned in the last chapter, from the inception of the armed struggle in the late 1970s right up to today a marked characteristic of the Tamil liberation movement has been the internecine fighting between different militant groups. There are numerous examples of people from the same villages, even from the same families, siding with groups in bitter conflict. During the Indian occupation the group popularly known as 'Three Stars', consisting mainly of the group EPRLF and breakaway fractions of the two groups PLOTE and TELO,[5] actively joined the Indian army in their fight against the LTTE. After the Indian withdrawal from Sri Lanka and the LTTE's takeover in Jaffna, these groups and a few others made common cause with the Sinhalese government forces.

In this situation people have at different times been able to identify each other as traitors to their cause or, something for which a need will always exist when a society is turned on its head, to settle old scores through such identification. During the Indian occupation masked local militants were used at sentry points to identify LTTE supporters. Stories told by refugees testify to the fact that, whatever happened afterwards, not knowing who put you in pain – your neighbour? your worker? your brother? – indefinitely increased the terror of the occasion. This terror of not knowing serves to generate a climate of radical epistemological uncertainty and to locate the ongoing social processes within a cosmos of doubt (Taussig 1984). Under conditions of extreme violence the constant reproduction of guesswork, rumour and denial may come to posit society midway between hyper-reality and fiction. While in Jaffna in 1988 I was allowed by the Chief of Police to examine reports forwarded by the Médecins Sans Frontières. They told a story of 'public disappearances', that is, the army denying knowledge of prisoners even *as and when* they were taken away in full view, their bodies turning up days later tortured to death or permanently disabled. During this period the Chief of Police and his people were not allowed to leave the Jaffna Fort and could do nothing to stop these abuses.

The breeding of informers and the circulation of information which has no known origin are directly related to the mechanics of power and the logic of terror. It is part of the dismantling of the familiar. As demonstrated by Scarry (1985), one of terror's main purposes is the taking apart of the victim's world as it normally appears to his or her consciousness. Torture, as a process embedded in the asymmetrical relationship between the torturer and the victim, centres on a transformation of the interconnection between body and voice; a process which, replicating war on a smaller scale, translates the hurt body of the victim into the torturer's voice of power. In order to accomplish this, in order to transform the hyper-individuated pain into a *representamen* of something else, of power, the victim's voice must first be taken away, reverted, brought back to a stage existing before the language in which his world appears – to the scream. Not only that, but his language must be destroyed *by* the world it normally represents; to the prisoner in captivity pieces of his world are brought to him as instruments of pain. The dreaded Special Task Force, a police commando-unit operating in the border zone, have a special predilection for what they call the '*Dharma Chakra*', Buddha's Wheel, a concept known and revered by all people in Sri Lanka. In *their* Dharma Chakra, prisoners are stripped naked and tied in a squatting position with their wrists around their shins and their ankles roped. A pole is then passed under their knees and they are rotated while beaten, causing injuries to their arms and legs. Tamil torturers of all convictions seem to favour the chilli, a familiar substance in all Tamil homes, either burning below the prisoner hanging upside down, the smoke causing pain to the eyes and making breathing difficult, or being forced into the mouth, the anus or the penis.[6] This un-making of the familiar externalises the disintegration of the victim's world through pain. His world is brought to him and destroyed in his presence in the very process by which it is being made to destroy him. Only when pain is total, when what began as being 'not oneself' has eliminated all that is 'not itself', is the scene prepared for the translation of body as fact into the fiction of the voice. Then, as Scarry comments,

... at least for the duration of this obscene and pathetic drama, it is not the pain but the regime that is incontestably real, not the pain but the regime that is total, not the pain but the regime that is able to eclipse all else, not the pain but the regime that is able to dissolve the world. (1985: 56)

CREATING ONE VOICE

On 29 May 1982, that is, before the civil war truly started, the Jaffna newspaper *Saturday Review* published an editorial which came to be prophetic. Commenting on the killing of two young activists in Jaffna by a group of armed youth it stated:

The political heat, denied an external outlet, is turning inwards now ... It is becoming self-destructive. The air is getting hotter with a new political intolerance. Brother is turning against brother; guns taught to shoot at targets, find that the targets are no longer there ... The truth is that there is a new underground force in the making, an underground force without ideals, which if allowed unchecked could even bring about a state of civil strife in Jaffna, and plunge the whole peninsula into chaos. This has to be nipped in the bud, and if there is one leader who has sufficient weight and authority to do this, it is Mr Amirthalingam ...

Mr Amirthalingam, in whom *Saturday Review* put their trust, was the leader of Tamil United Liberation Front (TULF), the party articulating the increasingly nationalist feelings of the middle-aged educated Tamils. His assassination in July 1989 by LTTE gunmen in Colombo represents not only the coming to power of a new generation in Tamil politics but also the culmination of a systematic elimination of all Tamil voices other than that of the LTTE itself. This process started with the assassination of the mayor of Jaffna, Mr Alfred Duraiyappa, in 1975, but accelerated from the early 1980s onwards. In those years in Jaffna early risers became accustomed to finding people tied to lamp-posts and executed during the night, often carrying posters round their necks telling of the crimes they had committed against the 'Tamil nation'.

The theatrical character of these power demonstrations is striking. By 1985 the Sri Lankan army was no longer able to maintain a regular presence in Jaffna but was confined to barracks except for military campaigns like the one which followed in 1986–87. This left the ground for militant groups to enforce their own law. A man, who at the time was a member of the Student Council at Jaffna University, told me the following story in Norway:

One day in front of the university a known LTTE man started teasing a girl student, making passes at her while people were watching. She clearly felt uncomfortable but he just kept on. This girl had a boyfriend who was also a student. When he intervened trying to stop him, the LTTE man pulled out a gun, put it to his head and killed him right there on the lawn. Then he just walked away like nothing.

Such everyday performances, and there have been many of them, should not be seen as separate from political dynamics. Excess is not accidental or supplementary to authoritarian rule; it is strategic and essential, rulers renewing their self-image in token displays of omnipotence. In their own small way such incidents are public rituals; making power tangible they assist the reorganising of reality.

With respect to the various militants groups, it should be said that their tactics have not necessarily been much different. However, since the LTTE have undoubtedly been better at it, it is on them that the focus must be. Read backwards, their effort of reorganising reality has in Tamil Sri Lanka followed four parallel tracks in the last ten to fifteen years:

The first is the systematic elimination of critical, or simply independent, voices. This process, which accelerated with the lamp-post killings, has continued steadfastly – e.g. the lawyer Annamalai was shot dead in 1989 because he spoke in favour of the US presidential candidate during a public meeting[7] – until in the 1990s inside the LTTE-controlled areas there is no opposition, no debate, no expressed opinion on political matters except that of the LTTE. Only when alone, and to outsiders, are people able to talk. While the killings of outspoken individuals over the years are too many to mention, there are two murders which, in the consciousness of many expatriate Tamils, seem to be particularly important, perhaps because the two people murdered were both young, not affiliated with any armed groups and had both been living in the West. They have therefore come to symbolise the futility of contributing something to their country through peaceful means. One is the 'disappearance' in 1988 of Mr Kanthasamy who left his comfortable London exile to go back and start the Tamil Refugees' Rehabilitation Organisation. The other is the killing of Dr Rajani Thiranagama, a young woman who, also living in England, went back to teach medicine at Jaffna University and work for the University Teachers for Human Rights (UTHR). In 1989 she was shot by gunmen in a Jaffna street on her way home to her children. While the responsibility for the acts has never been ascertained in a court of law, they are widely believed among migrants to have been orchestrated by the LTTE to eliminate actual or potential critics. When in 1990 I attended a one-year commemoration service for the killing of Rajani in Oslo, the attendance by Tamils was low because the meeting was seen as an implied criticism of the LTTE, something which people were reluctant to take part in.

The second track has been the elimination of clashing militant groups. There is, of course, no way for an outside observer to gain reliable information on the deliberations, not to mention the individual motives, of commanders in semi-clandestine guerrilla movements. It is, therefore, not possible to say what is behind the LTTE's wish to rule alone rather than co-operate with other groups representing a broader spectrum of the Tamil population. What we can establish is that by the 1990s the other militant groups have either been decimated or disbanded by the LTTE, or, because of rivalry with the LTTE, have chosen to join the government forces in their fight against this organisation. In December 1986 members of the EPRLF organisation voluntarily left the area after being disbanded by the LTTE in Jaffna. As mentioned they later came back to power with the backing of the Indian army during their occupation. Their rising unpopularity under Indian rule and the fact that many of their soldiers were killed after capture by LTTE at the time of the Indian withdrawal in 1990 have since made them an insignificant group in the contest for Eelam. What is of interest for this study, however, is that many asylum seekers fleeing to the West in 1986 and 1987 were former members of TELO and EPRLF.

The third track to oneness has been the elimination of dissent inside the LTTE itself. Stories told by former members of the organisation, now living in countries like Norway, point to a change in character of the LTTE from around 1985 onwards. The riots of 1977 and 1983 brought a flood of recruits into this and the other militant groups, many of them students both from Jaffna University and the universities in the south. Their main purpose being to provide their people with some kind of armed defence against an external enemy, the choice of which group to join was often a random one. This influx of idealistic youths provided groups with credibility and transformed the LTTE in particular from a marginal group of semi-criminals to an organisation which could claim national support. To many of these educated idealists, however, the internecine killings and the orders to attack civilian targets brought depression and despair. A few embraced the ideology and remained, some raised objections and were killed, and many eventually managed to leave the country and withdrew to a silent position in exile.

While the age of soldiers is going down, as may be seen from reading inscriptions on the tombstones at LTTE's burial places, all signs indicate that the LTTE has become an increasingly authoritarian structure. The most famous inside elimination has been the 'disappearance' in early 1994 of the organisation's deputy leader, Mahattaya, who among Tamil observers is believed to be the only person who could rival the leader Prabhakaran's own position. Two high-ranking LTTE officers, allegedly claiming allegiance to Mahattaya were publicly executed north of Vavuniya in May 1994.[8] Mahattaya himself has not been reported seen and is by most believed to have been killed in silence.

The fourth track to oneness, which it is important to realise belongs in this particular context, is the self-sacrifice of the organisation's own members. This spirit of sacrifice is often associated with two evocative symbols by observers. One is the glass capsule containing cyanide which all soldiers wear around their necks and which is to be used in case of capture. After biting through the glass the poison is swallowed and death, painful but relatively quick, normally follows. The cyanide is by no means a gimmick, it has been used again and again in entrenched positions, as when 15 members captured by the Indian army in 1987 committed suicide on the airfield in Jaffna before they could be transported to detention in the south. The other symbol is the Black Tigers, a suicide commando unit carrying out actions which for themselves have no alternative end to death. Since the day when, in July 1987, Miller, one of LTTE's most celebrated martyrs, drove a van packed with explosives through the gates of the army camp at Nelliady Central College and killed about a hundred soldiers, the Black Tigers have been responsible for a number of spectacular military actions and individual assassinations of political enemies, and have come to epitomise the LTTE's spirit of sacrifice.

This attitude to war has received worldwide attention and, for obvious reasons, has a psychological effect on the Sinhalese community in general and the confronting army in particular. After a battle in Welioya in July 1995, for example, the Sinhalese military spokesman, Brigadier Sarath Munasinghe, said to the press that he was appalled at the number of children killed in the enemy frontline:

'There were young girls and boys in large numbers,' he told Reuters. 'There is no respect of human life on their side. We can't sacrifice human lives like that.' (Reuters 31 July 1995)

As we shall see, to many Tamils in exile the willingness to die tends to redeem the LTTE of their sins. While people may criticise their killings and their tyranny, few are willing to denounce them completely. Many migrants, explicitly or implicitly, take pride in their daring actions and the widespread puzzlement over their recklessness about human life.

As for the LTTE as an organisation, in many respects they remain an enigma. To Tamils themselves the organisation has a mysterious, almost sacred aura of awe and danger; it is not *their* organisation in any meaningful sense of the term, it is a force which rules them; for good and for bad it has become their destiny. One may argue that much is to be learned about the interaction between LTTE and the Tamil people from descriptions of social dynamics in extreme situations like the German concentration camps during the Second World War (e.g. Bettelheim 1991). In spite of the large-scale migration, Tamil Sri Lanka is in many ways a closed society where a new generation is raised under conditions of extreme fear and terror. In the middle of Jaffna town in the 1990–95 period there was what can only be called a concentration camp run by the LTTE, inside which unspeakable events were said to take place. Living in Jaffna you knew what would happen if you raised your voice to object. At the same time, however, this picture is not complete because the presence of the outside enemy

cannot be deleted from people's minds. Somehow we must be able
to include in the picture Bettelheim's point (1991: 139) that in extreme
situations 'heroism can be the highest assertion of individuality'. When
the teenagers line up for training, one must assume it is with a
conviction that what each one of them sacrifices will return with interest
to the population as a corporate whole. This is relevant to the way
Tamils see their own situation: where to fight or to flee has for many
become the one dominant question.

4   MIGRATION TO NORWAY

The social background and internal relationships of Tamil migrants to Norway will be discussed at a later stage. In this chapter I wish to discuss, through a few empirical examples, three general characteristics of this migration. One is its social continuity, the second its present clandestine character and the third its 'nomadic' pattern.

For the social dynamic among Tamil migrants in Norway the fact that migration had already started when the war in Sri Lanka began is significant. In terms of inter-personal relationships what we see is a continuity from one type of migration to another. Despite the fact that Norway has had an immigration ban since 1975, present refugee migration cannot be properly understood without taking earlier work and educational migration into consideration.

For Tamil migration to Norway there are two institutions the importance of which cannot be exaggerated. One is Cey-Nor, a Norwegian fishery project established in the Jaffna area in the late 1960s. With its combined Norwegian and Tamil leadership Cey-Nor was a highly effective channel for communicating an image of the North to the local population in Jaffna. I will let Mr S, one of the first migrants to Norway, tell part of his story. Mr S accidentally met the Norwegian manager of Cey-Nor in Sri Lanka and was promised a job at the project:

When I arrived, the project itself was not yet started, and it turned out there was in fact no job for me. Instead I was assisted by the Norwegian manager in writing letters asking to be accepted as a student in the field of fisheries. In Norway my letter ended up in the office of Findus, the largest fish factory operating in the country. They wrote back to me saying there was no school, but if I wanted a job I should come to Hammerfest, a small town in the administrative district of Finnmark.

In 1971 I left Sri Lanka on a plane headed for Switzerland. From there I hitchhiked through Europe to Denmark. At that time dark people like myself

were not very common, and everywhere I came I received support from people
I met on the road. For example, I travelled to the northern tip of Denmark
in order to take the ferry to Norway. On arrival I found it was too late in
the fall, the ferry had stopped going. Completely broke I was housed, fed
and given ticket money for the long detour through Sweden by a Danish
family. On the coast-liner in which I entered Norway, I met a rowdy bunch
of fishermen going home with their pockets full of money. They took care
of me, took me ashore to drink beer, and when they finally stumbled off the
boat one of them stuffed one thousand Norwegian kroners in my pocket.
My meeting with Scandinavia was indeed a very happy one ...

What is most apparent from this part of Mr S's story is the change in
the context of migration to Europe from the early 1970s to today. To
imagine a Sri Lankan citizen being able to hitchhike from Switzerland
to Norway, with the many border crossings such a project involves,
would today be impossible.

The other Norwegian institution important to migrants are the
Folkehoyskole: these are private high schools that people attend for
one year. For some reason admission to these schools for Third World
students was left as a loophole in the immigration regulations after the
implementation of the immigration ban. Even though potential
students had to present an economic guarantee for living costs, many
young Tamils who would otherwise have tried to go as asylum seekers
found it more safe and in fact less costly to raise this guarantee than
to pay an agent to arrange a 'refugee travel'. When in Norway the
Folkehoyskole students had the possibility of being admitted into the
regular school system and to remain on a temporary visa until their
education was completed. In principle the conditions for holding on
to such temporary visas were very strict and dependent on school results
and educational progression. After 1983, however, Tamils soon realised
that if they dropped out of school, which many of them did, immigration
authorities found it difficult to force them back to Sri Lanka owing
to the civil war situation.

In the school year 1986–87 there were 338 Tamils in the
Folkehoyskole, compared with 286 in 1985–86, 167 in 1984–85 and
100 in 1983–84. These figures appear in a report on the situation of
foreigners within the Norwegian school system (Folkehøgskolerådet
1986).While the number is small, out of a total Tamil population which
in 1987 numbered 1881 according to official statistics, the percentage
is substantial. From a 1990s perspective it is interesting to observe that

what prompted the report were accusations in the media that the schools were 'cynically exploiting' Third World students by accepting them to Norway and then leaving them to an uncertain future. In defence the report points out that:

... pressure from applicants, often through personal appearance or through family and friends, contributes to a situation where schools accept more [foreigners] than they would otherwise have done ... Foreigners come in large numbers, only recruited through family and friends. (p. 7)

During the 1980s the Tamils were by far the single largest group of foreigners admitted to the *Folkehoyskole*. The network mechanism had the interesting consequence of helping to establish a much more decentralised settlement pattern for Tamils than for other immigrant groups in Norway. For the record, there is in my material no indication that Tamils have ever felt exploited by the schools. On the contrary, the liberal policy of school admission helped to establish the understanding of Norway as a basically 'good' country, an understanding gradually changing only in the late 1980s. The frustration which exists in relation to school admission, and it *does* exist, has been directed against the people who arrived and settled before the civil war started and who did so little when young people needed a place to go to. 'I could cry when I think how many could have come and received an education if they only had been told', one young Tamil said when we were discussing the *Folkehoyskole* migration. 'The truth is, these people (the early settlers) never wanted us here. They just wanted a nice little pond for themselves.'

The possibility of obtaining visas as *Folkehoyskole* students remained until 1989 when the same so-called 'criteria of possible return' started to be applied for student visas as they are for ordinary visitors' visas from the Third World. This meant that from then on an application for a student visa would not be granted unless there was reason to believe that the applicant could and would go back after finishing his or her education, something which excluded young Tamils. During the period in which it was available, however, the arrangement was very important for Tamil migration.

Let me return to the Cey-Nor connection through the story of another early migrant. Mr T left for Norway somewhat later than Mr S after a short-term spell of employment at the Cey-Nor project. Through a similar pre-arranged connection to the fish industry he settled as the first Tamil in another northern town, Innby. Through the detailed story of migration to Innby we may see how one kind of migration succeeds another. Mr T explains:

Shortly after I came to Innby, one other Tamil, Mr M from Kankesanthurai, arrived. He had been a sailor on a Norwegian ship. When he felt like settling down he applied to Findus for a job and was sent to the fish factory in Innby. We were the first two.

Mr M soon brought his wife from Sri Lanka. She secured a job and a working permit for one of her sisters who was already engaged to a Mr N. After arrival this sister, therefore, obtained a job and a work permit for her fiancé. Mr M's wife and her sister also obtained a job and a work permit for one of their brothers, and for the husband of a third sister in the family. After marrying, I myself invited two of my sisters to come and work in the factory.

This is how far it got before the immigration ban was implemented in 1975. From then on the securing of a job would no longer help a foreigner obtain a work permit. The *Folkehoyskole*, therefore, became important to bring in new family members, who, according to Mr T, would spend one year at school and pick up the essentials of language before starting to work in the local fish factory.

In 1976 I brought a third sister to Norway through the *Folkehoyskole*. The same year Mr M and his wife obtained a school visa for the wife's sister whose husband was already in Norway. It was difficult now, however, because the candidates for *Folkehoyskole* should really be between 18 and 25 years. To convince the school we had to explain how difficult it was for Tamils in Sri Lanka to obtain an education.

In 1977 I obtained school visas for three cousin children and for one child of the brother of my wife. Mr M did the same for one nephew of Mr N and for one nephew of the husband of M's other sister. In addition two Tamil youths unrelated to the two families found their way to the fish factory through the school system.

In the next few years a period of break-up followed for the small Tamil community. Mr T himself was accepted into advanced technical training and left with his family to settle in another town. Two of his sisters married and moved with their husbands. Mr M and his wife left the country. In the late 1970s M's sister, married to Mr N, died. After a few years two of Mr T's cousin children left to further their education in the southern part of the country. In the early 1980s Mr N's nephew illegally emigrated to Canada.

Despite all this, there has been a continuity until today. From 1983 on, when refugee migration started to gain strength, the process of rebuilding the community around the remaining members of the two families took place. Mr N stayed and soon married again. He is now the senior member of the community. In 1985 one of the younger brothers of his new wife moved in with them after finishing the *Folkehoyskole*. The brother of M's wife also married and two of his wife's nephews settled in Innby after having their asylum applications accepted. On Mr T's side, another nephew and a niece of his wife joined her brother's child after having been accepted as asylum seekers. Mr T's cousin child married a young girl who arrived as an asylum seeker after her application for marriage visa was rejected. Later, two of her cousins also arrived as asylum seekers and settled.

This story illustrates, I think, that despite the criticism raised against them, the earlier Tamil migrant workers have played an important role in helping the accommodation of later asylum seekers. The situation in Innby is not really special for a fishing community in the northern part of Norway. Surprisingly often we find that entrepreneurial individuals, most of them with a work history from the Cey-Nor project, have managed to incorporate a number of close and not so close relations into the local workforce.

BORDERS AND CONTROL

This early migration to Norway is part of a larger pattern of Tamil migration to Western countries. The writer V.I.S. Jayapalan (1991–92: 27) writes:

In the 1970s youths from the middle class constituted the dominating group of émigrés ... This wave of migration started with migration as part-time students and guest-workers to England, but soon spread via Germany and France to the peripheral countries of Europe.

The events of 1983 gave a new impetus to Tamil emigration from Sri Lanka. After this point the individual experiences of travel have common features. Increasingly, migrating has now become not only a passage from one place to another but a consciously planned act of subversion. Where the last checkpoint on the front line has been crossed the person is leaving one field of surveillance only to enter another.

A stay in Colombo, sometimes a very long stay, is always necessary to arrange the next steps. It is a precarious part of the journey. Sri Lankan authorities, for obvious reasons, keep a watch for militant infiltrators. All Tamils without previous residence must be registered at the local police station but even when going by the book life is not secure. At any time one may be stopped at a checkpoint and brought in for questioning. Lodging houses are regularly searched, not only for known individuals but for information: information on arrivals from the other side, on transport, troop movements and rumours. The uncertainty and physical danger of being a Tamil in the Sinhalese south is not the only concern however. It is also imperative not to leave traces. In long-distance telephone calls stories are told about deportations from European countries of people who have stayed too long in Colombo and who are therefore considered safe in their own country by Western immigration authorities: 'Don't get a permanent address', 'If you find a job, don't use your own name.' Here, already, the confluence and overlap of two fields of control, the Sinhala state and the future host government, can be felt.

In many areas of the world there exists a possibility for refugees to become 'official', to register with the UNHCR and wait in transit camps for Western delegations to come and select candidates for resettlement. In Sri Lanka this is not possible. Since they are still inside what is considered to be their own country, displaced Tamils are not, legally speaking, refugees. The two legal options are to apply directly to embassies for a visa that will rarely be granted or to withdraw to one of the squalid camps on the outskirts of the combat zone. The third possibility, the one so many thousands have chosen in the last ten years, is the illegal path, the journey outside, between and through bordered spaces achieved by breaking international regulations. Here it all depends on the individual and the guide they have chosen to give their trust and money to. The reason for its popularity is perhaps not only because alternatives are so few; the very act of going is a posing of agency against outside forces of restraint. In choosing this path, with its perils and its problems, the refugees become the 'doers' rather than the 'done to' and, like the Iranians in illegal transit described by Farmanfarmaian (1992), they have through this '... maintained a sub-systemic freedom and mobility that facilitated the exercise of their subjectivity, constantly challenging, negotiating and rupturing the systemic inscriptions that were aimed at containing them' (p. 92).

This adventure is of a different quality to that of the earlier work migration. Compare the following excerpts from two letters provided by an informant with the happy story of Mr S's hitchhiking experience through Europe:

14.4.92

God bless you.
Dear little brother, sister-in-law and son,
We started our foreign travel April fifth. We are in Yugoslavia now. Little brother. There was no time to send you a fax from Colombo. No one knew we were going.

Little brother. We are in Yugoslavia now. They first said we would be sent to Austria, the 14th or 15th we were told. Now we do not know if we will be sent to Austria or Italy. There are some problems with the route they say. If we land in Austria you can come and collect us, can you not? Call soon.

Your sister

It now seems we will be sent to Austria after all.

26.6.92

Dear sister-in-law, little brother and son,
May God bless you with good health.
We are now in Germany. We were never sent to Austria. We are well here. Little brother. It will be difficult to come to Norway. There are so many borders to cross. If I am lucky I will come some time later. You don't need to worry about us. God is with us. I am sorry you had to borrow money to get me out of the country.

Dear sister-in-law. Take care of little brother. My *Thali Kodi* [marriage necklace] is pawned, it is so sad. I received only 150 Mark. Now I have nothing. I don't know what to do.

Little brother. I will not ask you for money. Try to get back the money you paid to bring me to Norway. Send something to mother if you can.

I have no more news. May God be with you.

Sister

The key factor which makes the journey possible is a flexible information network which tells you how to make the first step and how to obtain the necessary expertise along the way. The general information is easily available, floating around in Wellawatte, the Tamil part of Colombo, or in any cheap hostel where displaced people are waiting for an opening.

The procedures to follow are reported back by the ones who went ahead: 'When you arrive in Kathmandu, you should buy a ticket to Guyana, transiting in Frankfurt. While the plane is fuelling there you can disembark ...'

What we see here is a confrontation between two concepts of geography. As opposed to the colonised space of the modern political map, bringing together heterogeneous localities into 'states' of epistemological representation (de Certeau 1984), asylum seekers rely on a revival of pre-modern spatial practices where named places appear as no more than memoranda prescribing actions. As against the map, constituted by bounded places in which to display the products of disciplinary knowledge, the narratives of contemporary migrants resemble mediaeval itineraries, manuals of spatialising operations indicating where to stop, how to proceed, which dangers to prepare for. Information is often surprisingly detailed. You will meet Tamils in Colombo who know they will have more difficulties if they end their journey at one Norwegian police station rather than another. Detailed knowledge becomes a vital possession. Without travel skills remembering when to do what and in which order enhances the possibility of success. If going without a guide you should be able to draw the transit scenes without thinking: 'When you enter the hall you must first reclaim your luggage at the barrier to the left. Remember, don't look confused, just bring it to the new security clearance at the other side of the hall ...'

In the 1990s the journey almost always requires assistance from relatives or professional 'agents'. For a long time the Singapore-Bangkok connection was among the most popular. Going to Singapore, where Sri Lankans can go without a visa, you do not leave the transit hall on arrival. Instead you arrange for a friend or relative in a European country to come to Singapore, buy one return ticket on a plane to Europe and one ticket to Bangkok, check in on the Europe ticket and meet you inside transit. There you take his or her boarding card for Europe while your relative goes on to Bangkok and flies back on a later plane.

Keeping to friends or relatives is always preferable. For one, it is less costly. While you can get a ticket from Colombo to Norway for one thousand US dollars, an agent might charge you twelve, fifteen or even twenty thousand. If you don't know someone who is already in the West and can help with the fare, a trip will involve the entire family: borrowing, selling land, accepting promises of future returns. What is more, while agents do have a heroic status they cannot be trusted. Their secret knowledge and capacity for command will put you at their mercy. Men hesitate to let their daughters and fiancées go with them. A ten-day journey also means ten nights. What goes on when darkness comes and there is nothing to do but wait? Stories circulate about Tamil girls being raped and dumped in brothels in Karachi, about the group of one hundred people left without papers at the airport in Tirana and about the three men from Nirveli found dead on the Czech border. What happened to them?

The problem is that agents are the only ones who possess the knowledge and are able not only to plan but also to assess reports, interpret rumours and make alternative plans. If an agent is caught or a group turned away at a European border the news will be back in Colombo by the end of the day. New routes will be discussed and prices negotiated. Before Rajah's grandmother, who was more than 70 years old, was apprehended at the German border and sent home to be detained for two weeks in the basement of Katunayake Airport, she had spent ten days touring the Far East and one week transiting in West Africa. Routes must be kept multiple, complex and flexible. If one point is blocked you must be fluid and adapt or you may use the rigidity of control against itself. Access to Norway, for example, is very difficult. Norwegian police check papers for outbound flights at the airport in Copenhagen. The Nordic Passport Agreement places the responsibility for border controls on the first country of landing in Scandinavia, and anyone caught on the plane coming from Copenhagen will be sent back to Denmark. However, nothing is impossible. What you need after crossing the German border into Denmark is a relative going the opposite way, from Norway to Denmark. When you meet, you take his used ticket, report to the Danish police that you are seeking asylum and after some questioning admit that you did arrive from Norway. In a few weeks' time you will be sent north according to the passport agreement.

When approaching the international airport in Colombo, however, such subtleties are a long way away. The long journey is ahead of you and requires concentration at every step; passing through the airport doors means entering an arena of total authority. Every official from the ticket agent to the stewardess on board embodies this authority, making judgements not only on your papers but also on your behaviour and possessions. The manipulation of the Western image of refugees as dressed in rags and looking destitute therefore becomes an essential part of preparations for the journey. A suit and white shirt is one possibility, jeans and leather jacket another. Western commodities must be used as signals to make officials relax. Whatever preparations the traveller is never in control, however, and passport examinations are the most critical of all critical moments. In order to leave Tamil refugees *must* necessarily break the rules on the use of passports, this abuse being a radical appropriation of the Western privilege of geographical mobility. Western passports are normally obtained from relatives already in exile or recirculated among refugees who are leaving one country to start the process over in another. Sometimes the photo will be changed, sometimes the passport may be used as it is, since to most European officials one Tamil looks much like another. This is only, however, a temporary protection and before the last landing both passport and ticket must disappear. Going to the toilet, tearing up the pages and flushing them down the drain is the last ritual act: it ensures protection of the route, the ones who will follow, and oneself against deportation to some country that has been traversed along the way. It is also the ultimate point of no return; if you go back now you do it as a prisoner. Stories are told about this moment: stories of endless joy to have come this far, of people drinking spirits for the first time to ease their nerves, of people throwing up from fear of what lies ahead, of what must surely lie ahead: guards, questioning and perhaps detention. 'I had never even been allowed to go to the temple alone', one girl told me. 'And there I was, all on my own, about to land in a country of which I knew nothing, to marry a man I had never met, without permission to set foot on the ground. I saw the lights from the city below and I would have given anything, pledged anything to be able to go back!'

THE LONG WAY TO NORWAY

Because of the internationally accepted principle that a refugee should seek protection in the first country in which he or she arrives, information about travel routes normally belongs to the most closely guarded part of a person's life. While to an anthropologist a refugee may speak freely about family relations, marriage problems and, if personally acquainted, also about political opinions, questions about how and by which route a person managed to arrive in Norway always tend to bring a certain uneasiness into the situation. What is clear is that from the perspective of a Tamil migrant certain places rank higher as migration destinations than others; Canada, England and New Zealand are probably the top three, Denmark, Norway and Switzerland are within group two, and countries like Germany, Italy and Greece are further down the list. What is also clear is that going directly from Sri Lanka to the country where you wish to settle is not always, not even *normally*, possible. In fact, since states favoured by asylum seekers tend to apply a strict immigration regime, almost invariably the countries with the highest 'rankings' are the least accessible. Norway, for example, is in air traffic contact with Sri Lanka only through transit cities where passports and visas are liable to be checked, so the possibility of being sent home involuntarily to Sri Lanka is therefore present. Furtermore, a stopover in one of these cities is enough, under the current interpretation of legal principles, to send the person back from the final destination to the transit country. To the refugee this situation has two consecutive consequences. One is that how close to your final destination you are able to travel directly from Sri Lanka is a question of economic resources. With enough money it *is* possible to buy papers and tickets which can take you to Canada or Norway; to most, however, the only way is to travel step by step; to go somewhere less costly first and then take it from there, one border at a time. The nine Sinhalese and eight Tamils found suffocated in the back of a container truck in Hungary in July 1995 after crossing the border from Romania is an indication of the dangers involved in this migration.[1] The other consequence is that, when finally arriving at their destination, many migrants will in fact have violated the condition of their stay, a situation that I will consider more closely in the next chapter.

As one illustration of this 'indeterminate' migration, I will reconstruct one documented case of migration to Norway based on a collection of letters. The letters are all written by one young man, Mohan, to his fiancée, Chandra, during a six-year period while he is in Europe with her two brothers, Sittu and Raj, his own cousins. What these letters illustrate is how long the road of migration often is and how problematic space, borders and mobility often become in migrants' efforts to maintain a sphere of social intimacy. However, by implication, they also show the resources of the international family network in

terms of information and practical assistance, invaluable in the adaptation
to a sort of refugee nomadism. The story of migration starts in 1980
when Sittu, the older of the two brothers, leaves Sri Lanka to settle
in Germany. What their original connection to Norway was is not
known, but as we see from Mohan's first letter, which was sent shortly
after his and Raj's arrival in Switzerland, at least some of the main
characters in this story had already planned to go to Norway in 1981:

July 1981

Switzerland

Dear Chandra,
Thank you for the birthday card you sent me. I will be here until 1985–86.
During this time I only have your letters to support me.
    Sittu and I often talk on the telephone. Poor man, he is living all alone in
Germany. In two months he will be leaving for Norway. I will also go there,
but not yet. There is no reason for that now ...

    Your Mohan

Only a short time after sending his letter Mohan and Raj decide to go
to Germany to join Sittu. However, they find that Sittu is about to
move on to France because of visa problems in Germany. Mohan and
Raj are able to find illegal work. Mohan does not like it in Germany
and the possibility of going to Norway tempts him, particularly after
one of his uncles has now gone ahead and another is about to try:

January 1982

Hamburg

To my dear Chandra,
I hope you are well. It is now seven months after my arrival in Germany ...
The day I received your letter Sittu left for France. It is sad, but what could
he do without a visa?
You asked what we are doing here. Raj and I work 1–2 days a week in a
store. When we don't work we watch Tamil video films and listen to music.
I don't intend to stay that long in Germany. Vanni-uncle ['our uncle from
Vanni'] wrote he was going to Norway. When was not decided yet. Colombo-
uncle ['our uncle from Colombo'] came there only 3–4 months ago. He told
me many details. I will surely go there some time if he can help. I will write
you about this later.

    Mohan

The next letter, written 23 months later, is sent from France where Mohan and Raj have now gone to join Sittu. One reason Mohan has not been able to write sooner is that the two of them were imprisoned by the French authorities after crossing the border illegally. At the time of writing Mohan has found work in France and sends money with the letter which he asks Chandra to forward to his parents. Both in this and the following letter he describes the situation in France as 'difficult' without elaborating. In a section which is not quoted he informs Chandra that her brother Sittu will get a visa to Norway 'in two days'. Mohan would like to visit home, which is one reason he too contemplates settling in Norway. We see how a decision is about to take form:

December 1983

France

To my forever beloved Chandra,
I am well ... I do not receive any letters from my family. I don't know why ... The reason I am thinking about going to Norway is to be able to go home soon. If you get a student visa it is no problem going home to Sri Lanka. The first 6–8 months you have to learn the language. In this period it is not possible to send any money home.

Your lover Mohan

March 1984

France

To my dear Chandra,
I will try to go to Norway now. The situation in France is becoming even more difficult ... Within Europe the situation in Norway is now better than in other countries. I fear it may become more difficult also there in the future.

Your Mohan

However, by January the next year, ten months later, Mohan is still in France. Sittu has been denied visa to Norway and has now gone to Germany from where he will try to make his way to Canada. Raj is in France with Mohan, but their relationship is no longer very good, Mohan tells Chandra. Raj is therefore contemplating going to Holland. The possibility of Mohan's younger sister Sitha going to Norway is now introduced:

January 1985

France

My dear Chandra,
Sittu is still in Germany, and trying to find a way to go to Canada. Raj is thinking about going to Holland, but nothing is decided yet.
I think Sitha will be going to Norway the coming August. Uncle and aunt came here from Norway and stayed for one week. They said they would apply for school admission for Sitha.

My love
Mohan

In June of the same year no one has moved and Mohan's sister, Sitha, has difficulties obtaining a visa to Norway. Chandra has now mentioned the possibility of going to Norway herself in the future, but Mohan wants to await his application for foreign national residence:

June 1985, France

To my dear Chandra,
Sitha will have problems getting a visa they say ...
It is good that you will come either here or to Norway. Sittu also wants this. Can you try to go to Norway in August 1986? Aunt and uncle in Norway will help with this if we ask them. I want to see what happens with my application here before I go there.

Your Mohan

The next letter is written ten months later. It is now more than six years since Mohan left Sri Lanka and since the two of them last saw each other. It is clear from Mohan's writing that this causes some strain in their relationship. It seems that Chandra has stated her wish for him to come and visit her. In passages which are not quoted Mohan informs Chandra that he has no papers with which it would be possible to travel to Sri Lanka. He discusses the possibility of their meeting in India. He says that he has applied for a visa to India, but that his application has been denied. He concludes that it will be too dangerous for him to go illegally.

Sittu has now managed to go to Canada and one of their uncles has followed suit. Mohan has asked Chandra if she thinks he should try to join Sittu there. Chandra, it seems, rather wants him to go to Norway. Mohan enquires about his sister Sitha's prospects of going. He also asks Chandra to find a bride for Sittu:

April 1986, France

To my dear,
I talked to Sittu on the phone yesterday. He said uncle had come to New York and will try to pass into Canada in 2–3 days. Please inform your family about this.

I too had planned to go to Canada, but I understand from your letter you don't want me to. Please tell me your feelings. I do not know if it is possible to get asylum in Norway. In Canada there are no problems.

I received a letter from home. They did not tell me if Sitha got a visa to Norway or not. Tell me what you decide about your own travel to Norway.

The couple XX will soon come to India to go from there to Canada. You should send a bride for Sittu with them. Try to choose a suitable sister-in-law for yourself and ask them to take her with them. It costs a lot of money but it is safe to go from India. It is the safest way for everybody. Do this if you can. Do not care about dowry, the important thing is that she is as kind as you.

Your Mohan

Then in July the same year we suddenly find Mohan in Norway where his sister Sitha has now already been living for some time. What stands forth from the correspondence is how life is now about to go in separate ways for the two lovers. Mohan tries to convince Chandra to come to him in Norway since it is not possible for him to visit Sri Lanka. Chandra, however, decides not to leave her studies at the university in Jaffna:

July 1986, Norway

Dear Chandra,
We are all well, and hope that you are too. We suddenly left for Norway and arrived here without any problems. Sitha is well. I met her after a long time. She is now working.

The reason I came to Norway is that it will be better for you. You can continue your education, and it will be easier for you to come here. You may prepare to come in 1987.

I will have to wait 1/2–1 year to get an answer to my application here. I could not travel from France in a legal way. Therefore I do not have my passport with me. Because of this it is impossible for me to visit you at home.

Your Mohan

December 1986

Norway

To my dear Chandra,
What to do if in two or three years it will be more difficult to come to Norway?
There are signs saying this may happen. I already told you this, but you don't
seem to care. If they [Chandra's family] will not let you go, you will have to
study and find a job there. I will stay here. Life will have to continue by letter.
I cannot go to Sri Lanka. I have told you it is impossible, I don't have a passport.

Mohan

Chandra's or her parents' decision not to leave Sri Lanka is hard for
Mohan. In his last letter his frustration with their separate lives and
with exile existence in general clearly shows through. At this point,
a little more than seven years after leaving Sri Lanka, his parents are
in India, Sittu is in Canada with one of their uncles, Raj is still in France
and Chandra and he remain separated. Mohan, as he says, 'does not
want to go back and does not want to stay abroad':

September 1987

Norway

To my dear Chandra,
I received your letter. Even if I had planned to answer immediately, it was
not possible for me. I am not able to write as much as I did earlier. That is
the way things have become.
    The people in Canada are well. My parents and my brothers and sisters
have reached India after going through great difficulties. Shall we never find
peace in this life?
    Uncle and aunt are well. It is only my family which has problems. Sitha's
[their cousin in Norway] birthday party was taped on video. I have a copy.
Tell me if you would like me to send it.
    The problems in Sri Lanka do not seem to end. My family has no hopes
any more. My little brother and sister will go to school in Madras. My dear,
I do not want to go back to Sri Lanka, I do not want to stay abroad any more
either.

Your loving Mohan

Let me tell you that the couple in question were, in the end, married
in Norway. After a few years they travelled to Canada to reunite with
Sittu and that part of their family. To conclude this story, let me include

here a last letter written to Mohan from his brother-in-law Sittu before Chandra came to Norway. With its emphasis on family unification, immigrant status and possibilities of work, all ideals which will be discussed in the next chapters, it may stand as an illustration of the hope of an end to a long journey:

May 1989, Canada

To Mohan, Sitha and the others. I am well.

Mohan, from what I have seen through these last years, it will be best if all in our families come here. It is possible to get a permanent visa here, and considering the future of the children nowhere will be better. If you come Sitha can come. You don't have to come illegally. If you come I can guarantee for mother, father and Chandra. If I guarantee for Chandra and she gets a visa she can guarantee for you. Then you can come as an immigrant. If you come you can guarantee for others in your family and take them here. One should act while the possibility is there.

I understand you have a good life in Norway, but here one can stay for life and build a future. When you are here you can buy a house. If you take a job you will have no problems. You can do anything here! Please think about it and write me.

Sittu

5 FIELDS AND BOUNDARIES

In this and the next two chapters I will look at certain aspects of exile life as seen from the viewpoint of refugees living in Norway. In particular I shall try to approach the paradoxes and contradictions which characterise the exile situation, but first I will indicate how I intend to do this.

In our meetings with refugees we face a situation where the lives of the people who choose to tell, or *not* to tell, their stories to us are often dominated by personal traumas and individual worries. Stranded in countries that they often did not choose to go to, among people they often do not know, they are left with the thoughts of those who remain with little chance of doing anything to help.

This pain which many refugees carry is important to recognise. It is not, however, what I focus on here, and for two reasons. One is, precisely, that to the majority of Tamil refugees the suffering which continues in Sri Lanka is more important than their own individual problems. The agony which always lies at the heart of refugee situations is, at least in this case, primarily the agony of others – not their own. The other reason is that the individual experience of suffering, to be understood, should be related to the society of which the individual is a part and to the wider political processes determining the individual's possibilities of meaningful life projects (Scheper-Hughes 1992, 1994). This, in my experience, is in fact what Tamils themselves do, and their life in Norway exhibits a determination in this respect which would make a focus on their private situations a distortion. Their efforts are directed towards making sense of what is going on in Sri Lanka and their own position with respect to these events. The terms in which individuals see themselves as part of their society of origin will be discussed in later chapters. Here I concentrate on what it means to be located at a distance from this society.

TIME AND SPACE

Even less than the study of relatively stable communities, the study of migration may settle with general accounts of traditions, institutions or frameworks of social organisation. There is a need to understand how migrants, as positioned individuals, give meaning to their situation in a divided but interconnected world. In trying this, I go a long way in accepting Barth's (1993) general methodological dogma that 'a critical step ... must be to discover the meanings, for the actors themselves, of their institutions and concepts' (p. 97). That is, we need to base our analysis on social and conceptual structures as these appear to individuals in their specific social locations.

Much has been said about refugees' relationship to time. In studies of Vietnamese refugees several authors have noted that people tend to compartmentalise time into three distinct phases – past, present and future – and have emphasised the need for analytical attention to the cognitive ordering of, and selective focus on, time variables in strategies of coping with exile. Beiser (1987) observes that '[d]uring periods of acute stress, refugees seem to focus on the present to the relative exclusion of past and future' (p. 437). Chan and Loveridge (1987), on the other hand, found that waiting in camps made refugees turned towards the past, while the present circumstances of camp life seemed to be of 'minimal significance' (p. 750). Knudsen (1990:127), while arguing for a cognitive model which develops through the chaining of elements from all three phases simultaneously, found his camp informants to be mainly oriented towards the future.

No doubt, on a psychological level the problem of integrating past and future is also fundamental to Tamil refugees. In particular, Beiser's understanding of the first exile years as a 'psychological moratorium' where an active effort is made not to let traumatic experiences of the past intrude the projections of tomorrow seems to me to be important. This may be one reason why past individual circumstances and personal sorrow are actively avoided as themes of conversation outside the immediate family.

At the same time, there are reasons not to overemphasise this time framing. In my understanding, which is social rather than psychological, Tamil exile life is more than anything characterised by 'simultaneity', moving not from home/past to exile/future through a journey in time but staying within a parallel time frame separated by distance and borders. One aspect of this is the interchange of information. While the situation in Sri Lanka seems to be of little interest to the Norwegian media, the whereabouts of Tamil refugees in Norway, exoticised through stories of human trafficking and political terrorism taken from the Norwegian tabloid press (Fuglerud 1997), has been given wide coverage in Sri Lanka. In the Anglo-Sinhala Colombo papers arriving in Oslo every Monday afternoon, this coverage has been twisted, systematically emphasising the Norwegian government's wish to deport refugees because of their subversive activity. Sometimes stories are outright false. Satchi, in Norway for 26 years and one of the few to speak freely against the new Tamil rulers from his exile position, suddenly found his name spread across a full-page story in the *Sunday Times*[1] entitled 'Tigers' narco connection', claiming that he had been raising 10,000 dollars for LTTE every month in Norway. 'This is what it took for me to lose my country', he commented to me. 'I will be arrested the moment I set my foot on the ground in Colombo. After going back and forth for more than twenty years, this is all it took. I can no longer go back.'

Tamil newspapers also cover the refugee scene, however. On several occasions the visits to guerrilla-controlled areas by Norwegian immigration officers, and their talks with political leaders in the LTTE, have been extensively reported on by Jaffna newspapers which are spread to and scrutinised by the exile population. To many refugees these stories are the main source of information on the Norwegian policy which decides their future. Home and exile refuse to be separated.

There is a general point here. The focus on refugees' cognitive ordering of time has often happened at the expense of their relationship to space. This is probably because time and space have tended to be conceptualised as separate and opposite dimensions. Time has been thought of as the matter from which history is made while space has the connotation of stasis; the neutral setting for time to happen. This perspective accords with the viewpoint of classical Newtonian physics. Here objects exist prior to their interaction, as does space, the arena for objects and interaction. In modern physics, on the other hand, basic ontological categories like time and space are not defined because they are seen as not having an existence in their own right. Rather, the underlying reality is seen as consisting of a space–time depending on the *interrelations* of objects. This conceptual development should be drawn upon to see that the space in which humans live and move is constituted by interrelations. Migrants find themselves within a complex web of domination and subordination, of solidarity and co-operation, within what Massey (1993) calls a 'power-geometry'.

Indeed, the first task that the refugee must accomplish is to reorient himself within this web. In the first phase after arrival the alterity of exile is often experienced in a very concrete way through the difference in physical environment. A more radical change in climate and nature than that between Sri Lanka and Norway is difficult to imagine and if one is going directly the journey may be made in less than twelve hours. One Tamil lady explained to me how, arriving in the middle of winter with the snowdrifts high against the houses, she believed that people in this part of the world lived in underground caves. A refugee counsellor in the northern part of the country told me how a young Tamil boy due to be settled in the township where she worked had desperately clung on to the aeroplane steps, refusing to come with her into town. Seeing the barren, snow-covered environment he was convinced he was being banished to somewhere outside human habitation.

These illustrations point to something more than initial confusion, they reflect a bodily experience of external existence. Since the early 1980s the politico-military situation in Sri Lanka has caused men and women of fighting age to be given priority by their families for the costly flight. The fact that nearly all Tamil refugees are scattered members of *one* generation is important to the understanding of exile dynamics; their social points of reference are elsewhere.[2] What will be said about exile networks below does not change the fact that most refugees lead a particularised and often very lonely life. In terms of self-identity, exile companionship and social interaction abroad cannot replace the individual's position within his own kindred. This interaction, the fragile redefinition of relationships, is instead itself an indication that the individual is re-placed on the outside of his own group. In exile, relationships are entered which would never take place at home but they are fraught with suspicion and rarely develop beyond a certain level. The situation at home, and the individual's position with regard to this situation, is always present. When he was moving to another town I asked Sri, a moderate LTTE supporter, how he would go about getting acquainted if he met a fellow countryman at his new working place. He answered:

I will begin by asking him if he has any news from home, that is our standard opening. Then I will ask him what he thinks about this or that of the recent development in Sri Lanka. If I understand he supports the movement I may invite him home. If he criticises the Tigers but is basically neutral, we may keep on talking at work. I am not a fanatic, I don't mind that. If I understand he is a member of one of the other groups, however, I will break off. I don't want to socialise with traitors.

Between 'movement' and 'non-movement' people these feelings are mutual. In dealing with fellow countrymen there is always the possibility that actions in Norway will have consequences in Sri Lanka. Tamil refugees are not fleeing a common enemy, the violence is within as much as on the outside. 'They are here, don't speak', newcomers will be informed upon arrival. 'LTTE is here, I cannot speak', informants will say, even when no one is around. From the late 1980s claims have regularly been made that one way in which the LTTE has controlled the flow of information to the Western world in order to provide their fight with national legitimacy is by reminding refugees that they have relatives left in Jaffna under LTTE 'guardianship'. Even Wilson, a founding member of the LTTE who was permitted to leave the organisation after a dramatic escape from Batticaloa prison in the early 1980s, found that after finally obtaining a visitor's visa for his mother she was being held back by his former friends in Jaffna. 'They just want to remind me that they know where I am', he said to me. 'They are afraid that after ten years in Norway I may be tempted to write a book or something.' In fact, from 1990 this effort to execute control beyond their own borders has been institutionalised through a very strict exit control in the Tamil areas of Sri Lanka, which includes the obligatory signing of a 'contract' by a guarantor staying behind. This person, who should be under 55 years of age, will be held responsible if the émigré settles permanently abroad without permission or in any way acts against 'national interests' as defined by the LTTE. In this respect the simultaneity of home and exile is very concrete and apparent.

In individuals' relationship to Norwegian authorities, on the other hand, this simultaneity tends to be interiorised. In several of his works Knudsen (1988, 1990) has drawn attention to the way in which Vietnamese refugees have been forced to construct and present life stories which secure future rights in host countries, turning self-presentation and control over biographical information into critical problems. To the Vietnamese, however, this situation has been limited to the period in transit camps. Having been accepted into Norway as part of an international agreement they cannot be sent back and their legal status secures their reunion with the immediate family. The asylum situation, on the other hand, is characterised by a lasting insecurity. As already indicated, in Norway many Tamil refugees have in fact violated the 'first-country' regulation on their way. To remain in Norway they must make up a story and stick to it. With the increasing emphasis on immigration control, from the 1990s there has been in principle no time limit on the revocation of a legal status if it is found that false information has been given; there is no question of putting the difficulties of flight behind. This situation increases not only a minimisation of interaction with Norwegians in general, and Norwegian authorities in particular, but also a sceptical reserve towards fellow countrymen. The idea that Tamils in exile tend to give each other away is part of the current self-understanding, a situation which prevents a communicative sharing of life histories. Most of my informants asked me not to tell their stories to other Tamils. One person asked me to keep secret the fact that he was receiving welfare money on two separate identities, not because he feared I might report him to the authorities but because if I told other Tamils *they* would report him. 'Tamils cannot stand seeing someone getting something for free', was his explanation. Another man asked me to take care of his passport when he was kicked out by his wife and had to stay with friends for some time. 'You cannot trust Tamils when it comes to passports', was his laconic comment. This understanding, it should be observed, is not without a basis in actual experience. When the possibility of sending home Tamil asylum seekers came up for renewed discussion in 1994, a frenzy broke out in one of the small northern settlements. It incited people to go to the police on their own initiative and provide what little information they had about their neighbours. Within a few days local immigration authorities were able to establish that, of the 120 Tamils resident in the village, more than 40 had been living in Switzerland before coming to Norway. Refugees become conscious of the role of contingency in history and therefore do what they can to cover their tracks. 'We all lie to each other', one informant said to me.

We lie not only about the routes we came and about our political background, but about where we come from, about our families, the number of brothers and sisters, where they stay, about anything. Lying is our only security. Even if we know that others are lying and they know that we are, we don't want to be caught telling the truth ...

There is reason to believe that this situation may carry consequences in terms of self-identity. In Gidden's's interpretation of the concept (1991), self-identity is 'what the individual is conscious "of" in the term "self-consciousness" ' (p. 52). It is about gaining a sense of who one is through an intersubjectively founded story of how one has become and where one is going. Self-identity, therefore, requires the communicative sustaining of a biographical narrative which makes a continuous, reflexive self-understanding possible. 'Alienation' (*fremmedgjøring*) is a term often used by refugees themselves to describe their situation. To a non-professional observer of the human mind, a lack of 'biographical continuity' does seem to be a problem within the refugee population, especially among the very young, often expressing itself as a kind of paralysed non-activity and the inability to make clear, even to himself or herself, the series of decisions and events which led them into exile.

This aspect of the exile situation connects to larger configurations within Tamil cosmology. The dichotomy of 'inside' (*akam*) and 'outside' (*puram*) is a basic theme in Tamil art and ritual. We find it in the old Cankam poetry where the contrast between *akam* interior, kin, settlement, well-matchedness, and *puram* exterior, non-kin, uninhabited areas, ill-matchedness, is linked to two separate codes of conduct conceptualised as 'love' and 'war' (Ramanujan 1985). We also find it in a variety of rituals aiming to establish and maintain social and divine order, fighting the evil, disrupting forces of uninhabited areas like deserts and jungles (Pfaffenberger 1982, Tanaka 1991). Before discovering the rituals which make orderly living possible, it is believed, people led unhappy lives dominated by illness, fighting, infertility and poverty. Breaking or moving out of the reach of rituals securing this order makes a person susceptible to *tosam*, deep, afflicting disorders of the body's natural harmony. What needs to be stressed in this context is the inherent social character of *tosam*. The breaking or circumventing of ritual rules is not a question between a person and divine forces alone. It is by putting oneself outside the social context in which cosmological principles are embedded that one may inflict *tosam* upon oneself. Daniel (1989) has captured this essential point in his analysis of suicide among internal Tamil migrants in Sri Lanka in terms of *tanimai tosam* – 'aloneness disorder'. Claiming that 'aloneness' is a culture-specific and 'darkly experienced' (p. 76) state of being, he points out that:

Paradoxically, 'aloneness' is not being alone, in the strict sense. It is being disconnected from other human beings with whom one ought to be connected. The corollary of such disconnectedness is finding oneself in the company of undesirable entities, abnormal persons and powers. The social bonds and one's bondedness with the social prevents the intrusion into society and the socialized self of such 'alien' persons and powers. (p. 78)

This vulnerability of the disconnected individual is an underlying theme of exile life. In the fall of 1995 in Indian and Sri Lankan temples Hindu gods started drinking milk fed to them in spoonfuls by devotees, leading to milk shortage in large parts of South Asia.[3] Being understood as a sign of grace and protection, the feeding procedure was also tried at the small improvised temple in Oslo (see next chapter). The fact that it did not work was attributed by some to the Tamil community's moral decay in inauspicious surroundings. This marginal position is the theme of one of the few, and certainly one of the best, literary works produced by a Tamil writer in Norway, the short story, 'Chekku Madu' (literally, 'the Oil-mill Oxen'), written by the poet V.I.S. Jayapalan.[4] The story is about Kumaran, a former student from the prestigious University of Peradeniya who ends up slaving over a dishwashing machine in a restaurant in Oslo, which to Kumaran is a live being with which he communicates. While lonely and suffering, waiting for an opportunity to marry his boyhood sweetheart, Kamali, who is now in India, Kumaran is attacked by a malevolent spirit, a *pey*, which takes up residence in the kitchen of his cheap lodging:

Every time he returned to his room he found dirty, smelling plates in the corner of the kitchen. Every night the *pey* disturbed him by throwing kitchen utensils around the house. In the mornings, however, there was nothing on the floor.

In the text Kumaran's work in the restaurant is an emblematic expression of Tamil migrants' social devaluation in Norway:

When the owner of the restaurant learned that the well-built jobseeker was a Tamil, he immediately understood that he was the right man for the dishwashing machine. The machine, with its long-standing relationship to

Tamils, spoke Tamil. Kumaran, on the other hand, served the machine loyally and fulfilled its wishes even before they were uttered.

Through Kumaran's assurances that he who cleans the dishes of others must be trusted to maintain his own cleanliness, the reader is led to understand that his position at the lower end of the economic ladder is precisely the problem, as cleaning leftovers from others is the most demeaning work according to traditional Hindu thinking:

Once a guest came on a surprising visit. The guest, a friend from the university, made Kumaran angry when he took the side of the *pey* as soon as he entered. He suggested that the one who piled the dirty dishes in the corner was not the spirit but Kumaran himself.

'How can you say that I don't clean my own plates, I who wash dishes for the whole of Oslo?'

Kumaran chased him out.

For Kumaran the *pey*'s attack is made more serious by the fact that in Norway he has no access to ritual purification and no family around to protect him. It is his location outside ritually ordered space which makes him vulnerable to attacks:

Kanagamma [Kumaran's mother] and Kamali became very upset when they heard about Kumaran's situation, and they sent him a protective thread to tie around his wrist and some holy ash from the Murugan temple in Madras. This was first-aid protection. They also wrote that they would go as pilgrims to the most important temples in Tamil Nadu to pray for Kumaran's protection.

The Indian – as opposed to Sri Lankan – origin of the sacred remedies is of some interest in the story. It serves to pose the opposite forces of auspiciousness and inauspiciousness dramatically against each other:

Kumaran, being an average Sri Lankan Tamil, looked upon himself as superior in most respects. Only with regard to religion and Tamil culture was he willing to admit the superiority of Tamil Nadu. That the things he received from his mother and Kamali were sent from there made him very happy. Having tied the thread around his wrist he challenged the pey:

'Come now if you dare!'

The evil spirit did not show for a few days, but the night after he had written to tell about the improvement the trouble started again. In addition to the usual noise of dishes thrown on the floor, the *pey* now started talking to him in a low secretive voice. Kumaran started to shiver when he realised that just as malaria can become resistant to medicine the *pey* had become immune to the sacred remedies.

'Chekku Madu' amounts to an interpretation of the meeting with the West in cultural terms. *Peys* are attracted to pollution (*tudakku*), in particular that kind of pollution which results from specific acts or conditions. To draw a parallel, one of the main 'conditions' which attract *peys* is childbirth, and the elaborate rituals which are traditionally performed on the fifth day after delivery (*kottipey kalippu*) are designed to lure away the *pey* from the mother. Here the midwife prepares a 'meal' of all elements considered polluting in the delivery situation for the *pey* and brings it to a desolate place where, wrapped in a bundle, it is placed in a tree. She then marks out a space around the tree by drawing a circle around it with a knife, thus fencing in the *pey* inside this area.

Though different, it is possible to argue that these situations do rest upon the same logic. As observed by Marglin (1977), in Indian cosmology what we may call 'act pollution' is fundamentally connected to a breakdown of the boundaries which uphold physical or social wholeness. In the same way that childbirth implies an 'opening' of the body, migration means exposing the social body to dangerous influences from the outside. This understanding is supported by the thorough body-cleansing rituals which many migrants undertake on a regular basis and the protective quality attributed to Tamil food. However, Marglin's argument is more complex than what has been outlined, because pollution as a result of boundary transgression is always relative to social hierarchy. In other words, the danger of pollution varies according to the position from which one faces the outside. This complexity is of importance in the present context because what migrants fear, I will argue, is to be placed in a position of submission *vis-à-vis* Norwegian society. This argument will be continued in Chapter 7.

FIELDS AND NETWORKS

In one of his works Fredrik Barth (1978) has pointed out the, perhaps obvious, fact that scale is an important aspect of all social interaction. 'Scale', the question of size and numbers in social systems, is different from the micro-macro hierarchy. The study of local communities is different from the study of small-scale systems and the study of large-scale systems is different from the study of interconnections between local communities. Scale is a property of systems within which inter-action takes place.

The reason for pointing this out here is that migration makes it difficult to delimit the boundaries of such systems. Systems interact and overlap to an extent where it becomes difficult to say which is which. For example, it is a well-known fact among Tamils that in Norway the local LTTE people were for a number of years allowed to monopolise positions as interpreters for the immigration police. That interaction between a police officer and a refugee in a situation of interrogation is on unequal terms, defined by the context and scale of Western immigration, is readily understandable. But when the refugee is afraid of telling his story to the police officer because of the interpreter's connections to the militant opposition in Sri Lanka and this interpreter is employed by the Norwegian police, where do we draw the boundary of the system?

To formulate this point in more general terms, most studies of migration still rely on a concept of 'community', with its implied meaning of a common set of rules and values, identifying a discriminable population with a single bounded territory or place. By so doing writers assume that the social interaction in which people take part will be more intense and/or more 'significant' within this space than across its borders. One way or another they also assume that residents will treat the place of the community as the most important context of their actions. Consequently, as a movement from one place to the other, migration has often been treated as a change from one significant environment to another and as a process in which migrants either assimilate to a dominant way of life or forge their own synthesis out of two separate cultural wholes. This socio-spatial framework no longer seems an adequate representation of the social dynamic involved in migration to the West. Home and host countries, the places of putative communities, often seem in analytical terms no more than *sites* in which circuits of people, values and information intersect with local ways of life (Rouse 1992, also Foucault 1986). I argue that the complexity of life in Norway, involving disjunctured discourses on personal and cultural identity, results from the overlap and interaction between two processes: the bureaucratic management of identity labels in the host society and the social transformation and cultural redefinition among the Tamil population.

The complexity of exile life is experienced as social fragmentation. Unlike the Pakistani migrant worker community or the Bosnian refugees for example, the Tamils have not so far been able to establish organisations which could represent their interests *vis-à-vis* Norwegian society with any kind of legitimacy. The occasional consultations with national authorities – police, immigration, parliamentary politicians – have been set up by one of the few 'brokers' within the community, only temporarily licensed to speak on behalf of a larger circle. On a local level there has been a tendency for the *sanghams* ('welfare organisations') to split very rapidly into fractions and remain ineffective, often due to rivalry between followers of different candidates for leadership. This untidy picture has been emphasised by internal conflicts, occasionally developing into fist fights and public accusations of blackmail and death threats.

These internal fissures are of utmost importance to the situation of the Tamil group as a whole in Norway. Besides immigration policy itself, they are the main reasons for what I will later describe as a position of cultural withdrawal from Norwegian society. The split between those who support the LTTE and those who do not is undoubtedly the most important of these fissures. To the non-LTTE people any information on their home country, every explanation of why they are in Norway, exposes them to accusations of betrayal. It is not the only fissure however. What makes the situation so complex is that other divisions tie in with this one, old divisions from the home country and new divisions emerging from exile itself. These also need to be taken into account.

In terms of inter-personal relationships social fragmentation is not readily apparent to outsiders. To a Norwegian the first impression of Tamil life is one of dense sociality. When doing fieldwork you never really have to organise anything, you just sit down somewhere and things will begin to happen. Visitors come and go, food is brought and shared, telephones are ringing, and before you know what is going on you are on your way to something or someone that people want to show you. Things can be and are taken care of. Travelling with Mr J, my guide to the Norwegian Tamil world, I was always impressed about how he would be able find a place to sleep the next night by placing a few calls. One time when we were on the boat from Hammerfest to Båtsfjord in the middle of the night, two villages on the northernmost coast of Norway, he picked up the phone and in one call arranged for someone to meet us at four o'clock in the morning. Knowing that he did not know anyone personally in Båtsfjord I asked him how he had managed to do this and was told he had called a friend back in Oslo who had a friend who had a cousin in this place. As it turned out this cousin had just been reunited with his wife from Sri Lanka and did not think it suitable to receive visitors, so he sent someone else who could accommodate us. It was all arranged within two hours.

This aspect of organisation, the mutual offer and expectation of assistance, is an important part of exile life. It is the safety device without which refugee existence becomes a life-threatening adventure. You can observe this sitting in the hall of any refugee reception centre. The most valuable thing that people bring, the object most closely guarded, is normally a well-worn notebook with telephone numbers. This book is what they stake their future on. As you spend time with people and overcome your first impression of chaotic intermingling, you will, however, soon notice that the same faces appear. The relationships of reciprocity are not based in common identities as Tamils or refugees, they are mainly sets of *dyadic* relationships, forming on the aggregate level what Granovetter (1973) has termed 'clustered networks', sets of overlapping personal networks with limited outside contact, seldom counting more than ten or fifteen people.

These networks form three interrelated social fields within the Tamil community in Norway, 'social field' being understood as a relatively bounded system of inter-communication with a dynamics of its own (Grønhaug 1978). These fields are based on three different but partly overlapping principles organising rivalry between factions:

One field is constituted by what Kuntz (1973) has termed 'vintages' of flight. Disregarding refugees' legal, definitional requirements, what makes people flee are not outer conditions as such but individual inter-pretations of events and self-perceived dangers or motivations. Becoming a refugee is a matter of translating external pressure into individual decision. Individual action, however, is not normally without a pattern. Refugees have a tendency, as the situation ripens, to leave the country in distinct sets, each clinging to the moral and political justifiability of their action and sceptical of those who departed earlier or stayed longer. While to outsiders the 'vintages' internal to a group of immigrants may be imperceptible, the exact time of departure from home will be to the refugee himself and to the group in general a significant identity marker. The week, month or year of flight, as the case may be, will connect him not only to other members of his vintage but to the larger political currents and counter-currents at home and will, in exile, become a document of identification. Vintages, in Kuntz's words, become 'fate groups'. Among Tamils in Norway one may identify three main 'currents': firstly, the early migrant workers leaving Tamil Sri Lanka in the period 1968–80, secondly, the early refugees leaving in the period 1980–86, most of whom were granted refugee status in Norway, and thirdly the asylum seekers leaving after 1986. This pattern corresponds to the back and forth of intra-ethnic war. Vintages constitute the main field for relationships of equality and mutual acceptance, in other words, of friendship and daily company. Often such relationships have a 'touch' of family to them, but, if so, they are seldom found among close family members placed in hierarchical positions like brothers or nephews and paternal uncles. They are either found between cross-cousins, who are equals, or, more often, between people who do not know the exact connection but who will say 'he is on my mother's (or father's) side'.

The next field is organised directly on the basis of politics. Although actual participation in organisations is limited, comprising no more than an estimated 5 to 10 per cent of the population, the divide between circles feeling allegiance to the opposite sides of the intra-ethnic conflict is strongly felt. While most early migrant workers were not politically active and politically active non-LTTE asylum seekers have been members of a number of separate militant groups, the divide among Tamils in Norway has been on an LTTE /anti-LTTE basis. LTTE is today the only militant group with a properly working organisation in Norway, keeping offices in the main cities and having more or less official representatives in most Tamil settlements. This representation has meant that it has not been possible to resolve questions of belonging and cultural identity. Establishing the exact influence of LTTE activity for different groups of people is a sensitive and very difficult matter. It is clear, however, that for ordinary people going about their own business, proof of sustained 'national' identity has been demanded in accountable form through regular money-collecting visits by representatives of the movement. For people with intellectual or political aspirations the problem is more acute. Since 1988 when local LTTE people attacked and almost killed an EPRLF speaker during a public meeting in Oslo, the split and rivalry between the LTTE and anti-LTTE factions have been a recurrent theme. The population is stretched out along a scale with activists at both ends and the majority moving uneasily in between. Since LTTE's understanding of its own role includes being the sole representative of the Tamil people, their activity is something that all exiles are forced to take a stand on. This also include the migrant workers who by virtue of their seniority and language skills are often sought to act as middlemen in dealings with Norwegian authorities. To LTTE every initiative being taken outside its own organisation is suspect in character, as in the late 1980s when they tried to stop private individuals collecting money for war victims in Jaffna without going through their organisation. Such initiatives, however limited, are always seen to have political implications because, one way or the other, they will project an image of who and what the Tamils are, definitions which are at the root of internal conflicts. 'All Tamils have Tiger heads or Tiger tails,' is Mr J's expression; if you do not conform you are watched. As a writer twice detained by LTTE in Sri Lanka and once freed from the execution field itself by a cadre who happened to like his poems, he is entitled to speak his mind.

The third social field is structured on the basis of traditional loyalties, especially family, caste and village membership.[5] Most Tamils resident in Norway come from a small middle- and upper-middle section of the caste spectrum and from a handful of villages in Jaffna. Since caste is a very sensitive question and an area where incorrect information is readily given, an accurate record is not possible. As a rough estimate, however, members of the Vellalar, Karaiyar, Ceviyar, and Thimilar castes probably make up more than 80 percent of the population in Norway. Many come from Jaffna town and from the villages of Karayoor, Arialai, and Navanthurai. More so than the others, this field is important to the *act* of migration; this is where money is lent and passports borrowed, where marriages are negotiated and where responsibility for children, dispatched from the war zone on their own, is transferred. It is also where the *continuity* of migration lies. Most networks within this field has its own 'genealogy' with a revered founding father or mother who in exile may be sought for assistance or to mediate in internal conflicts between members of their 'lineage'. Relationships within this field are not necessarily between close relations, however. More often they are between a classificatory relatives, or, as in one case I am familiar with, between a number of asylum seekers and one lady who has dedicated her life and money to help *all* caste members of her village come to Norway, disregarding any personal connections. Neither are they primarily friendship relations but relations of authority and respect, modelled on the hierarchical structures of the family.

Some remarks should be made to fill in this picture. Firstly, we should observe that some social and cultural traits do *not* constitute separate fields. Religion, for example, is largely irrelevant for organisation outside the immediate family, although exiles are divided between Catholics and Hindus. To some extent this is because religion is subsumed under other fields, e.g. Catholic Karaiyars and Catholic Vellalas being considered separate endogamous sub-castes under their main castes. Income and wealth, at least so far, do not seem to constitute a field in its own terms either. While financial resources may give personal prestige, such resources do not structure interaction.

Next, it should be noted that social fields are not *groups*, they are all based on *contested* internal hierarchy. By saying this I simply mean that within each field, while there is no agreement on the ranking of membership categories, there is an agreement on what the competition is about, which is precisely which field-specific criteria for leadership should apply. That is, in field-structured competition a claim for superiority based on one specific position within a social field will be refuted by the counter-claim that this position is not valid or is in fact not the superior position.

Thirdly, we should observe that seen as part of one or more social fields the individual is situated within systems of social interconnection which are not necessarily coextensive with the geographical unit within which he lives. In the present case it is significant that all three fields in Norway connect directly back to Sri Lanka in the sense of sustaining natural bonds between actors in Norway and positioned groups in their home country. By referring to these bonds in their local struggles for dominance all actors draw upon contextualisations of past Sri Lanka (Ceylon) or present Eelam in their quests for legitimacy.

Finally, in terms of traditional theories of role allocation, the constitution of revolutionary politics as a separate social field, which is connected to the loosening of inter-caste hierarchy, introduces a complexity of social organisation unknown to pre-war Jaffna. The *degree* to which this is so is, however, not easily determined. In Norway, while scorn and mutual distrust have been part of the relationship between migrant workers and refugees as membership categories, in terms of inter-personal relationships seniority of stay will normally override this. That is, while a refugee may refute the early settlers' claim to leadership in general, he will seldom oppose his own senior relatives.

Undoubtedly, a certain overlap between caste and political allegiance does exist. The foundation of this is the Karaiyar caste's loyalty to and control over the LTTE. In Norway it seems to be the case that political allegiance among the majority of 'urban middle-class' Vellalars, this designation referring to their position in Jaffna, not in Norway, is largely a matter of personal feelings and choice, while the stances of micro-castes like the Ceviyars and the Thimilars tend to be influenced by their different traditional relationships to the Karaiyar caste. Like the LTTE leadership in Jaffna is heavily dominated by the Karaiyars of Valvettithurai, the LTTE leadership in Norway is dominated by Ceviyars of Arialai, and many fellow migrants focus on this fact in judging their actions. Several informants argue that the LTTE's national project is nothing but a clever strategy of caste-climbing. Whatever the truth in this, I find it important to note that the LTTE's violent trajectory may be, and in fact is, construed alternately as a continuance of inter-caste rivalry and as a true revolutionary politics incorporating all members of the Eelam-Tamil nation.

This last point indicates that in model situations there may be a considerable overlap between different social fields. Bergen, a town on the west coast of Norway where the most established Tamil settlement is found, presents one such example of field intersection. From a tightly knit group of migrant workers, comprising no more than ten to fifteen people of different castes and families in 1975, the Tamil population today has grown to about 700 people, most belonging to three different extended families headed by members of the original group of migrant workers. Comprising both Hindus and Catholics the early settlers have been able to build or gain influence in already existing, religious institutions to support their own senior positions *vis-à-vis* the refugees. While these seniors meet to resolve conflicts and discuss matters of common interest, one section today supports the LTTE while two do not. This split has taken place according to caste.

The situation in Bergen is, however, unique among the Tamil settlements in Norway and in general the exile situation undoubtedly imposes an extra complexity on social organisation. In other words, the proper dynamics within each of the fields cannot be described without taking the Western refugee regime and its national manifestations into account. Most important in this respect is the splitting of families as a consequence of immigration practices. This happens in every refugee situation, but I do think the *degree* of split between different countries, due to their reliance on the 'jet way' to the West, makes the Tamil diaspora rather unique among today's refugee populations.

Furthermore, compared to other groups of immigrants the Tamils have a uniquely dispersed settlement pattern inside Norway as well. While the general tendency is for immigrants to concentrate in the four or five largest cities, Tamils are well represented in smaller townships. Besides their own initiative in seeking out pockets in a difficult labour market, there are two main reasons for this. One is the tradition of work and *Folkehoyskole* migration in which individuals, through family connections, were recruited to peripheral localities (see Chapter 4). The other is the state-organised settlement of refugees, under which these, as individuals, have been provided house and work or welfare in outlying communities. Through such different trajectories incompatible Tamil statuses are often brought together: high and low caste set to work together, members of opposing militant groups made to share the same house, etc. In these situations statuses from different social fields provide a register through which agents contextually may negotiate their intra-ethnic identities. Often such negotiations seem to result in disagreement over which set of statuses is to be considered valid. That is, while one person may claim a position in terms of representing some political group, another may base his own claim in caste membership or in a longer period of residence. Equally important to social dynamics, however, is the fact that in dealings with the surrounding society, especially the public sector, *compatible* statuses are often made irrelevant and replaced by statuses derived from government classification. Categories like 'migrant', 'student', 'asylum seeker', etc. reflect the social and political climate in host countries, not a difference between people accorded these statuses. A Tamil accepted as a student five years ago would today have to apply for asylum. Of two comrades fighting side by side in Sri Lanka one may be afforded refugee status, the other immigrant status if any. But if classifications say something they also do something. Official taxonomies carry implications on the distribution of privileges, and the different ways of incorporation do affect individuals' relations to each other. Categories, created to be manageable, are filled by people who are all within the same national space and who take part in the same social dynamics.

SPACE AND HISTORY

Exile provides an element of ambiguity to cultural reproduction which will also be discussed in the next two chapters. It does so mainly in two ways: on the most concrete level the geo-political situation makes Tamil exiles' participation in Jaffna's local affairs difficult at best. If granted asylum or a permit of residence, refugees are requested to trade their own national passports against travel documents which do not allow the holder to visit his or her home country. Under conditions of war the Tamil areas have been inaccessible by telephone and for long periods of time by mail. Field-structured action, therefore, has a sense of 'doing-what-one-imagines-others-would-think-is-the-right-thing-to-do' about it. While this is most obvious with regard to the field of traditional loyalties, it is also apparent with regard to politics. When one gets to know them the individuals manning the LTTE offices tend not to deny that their connection to decision-makers in the organisation is marked by distance and poor communication, and that explaining and justifying these decision-makers' capricious policy of violence is not always an easy task.

On a different level of abstraction the problem of space takes us back to the question of time. The 'simultaneity' discussed above is not a neutral calendar time moving at its own pace but is in itself a construction assisted by distance. By seeing themselves and each other in terms of processes at home, 'home' also becomes a way of speaking about themselves in exile. The 'betrayal' of the non-LTTE groups when joining the government forces is a way of ascribing identity to agents in exile; judgement on LTTE's actions in Sri Lanka is also a judgement on their presence abroad. In this construction space and time merge.

That past, present and future are somehow interwoven is a familiar conception. The only way to create a coherent present is to connect it to a past through which it was produced and from there to work one's way forward to a correct image of the now which one seeks to understand. In this cognitive process 'history' is understood selectively; past events are emphasised by a present which allows them to stand as causes for what is. As Connerton comments:

We experience our present world in a context which is causally connected with past events and objects, and hence with reference to events and objects which we are not experiencing when we are experiencing the present. And we will experience our present differently in accordance with the different pasts to which we are able to connect that present. (1992: 2)

Political discourse exists at two levels among Tamils in Norway; one external, directed to and moulded by Norwegian society, and one internal, protecting itself behind a common ethnicity. The second is embedded in a multi-vocal historicist discourse on the recent Tamil past where people speak to each other and themselves about the present by way of causal interpretations. This discourse is mainly articulated as comments and judgements on political or military events – that is as related to news from home. The imputation of moral legitimacy, or illegitimacy, to such acts and events serves to locate commentators within what Connerton calls separate 'narrative homes' (1992: 19), that is within interpretative frameworks which are different from those of other positions or homes. The very fluid situation in Jaffna for the last decade and a half, with large gaps in information and without any authorised version of the period having had the chance to take form, naturally provides a rich material for such historicist constructions. The whos, and especially the whys, are always in the forefront of people's minds – why was the ceasefire broken? Why was Mahatiya dethroned? Why was Amirthalingam killed? – and will be answered differently from different narrative positions. Let me provide one example which is informative of this space-time interconnection:

In May 1994 rumours started to circulate in Norway about the LTTE's leader, Prabhakaran. Debates behind closed doors became heated at times, some arguing that the LTTE in Norway should now be boycotted. What the rumours said were two things: one was that after a faction broke out of LTTE and established the organisation PLOTE in 1979, Prabhakaran, lacking resources of his own, had temporarily joined the organisation TELO which was then under leadership of two militant leaders called Kuttimani and Thangathurai. Together with them he was supposed to have taken part in a famous armed robbery of the Neervely Bank in Jaffna. The second was that subsequently Prabhakaran had personally tipped off the Sri Lankan police

on the whereabouts of Kuttimani and Thangathurai, this information
leading to their arrest and, as a result of this arrest, their death in the
Wellikade prison massacre (see Chapter 3).

Since this information referred to events of ten to fifteen years ago
it was at first unclear to me why it caused so much agitation. What I
failed to understand, of course, was that the facts under discussion were
the foundation of a sequence of political and military developments
involving the killing of a large number of people. Co-operating with
other militant organisations is punishable by death in the LTTE; that
Prabhakaran himself should have worked under TELO orders
questioned the legitimacy of a large series of acts committed by, and
on, members of the exile community and their relatives. That he
should have betrayed his former superiors by tipping them off to the
police was almost inconceivable. What made it worth discussing was
that this rumour was corroborated by another intertwining story.

On 1 May 1994 the writer and publisher, Sabaratnam, was killed
by unidentified gunmen at his home in Paris. Critics of the LTTE in
Norway pointed out to me that shortly before his death Sabaratnam
had written an article in the Canadian magazine *Thayagam.* In this article
Sabaratnam had observed that all who participated in the Neervely
Bank robbery, except Prabhakaran himself, were now dead, killed either
by the Sri Lankan authorities or by the LTTE. He implied that
Prabhakaran saw it in his interest to remove the other participants in
the action in order to conceal his own co-operation with TELO.
Sabaratnam had promised to return with another article disclosing the
real story behind the robbery and the capture of Kuttimani and
Thangathurai, but was killed before this could take place – allegedly
by the LTTE itself. By the adherents of the *Thayagam* version, the killing
of Sabaratnam and Prabhakaran's betrayal in the late 1970s were seen
as closely connected events which should make people turn their backs
on LTTE activities in exile. Not only did Prabhakaran's tip-off
constitute a collaboration with the enemy, but the killing of Sabaratnam
reached the lowest possible level of human baseness. It was claimed
by people familiar with the early history of the militant movement
that in the mid-1970s, years before the Neervely robbery, when
Sabaratnam himself was a political activist in Jaffna, he had taken
Prabhakaran into his house while he was wanted by the police and
had kept him in hiding for several weeks, putting his own life in danger.
Repaying this old debt with murder constituted a breach with the

militants' most fundamental 'code of arms' and, by implication, left his organisation, LTTE, without any legitimate claim for support.

What we have, then, to establish the legitimacy or illegitimacy of LTTE's position in Norway is a 15 years' time-span and the geographical locations of Jaffna, Toronto, Paris and Oslo interwoven.

Through the ascription of responsibility for actions and the location of such responsibility within descriptions of sequential developments, 'narrative homes' come to denote discrepant spheres of morality. The relationship between social fields and narrative positions will be discussed in later chapters. Here I would like to suggest that there are two ideal positions, each with its own separate organisation of the past. As both see the present as the result of a disruption in the continuous unfolding of history, these two positions are structured around the question of where this break is to be located. 'You must understand, we are a religious people', Bastianpillai, one of the early migrants, told me, serving coffee in his comfortable house in Bergen;

Under normal circumstances all this killing would be unthinkable. Education and intellect used to be our pride. Look what the world is saying about us now. This is something new. We do not understand what has become of our community.

Viji, a young refugee who had arrived in Norway as an unaccompanied minor, expressed a different view. Not accepting me as a visitor to his lodgings, he had agreed to come to my office and explain what was going on in his home country: 'Before, the Sinhalese fascists could do whatever they wanted to us,' he said, 'now we have shown them.' When I asked him why this 'showing' was a necessary task, he embarked on a long story of how Tamils had been mistreated when brought over from India by the British in the last century. When I asked him why he wished to take on the Sinhalese for something the British had done, and if the Tamils brought to work on the tea plantations were not, strictly speaking, a different people from his own Jaffna countrymen, his view was very clear: 'British, Sinhalese – the same, Jaffna Tamils, Indian Tamils -the same!'

In their own choice of words these views reflect a difference between seeing the present struggle as a breakdown of morality, and the present exile as a way of preserving former excellence, and seeing this struggle as the logical consequence of long-term outside dominance. These positions are both strongly influenced by distance, because they imply a process of abstraction which is rare among people engaged in the day-to-day cataclysm of the conflict. By ascribing motives and moral attributes on the basis of general categories, actions are read, so to speak, in the light of historical and cultural totalities. This cognitive process is significant for ethnic dynamics in exile.

6   MONEY, MARRIAGE AND MEANING

In this chapter I start by considering one example of Tamils' economic activity in Norway. In the public media this activity is often portrayed as an 'integration' into Norwegian society. It is my argument that an understanding of the Tamil economic profile should be sought in their own cultural logic and in the ties which connect them to Sri Lanka.

According to official records (KAD 1994) Tamils are the group of immigrants with the highest rate of employment and with the lowest level of welfare support in Norway. One reason for this situation is the acceptance of the kind of work which is not in demand. In Oslo, according to a recent statistical survey (Djuve and Hagen 1995), only 1.3 per cent of Tamils' income comes from welfare, as compared to, for instance, 41.7 per cent among Somalis and 37.5 per cent among Vietnamese. In fact, the Tamil level of welfare support is lower than among Norwegians (2 per cent). In the capital Tamils' main employment is cleaning and, like Kumaran in Jayapalan's short story, washing dishes in restaurants.

With respect to employment, compared to other immigrants Tamils have another characteristic, which is their willingness to leave the anonymous security of the larger cities in order to look for economic opportunities. Their settlement in the northernmost part of the country is one example of this. If you start in Oslo and go 2000 kilometres north, about the same distance as Oslo–Rome, you will come to the small town of Alta, one of the main towns in Norway's northernmost administrative district, Finnmark. If you continue by car or bus you will soon see the last trees pass by. You now have six to twelve hours of driving ahead through the barren Arctic landscape before reaching one of the many small and isolated fishing communities facing the Barents Sea. This is what Norwegian tourist authorities call the 'land of the midnight sun', seldom mentioning that three or four months of the year will be completely dark, that supplies are often scarce in winter because storms make transport difficult or that snow in June is the rule rather than the exception. In this rather inhospitable area Sri Lankan Tamils have won a reputation as workers in the factories where fish is cut and packed. Even if the numbers are small, seldom more than 50 to 100 in one village, statistics will show that in several villages Tamils represent 5 to 10 per cent of the total population. By the sheer extreme in their natural and social surroundings these settlements give us a general idea about Tamil life in Norway.

Finnmark is an interesting case because it shows how a group of immigrants which is rather marginal within the national context can establish a strong local position through its social characteristics and the incentives which cultural imperatives provide. Since the mid-1980s Tamil refugees have replaced many of the Norwegian seasonal workers and most of the Finnish short-term migrants who until this point had been important to the fish-processing industry. This is mainly due to their internal organisation and to their flexibility as workers. The fish industry is very sensitive to changes in the supply of fish for processing, something which makes organising the labour force a real challenge. If the supply of fish is good the management needs people who can work 18 hours a day and who will attend jobs where they are most needed. If the sea turns 'black', as they say, and the supply is suddenly turned off, there is a need to reduce costs quickly by dismissing personnel. Seen from the management's point of view, Tamil workers are ideally suited to this situation, a fact which is openly admitted. One factory official pointed out to me that in 1987 the normal amount of fish cut by a Norwegian in a day's work would be three to four hundred kilos. Most Tamils, on the other hand, will cut close to 1000 kilos in a normal day and afterwards might ask to work overtime. In fact, the Tamil workers have helped to raise not only the level of expected output, but also through the money they bring in – the work is done on piece-work contracts – the social reputation of fish factory work as such. In particular, the flexibility is enhanced through the decreasing importance of gender roles within production. Being without previous experience in fish factory work the Tamils lack the prejudices found among Norwegian and Finnish workers. Traditionally, the cutting and handling of fish has been regarded as 'women's work'. Men would work at the factories but only as overseers, or outside in loading, transport, etc. Even at times of acute labour shortage it would be difficult to shift the workers around to finish cutting for a special delivery. Today this is changing. Tamils have shown that a good cutter can reach a monthly salary of 25–30,000 Norwegian kroners, 4–5000 US$, an amount of money that most unskilled workers in Norway will find highly attractive. Most important, the Tamils keep discipline within their ranks and seldom complain about the treatment they are given. Making use of their internal organisation as a resource in their own production, there is a tendency for factory managers to hire only Tamil workers related to people who are already employed. In this way any problem created by a worker will backfire on one of his own relatives.

The story of Tamil settlement in the north is interesting. For the Tamils themselves it is, however, not necessarily a happy story. There are, I think, reasons to challenge the understanding that these settlements in any way reflect an adjustment to the surrounding society. On the contrary, they stem from a dire economic need pertaining to the organisation of family affairs in a situation of war. Many young people's careers in the fish industry take place at the expense of further education and a fuller participation in both Norwegian and Tamil society. If you invite *Lakshmi*, the goddess of prosperity, into your house, *Saraswati*, the goddess of learning and wisdom, will leave, the Tamils say. Among refugee counsellors it is a common complaint that motivating Tamils for language and work training courses is difficult, all they think about is making money. Life in the north is hard. The cold and darkness in winter bring depressions; in the summer the bright light at night-time makes sleep difficult. The climatic conditions are perceived to be 'unnatural' (*iyatkaikku maraaka*). To those who remain in factory work for too long the repetitious nature of work operations tends to create physical problems. The heavy reliance on a few fellow countrymen carries little variation in social life. Interaction with Norwegians is mostly limited to working situations. For such a large group living in a foreign environment the Tamils' most conspicuous characteristic in these communities is their invisibility. Their use of public space is limited and mainly confined to organised events. Though squabbles over scarce resources like jobs, houses, and local women have occurred, the main reason is not ethnic tension but the part that these arid areas play in their own life projects. One Norwegian lady from a village where Tamil settlement is of rather recent origin expressed her understanding like this: 'When they came in 1988 they laughed and played almost naked in the snow. Then they disappeared into the factories and we have never seen them again.' The question must be asked why they take upon themselves this burden of hard labour.

'WORKING FOR MY SISTERS ...'

Detailed studies of residence patterns among immigrants tell us that out of the Tamil asylum seekers having settled in northern Norway after 1976, only 7 per cent of the men and none of the women were still living there seven years later (Sørli 1994). The work in the fish industry is, therefore, not necessarily a lifetime career. As shown by the history of migration to Innby (in Chapter 4) it has served mainly as a stepping stone into a more 'regular' exile situation. In particular, this entails paying debts and covering the basic needs of parents and siblings at home. The capital lost through the flight must be regained and the responsibility for their original families must be taken care of before they can go on with their own lives. A few years in the north is one way of solving these problems.

The first years' earnings from factory work seem to go mainly in two directions. For the asylum seekers the first priority is to repay the loans and credits which have gone into paying transport to Norway. As indicated in Chapter 4, transport from Sri Lanka easily runs into 10–12,000 US$ and financing normally involves both assistance from the extended family and borrowings from unofficial credit institutions. Some of these 'institutions' have representatives in Norway who will see to it that the money is repaid.

Besides this, what is foremost in most people's minds are questions of family and marriage. In one of the townships where I did fieldwork, out of 43 Tamil men, four of whom were already married and five were under 18 years, 16 had applications for reunion with a wife or fiancée under consideration. If already married, a way must be found to pay the fare for spouse and children and for their support in Norway. If not married, sooner or later the question will arise. Establishing a family in exile is, however, a complex process where the demands of Norwegian authorities and the native family at home must both be accommodated. In migrants' relationships to the Norwegian immigration system the questions concerning family reunion are among the most difficult. It is also where the differentiated distribution of privileges according to legal status is most readily apparent. While holders of refugee status are automatically granted reunion with their spouse and children, and students are normally permitted to bring their families for the duration of their stay, holders of 'foreigner's passports', that is asylum seekers who have been granted residence on humanitarian grounds, are required to document their ability to support their families before reunion is granted. Tamil refugees are acutely aware that, apart from a handful of individual exceptions, none of their countrymen arriving after 1987 have been accorded refugee status. Comparing their situation to that of the Vietnamese and the Chilean refugees they interpret this fact as a non-recognition of their difficult background. Before 1991 the requirement of economic support was permanent, but under the new law it is lifted after three years of residence. For married men this period of waiting is, of course, intolerable and most are willing to do anything to shorten it. The requirement of support is also there for reunion with a future spouse and, in this case, the applicant will also need to show that there is a 'real' relationship, something which is often difficult because the two parties may not know each other before the engagement.

The great majority of marriages contracted in Norway are arranged marriages, generally between one party in Sri Lanka and one party in Norway. So-called 'love marriages', unions entered without a prior agreement between the native families of the two people, do occur but not often. Implicating a major break with tradition and the wish of parents, such marriage is for many young people more of a tempting attraction, a contemplated possibility rejected when it comes down to going ahead with it.

What separates 'arranged marriage' and 'love marriage' as two types of union is not primarily the consent of parents as such but an agreement between the families concerning marriage benefits, in particular the dowry to be brought by the woman into the marriage. Through dowry the phenomenon of migration connects to the very core of Tamil culture, and I will return to this question in Chapter 8. Here we may observe that while dowry practices are fought by the LTTE in Jaffna, dowries are inflating within the exile community. A complaint often heard by male refugees is that dowries are reaching a level where it has become difficult to establish families. This worry reflects a situation where brothers have been delegated moral and economic responsibility for their sisters' marriages by their parents. In the anthropological literature the dowry has generally been regarded as a *pre-mortem* inheritance to the daughters of a family (Comaroff 1980). In the prevailing war situation it is normally a chosen son who *pre mortem* inherits the realisable capital of the family and invests it in migration against taking further responsibility for his native family upon himself. This implies, *inter alia*, that he must procure his sisters' dowries before establishing a family on his own. The amount of money involved in a dowry will normally be 20–100 000 US$ according to the status of the husband; for a migrant with two or three sisters the task is formidable in Europe's present labour market, even if aiming only at the lower end of the scale. Let me present one individual story, told to me in consecutive parts, focusing on its economic aspects:

Benjamin was 29 when I first met him in one of the small fishing villages in northern Norway. Originally he was from a village in the central part of Jaffna where he was born as the third of five children of a reasonably wealthy landowner.

Benjamin's elder brother had joined one of the guerrilla groups early in the 1980s and was soon killed in an encounter with government forces. On his death Benjamin joined the same group, but when the in-fighting started in the autumn of 1986 his parents took their savings and borrowed the rest to pay an agent in Colombo 12,000 US$ for organising Benjamin's transport to Europe on a false visa to Germany.

After arriving in Germany and spending the next few months there, Benjamin decided to try his luck in Norway, together with a boy from his village. Borrowing money on his own this time, he paid an agent to take the two of them by car through Denmark and Sweden. They arrived in Norway the day before New Year's Eve 1986 and applied for asylum at the local police station the next morning. Benjamin was granted residence on humanitarian grounds by the summer of 1987. After one year of unemployment in Oslo he was offered a job in a fish factory on the northern coast through a distant relative on his mother's side.

Two years later Benjamin had repaid the money that his father had borrowed to pay for his travel from Sri Lanka and his own debt incurred in Germany – a total of about 14,000 US$. Doing this, however, had been one of his least problems. Since the farm provided no income, he had to take responsibility for his sisters' situation. His one older sister was already engaged to a local boy at the time when Benjamin left, the dowry having been negotiated and agreed. Together with a piece of land, the relatively modest equivalent of 10,000 US$

was promised in delayed payment. Since Benjamin was now the only breadwinner in the family, and the family savings had gone into his travel, it fell upon him to settle the matter.

Benjamin decided to bring to Norway the elder of his two younger sisters. He thought that if he brought her over she could perhaps help support the rest of the family. This later proved to be correct and the sister turned out to be a very industrious and hard-working girl. To get her to Norway Benjamin proposed a marriage with the young man who had accompanied him from Germany, a man known both to his sister and his parents. The man agreed, but initially demanded the equivalent of 16,000 US$, most of which would be transferred back to his own family. After some negotiations, involving the respective families in Sri Lanka, the two friends agreed upon the amount of 20,000 US$, half paid immediately through a bank loan, half paid over two years, out of which the groom should cover Benjamin's sister's transport to Norway.

At this point, a year before we met, Benjamin had been in Norway for about four years. In addition to supporting the daily expenses of his family he had, on his salary from the factory, paid 34,000 $US during the last three years in debt and dowry, and he owed his friend an additional 10,000 US$. He was 28 years old then and had for some time wanted to marry himself. After repeatedly asking his mother to assist in this matter, he finally received a message on his sister's arrival in Norway that there was a girl whose family was looking for a husband and that his parents would look into the matter. After that, he heard nothing for eight months. While waiting, Benjamin worked hard, looked for a house and tried to save money. He knew that for a fiancée to be granted an entrance visa to Norway he would need not only a job to support her but also what immigration authorities judged to be a 'suitable' place for them to live. This was a major problem because the few houses in the village which could be rented were owned by the fish factory which preferred to pack them with single workers. Benjamin too, for the time he had worked there, had lived in a four-bedroom house, owned by the factory, together with five other men. Not only would it not be accepted by the immigration people, but it was not a place to accommodate a wife either. He realised that in the case of marriage he would have to buy a house.

News about the marriage proceedings was finally brought to him by his youngest sister who had managed to leave the war zone and had taken the three-day trip to the capital to call him on the phone. She started by telling him that the family of the girl in question had agreed to propose and that she – Benjamin's sister – would mail a picture of the girl in question to him while she was in Colombo. There was a problem, however, the sister explained, in that an acceptable dowry from the girl's family would not be obtainable until next year. Benjamin's parents had insisted that the dowry should be paid in cash, and this money would have to come from the girl's two brothers who were now in Canada. Then his sister went on to say what Benjamin understood was the real message of the conversation. Because of their two sons' connections to an opposing militant group, the family had difficulties under the LTTE regime established after the withdrawal of the Indian forces in 1990 and the parents wanted to marry her out of the country. Crying, she begged him to send her the money for the dowry to be placed in a bank until the matter could be settled.

This, then, was the dilemma facing Benjamin when I first met him. Should he disregard his sister's prayer and take a loan to buy a house so that his future wife could come as soon as the dowry arrangements were sorted out? Should he buy the house and try to arrange his own marriage, insisting against his parents' wish that the dowry could wait? Or, should he, like they probably all wanted, not buy the house and take a second loan for his youngest sister's dowry? In that case, if he had to repay this loan before buying a house, when would he be able to see the woman he wanted to marry?

What is of general interest in this story is the way in which the process of international migration interacts with local dowry customs. There is in Jaffna a strong preference for marrying children out of the country, particularly daughters. The fact that potential husbands are themselves already in the West makes the task of raising capital no less demanding; indeed, quite the contrary. Instead of one dowry helping to finance another, floating as capital within the system of family networks, the cost of illegal transport now siphons off this capital to greedy travel agents. The fact that many Tamil refugees experience the Scandinavian, bureaucratic system for receiving refugees as close to unbearable with its language programmes, work training courses and limited possibilities for making money (Steen 1993) is therefore not surprising. After 35 the prospects of establishing a family decreases rapidly, even for a man.

To parents in Jaffna and brothers in exile, marriage in the West represents the possibility of a future without war for daughters and sisters, especially so with the increasing difficulty of going as refugees on their own. Actually finding spouses may, however, be a problem. The economic element does not make marriage a limited market transaction in a Western sense. Tamil marriages resemble what Mauss (1969) termed 'total prestations', transactions where social existence is put at stake through the contraction of continuous and obligating relations of reciprocity. As such they presuppose information which makes possible a calculation of the risk involved: information on caste, family background, personal characteristics, economy and – often – the legal status in a host country of potential marriage candidates. Let me continue Benjamin's story:

When representatives of the local LTTE commando knocked on the door of Benjamin's parents, they made it clear that they saw their remaining daughter as a suitable contribution to the cause for people who not only had traitors in the family but also used to exploit the low-caste workers of the area. In other words, they wanted her to join the forces.

Instead of taking the risk of sending their daughter on her own to Norway, the parents contacted a professional marriage broker in Colombo, explaining that they were willing to pay a generous dowry to a husband with citizenship in a European country if the settlement could be made quickly. In less than six weeks the broker brought and presented a suave, well-dressed young man who, they were told, was living in France working for Air France as a pilot. Trusting the broker, and realising that Benjamin could in fact not carry another burden, the parents prepared the transfer of ownership of most of their farmland for onward sale through the broker's firm. When the broker and the groom arrived, the papers were signed and the marriage ceremony arranged in a matter of days. Soon after, the couple left and the parents had no news from their daughter for four months, until they received a letter, mailed in India, saying that her husband was not a pilot, had no visa to France, had not been sober since the wedding and was treating her badly.

This could have been the end of the story, but because of Benjamin's connections to militants hiding in India it was not. Receiving the news about his sister, Benjamin asked his former colleagues to trace the couple and, when they did, he went to India himself to see them. With a gun to his head, his sister's husband told them that he was in fact a distant relative of the broker and that this man had offered him one-third of the profit from the land sale to play the part and marry the girl. The rest the broker had kept for himself. He had been in the process of migrating to Canada when the assignment came up and had now taken the money and left. After hearing the story Benjamin offered to bring his sister to Norway. Crying, she told him she was already pregnant and saw no future without a husband. She therefore preferred to stay with him.

In a situation where the Jaffna community is spread across five continents, personal information becomes all the more necessary but often very difficult to obtain.

REPRODUCING BOUNDARIES

Village life in Norway provides insights of general importance. What emerges in these northern miniature laboratories is the close and complex relationship between outside and inside. Even in Finnmark, where people may drive 300 kilometres on a Sunday to see a Tamil film shown in the next village, social divisions are reproduced: 'vintage', politics, family/caste. The dynamic behind this reproduction is similar to the one found on a national level, only replicated on a smaller scale. However, precisely because intra-ethnic avoidance is impossible here, and the external imprint of ethnic identity categorical, it becomes apparent that this reproduction of internal boundaries must be located in a larger setting. In the village life is unambiguously divided between Norwegian and Tamil contexts: *work* Norwegian, *home* Tamil, *week* Norwegian, *weekends* Tamil, *day* Norwegian, *evening* Tamil, *public* Norwegian, *private* Tamil, and it is in, or in relation to, contexts defined by Norwegian standards that internal divisions are being played out. Inter-ethnic socialising is largely limited to public events of one kind or the other, events which through debates on whom to invite, and by whom guests should be spoken to, tend to bring out conflicts otherwise suppressed. Conflicts in exile are mainly rooted in controversies of representation, in disputes over the object to be presented to the outside interpretant.

For Tamil migrants in this area participation in Norwegian contexts is different from that of the Saami minority, in the same area, so well described by Eidheim (1971). While most Saami, due to language skills and physical appearance, may *try* to engage in interaction without giving weight to their cultural background or ethnic normative standards, individual 'passing' in this sense is impossible for a black Asian with a foreign accent. Although he is normally recruited into the community as an individual worker, to most local Norwegians he has no social markers other than his Tamil-ness and the fact that he is understood to be an 'asylum seeker'. In public discourse – at work, in pubs, even by the administration – Tamil residents are invariably designated by ethnic identity alone. Even when favourable, which it is by some and not by others, report is seldom or never in individual terms. Correspondingly, little effort is made by Tamils themselves to enter personal relationships with local residents or to comply with Norwegian standards in general. Against categorical ascription anonymity is seen as the most effective defence. 'Tamil-ness' inhibits personal associations with local residents but it also prevents the person from being held responsible for the next man's political opinions or idiosyncratic whims. In working places the Tamil language is consciously used because with the imposition of radical difference goes a tactics of cultural withdrawal. Awareness that all actions and all statements will be understood metonymically makes silence a norm. Because external ethnic categorisation makes contacts with the surrounding community sensitive, efforts are made to control and limit such contacts by others. It is when someone *has to* speak, when a representative *must* be chosen, that conflicts flare up.

This is not to say that in contexts which are strictly Tamil social divisions play no part. What is apparent, however, is that people normally *are* able to live together and that, considering their backgrounds from a country at war, violent conflicts are surprisingly rare. Life among the single men in these villages is an illustration of Bruner's point (1990) that the most interesting aspect of conflicting interests is not how much they separate us, but how 'much more often they are neutralised or forgiven or excused' (p. 95). With the exception of the few who are *active* LTTE-members and who, for reasons obvious to the Tamils are treated with distance and care, the main internal, interactional boundary in these temporary settlements is not one of political affiliation or regional origin but the one between married and unmarried men. Among unmarried men there is a fellowship based in social marginality, not primarily in relation to Norwegian society but to traditional Tamil standards. While not perceived as a religious precept, the Hindu ideal of the 'householder' (*grihasta asrama*) is very strong among most Tamil men. Only as a married man do you become a full member of society. In social terms the unmarried community represents a contextual and temporary suspension of the internal boundaries discussed in the preceding chapter. While recruitment to the village is through dyadic connections, once you are there there is a spirit of communality given shape by the consumption of pizza and beer. To portray this fellowship as 'communitas' in Turner's sense (1974) of the word would be to exaggerate. Rather it is a deliberate under-communication of hierarchical difference. Interaction seems to be consciously designed to avoid any pretext for re-aligning into groups of split interests. When something needs to be discussed all factions are consulted, houses are conspicuously declared open for visiting in the evenings, assistance is demonstratively offered. In this context behaviour in the presence of guests differs radically from the many composite households where married couples have taken in younger unmarried relatives. There, unless directly asked, only the male head of the house speaks, women and dependants deferring and taking their seats in the background. Among singles anyone is free to speak, no one is in a position to restrain the action of another. Naturally, there are also among unmarried men aspects of leadership and following, but rather than enduring hierarchical relationships there is in this context a focus on instrumentality and industrious individualism; leadership is transitory and context-specific, leaders are first among equals and the man chosen to speak is the *kettikarar*, the man who is skilful and clever and who is able to prove it in action (see David 1977).

In spatial terms the unmarried Tamil context constitutes a variant of what Foucault (1986) has termed *heterotopia*, a site 'capable of juxtaposing in a single real place several spaces, several sites that are in themselves incompatible' (p. 25). Here the villages and regions of Eelam are moulded in conversation. What else is there to talk about than memories of parents, village, school, the quality of soil, men and village women? Marriage, of course; hopes of family life, proper food and a sizeable dowry putting an end to economic problems. Certainly not politics or pain. A refugee counsellor told me she felt proud when she managed to bring the then only Tamil psychologist in Norway to hold a meeting in her community. It would be an occasion to work on traumas and heal wounds, she thought. After sending personal invitations to about fifty residents, only one person appeared at the meeting. Hours and days may be spent in front of the video, watching Indian films sent by mail from Oslo. Representations of Norway are incorporated into the single context, however, often in the form of jokes expressing non-acceptance of the Western bureaucratic morals at the base of their own vulnerable position:

A man working in town was asked by a Norwegian policeman who was his neighbour if he could buy two bottles of liquor for him at the town liquor store. 'I have a lot to carry today,' the man said, 'can I bring you one today and one tomorrow?' 'No,' the policeman answered, 'the reason I asked you to bring two is because you will be deported tomorrow.'

Like a mirror reflecting in its concrete surface the simultaneous visibility of absence and the absence of geographical viewpoint, the unmarried context reproduces both its own heterotopical place and the space surrounding it .

The divide between unmarried and married men is not one of conflict. It is based in the recognition that when getting married the single men become unsuitable company for the married couple. Marriage is always accompanied by a change of lifestyle. Single men say in jest that the main reason why they drink and smoke, both improper habits from a Hindu point of view, is so that they can stop when they marry. On marrying a man steps out of the utopian fellowship of the heterotopia and back into Tamil society proper. Through marriage I have seen men transformed literally in a matter of hours from rowdy youngsters to pillars of social order. Before marriage a man can be anything: a deceiver, a scoundrel, an outcast, and the single context incorporates this lack of information by basing its fellowship on the principle of 'as if', accepting what people choose to tell about themselves. Through marriage, through a properly arranged marriage that is, a man is *judged* by society; his background is laid open, his character decided, his 'value' is set. He becomes a man of authority – of relative authority, it is true, but always in command of his wife and future children – with his family's name to protect. He becomes a representative and caretaker of the finely graded quality which is the traditional Tamil society. With the exception of political representatives *per se*, married men, men outside the utopian fellowship, are thereby normally sought as spokesmen, selected through processes of choice recurrently breaking open the fragile community of silence.

What we have is a very complex process of fusion and fission, revolving around who has authority to speak on behalf of whom. This process is not without its logic, however, and the distinction between married and unmarried men, and the exception of political representatives in accepting this distinction as relevant, is part of this logic. As will be further discussed in later chapters, it is my argument that the divisions and conflicts between actors can be reduced, on an ideological level, to an opposition between the acceptance or non-acceptance of traditional structures of authority. Claims for authority based on representing pre-war society on the one hand, and LTTE's parallel claim to represent the future liberated nation on the other, constitute opposite poles on a scale representing two different forms of legitimacy. The traditional end of this scale is not simply caste in the *sastric* sense, but – within the limits set by a merger of caste dynamics and capitalist values to be discussed in Chapter 8 – caste *cum* education, *cum* wealth, *cum* success in general. In fact, one more '*cum*' may be added, because the only ones who have been successful in a Norwegian setting until today are the few migrant workers who have been living for 20 years or more in the country. Thus Bastianpillai, insistently anti-LTTE, Christian, and originally of a modest caste origin, emphasised how during his son's confirmation 60 to 70 people had come to present gifts despite the fact that he had *not* invited any guests. This is a proper patron approach to life, replicated on a non-Vellala level, and it is part of what the bound mode symbol *varicai* is about: to allow others to pay respect to you.

Within each of the three fields mentioned – vintage, politics and family/caste – there is one position which speaks unambiguously from one end of the acceptance–non-acceptance scale and several which do not. That is, on the one hand you may claim a position on the basis of being an early migrant or on the basis of traditional statuses, while being a member of one of the anti-LTTE parties. You may even do so while passively supporting the LTTE. What is *not* possible is to base such a claim simultaneously on traditional authority and on LTTE membership. On the other hand you may legitimately dispute the LTTE claim for leadership, but not on the basis of membership in the non-LTTE parties. It can only be done from the vantage point of being an early migrant or on the basis of (high-) caste status. The role accorded to married men in dealing with Norwegian society in the northern villages amounts to holding a position, in this particular setting, at the traditional end of this scale. As I will try to show, however, in exile the middle positions in this picture are not only the most important but also the most interesting.

BONDS OF AUTHENTICITY

In discussing marriage under present circumstances, we must keep in mind how the war situation has affected the sex and age composition of the Tamil population. The Tamil settlements in the north are predominantly male, as is Tamil migration to Norway as a whole. Of the 3087 asylum seekers from Sri Lanka arriving in Norway between 1985 and 1992, 2535 were men and only 552 were women (UDI 1992). Neither is the sex discrepancy noticeable only in exile. According to a survey conducted by the northern district administration of Sri Lanka, in 1994 in Jaffna women outnumbered men six to one.[1] In other words, the question of marriage must be seen in a perspective where 'exile' is predominantly male and 'home' represents the older generations and young women.

The reason why marriages normally involve one party in exile and one party in Sri Lanka is not simply the sex ratio. When it comes to marriage most men are sceptical towards women who have lived in the West outside the direct control of their parents. There is a feeling that through their interaction with Norwegian society, women may, literally speaking, no longer embody the virtues expected from a Tamil wife. This is a question which is not limited to sexual purity as such, pre-marital sexual abstention is mostly taken for granted, but rather it has something to do with the male conceptualisation of femininity as contained in *karpu*. *Karpu* carries the meaning of 'chastity' and 'conjugal fidelity', but it also has a wider reference. It refers to a code of social conduct in which the segregation of sexes and the restricted behaviour of women are central elements, expressing themselves in an extreme female prudishness. Most young men want to marry a woman who is like the women in Jaffna, and this quality can be read straightaway through her body language:

To be morally pure, virtuous and obedient are considered as the highest form of ethical ideal prescribed for women. Shyness, timidity, ignorance, passiveness, obedience are regarded as ideal patterns of behaviour, or rather, the essential qualities of 'femininity' ascribed to virtuous women.

This was written by Adele Ann (1994: 56), an LTTE intellectual, married to the organisation's long-time political adviser, Anton Balasingham. The LTTE are fighting this ideal of femininity and one thing Tamil men in exile fear more than having to marry a 'Westernised' girl is, incidentally, to be set up for marriage with a female LTTE fighter.

In Tamil culture marriage has a pronounced symbolic quality, expressing in condensed form the underlying principles of traditional society. First, the process of negotiating marriage activates the three main mechanisms structuring inter-personal relationships in hierarchical orders: *gender* (as man superior to woman), *age* (as the older generation superior to the younger one) and *caste* (as pure superior to impure); the union which is the outcome of this process is a tangible expression of these hierarchies. Second, these mechanisms are set within, and validated by, a larger cosmological configuration which is explicitly replicated in the institution of marriage. During the marriage ritual itself the couple are exalted, honoured and worshipped as a divine couple (Dumont 1980, also Good 1991) and the platform on which the couple sits is to be regarded as a temporary temple. Furthermore, marriage involves 'taming' the female power, *shakti*, by conferring upon the bride the status of *cumankali*, the properly wedded woman and potential mother of sons. The *cumankali* is the most auspicious being in the Tamil universe, and has the power to bring health and wealth to her man, to save life, to alter events. By partaking, through her sex, in the active, female principle of the universe the wife and mother can bring prosperity (*palan*). The precondition for this is that her sexuality, her innate force, is controlled, bound and directed to the creation of order (Wadley 1980). The auspiciousness, therefore, is not a consequence of her femaleness as such but depends on her relation to others: on her being controlled by her father before marriage and on her loyalty to her husband after marriage. Chastity (*karpu*), to the *cumankali*, is unconditional and is symbolised by the *thali*, the gold ornament which her husband ties around her neck at the wedding and which should never be taken off until his death. When her husband dies and the *thali* is removed the woman becomes a widow – an acutely inauspicious being. The tying of the *thali* is the symbolic core of the marriage ritual and is what legitimises sexual union, confers upon the wife a code of obedience and, in a sense, entrusts her with the prosperity and well-being of the family. To the male migrant, marrying a partner from home carries the feeling of linking up to this Tamil heritage, of drawing nourishment and blessing from tradition and from the traditional woman. Correspondingly, marrying an exile spouse, especially in a 'love marriage', is seen as breaking the bond of tradition, of breaking loose from the authority and auspiciousness which lies at home, embedded in the family network. It is worth noting here that marriage is the single occasion among Jaffna Tamils in Norway where caste considerations are admitted as legitimate and necessary. While *consciousness* of caste is always there, this is never openly made to carry interactive implications. Asking someone about his or her caste is considered highly improper. In political considerations caste is either simply taken for granted on the basis that all implicated parties already know each other's background or it is euphemised as 'village origin'. This means that marriage is the only opportunity for consolidating an important part of personal identity and, because of the floating conditions in exile with its inaccessibility of reliable information, it can only be properly validated from home.

In this respect marriage is part of a larger picture where the process of cultural authentication always leads back to Sri Lanka. In answer to my questions I have repeatedly been told, 'If you want to learn about Tamil culture you must go to Sri Lanka. We are stranded people without knowledge.' This feeling that the 'real' culture rests at home is probably a common phenomenon among exiles. What I wish to point out is the doubleness inherent in this situation. Tamil society in what I will here call its 'traditional' form would have, so I understand, the potential of recreating itself in exile. This, in fact, seems to have happened in the Tamil settlements in Malaya under British rule (Ramasamy 1988) and in London in the early post-independence period (Steen 1993) where close communities were built around temple institutions. On the other hand, when the initiative was taken to establish a Hindu temple in Oslo in 1991, this was seen by many asylum seekers as a strategy by senior migrants to bolster up their own position in a turbulent social situation. The problem seems to be that recreating a Tamil community in its traditional sense would necessarily imply recreating it as a hierarchy of seniority and caste, an idea not appreciated by all. As far as seniority is concerned, I find it interesting to note how rarely you find elder and younger brothers, or fathers and sons, living together in exile. Out of the 196 unaccompanied minor Tamil asylum seekers arriving in Norway between 1986 and 1992, *not one* in 1993 had applied for the family reunion with their parents to which they were entitled.

This is, no doubt, partly because of the immigration policy practised by Norway. I do suggest, however, that the experience of war and migration has introduced feelings of ambivalence towards traditional structures of authority and that this may also be part of the explanation. There is a sense in which the structure of family connects to the contested nature of caste in Tamil society. The reason servant castes in Jaffna are termed *kuttimakal* – 'children of the house' – is because family relations are built on 'feudal' authority, on bound mode symbols, in particular *anumati* – the 'giving permission to'. As expressed by Kakar (1981: 117), in the traditional Hindu family:

> Regardless of personal talents or achievements, or of changes in the circumstances of his own or other's lives, an Indian's relative position in the hierarchy ... his obligations to those 'above' him and his expectations of those 'below' him are immutable, lifelong ... Among brothers, authority attends seniority, so that men and boys, while deferring to their father as his sons, owe some of the same respectful compliance to their elder brothers.

Suggesting that the war and violence, the serving as guerrillas – or simply *seeing* soldiers taking the same orders with similar weapons and in similar uniforms – may have removed some of the taken-for-grantedness pertaining to this hierarchy is hardly pushing the matter. In discussing the lack of organised Tamil community life in Norway with one informant, I remember being struck by one of his comments. Pointing out that the Pakistani community in Norway is composed of several generations seeking to rebuild a 'natural' community in exile, he phrased his point like this: 'With us it is different. When we leave Sri Lanka we close the door behind us. We are free!'

In fact, while I do think migration is an agent of change, invoking this change may not be necessary to bring out the *différance* inherent in migration.[2] Another informant reflecting on his situation metaphorically compared himself to Aiyanar who is the second brother of Ganesh, the Hindu god with the elephant trunk. I did not understand the meaning of this reference, I must admit, until two years later when I read Obeyesekere's (1990) discussion of the Hindu Oedipus myth where Aiyanar is the son who, when running away, renounces his mother's affection in order to escape the castrating authority of his father Siva. Ganesh, on the other hand, whom most Jaffna Tamils give prayers to in exile, accepts his castration in order to remain in his mother's loving presence. In my understanding, the freedom from what

your heart desires, the longing for what you cannot have and would
not have if you could, are fundamental aspects of Tamil life in exile.

As for religion, with the exceptions noted, Hindu religious life in
Norway is largely unorganised and it is difficult to avoid drawing the
conclusion that it is so because most people prefer it to be that way.
Negative feelings against the Oslo temple project were clearly based
on a fear that the group of senior, well-established migrants should
claim the traditional roles of temple patrons, trying to exercise internal
control based on traditional criteria of rank. As shown by Appadurai
and Breckenridge (1976), temple honours, resulting from privileged
interaction with the deity, confer upon recipients the pivotal status
of *yajamans* ('sacrificers'), the distribution of outcome from religious
transactions to other worshippers depending on their goodwill. In our
context control over temples would amount to trying to make religion
an inclusive identity over and above participation in the social fields
discussed previously. While embracing aspects of tradition drawn
from Sri Lanka, there is a certain reserve against transplanting
institutions. Marriage rituals, for example, are normally not performed
'by the book'. A proper Vellala marriage demands the active
participation of a large number of castes (e.g. Ohno, Sanmugadas and
Sanmugadas 1985). In fact, together with temple festivals, marriage
rituals are *the* occasions where the differentiated services of ranked
castes may be seen to constitute a 'whole' in Dumont's sense (Ryan
1980, David 1977). The minimum required caste participation in
marriage would be for a Brahmin to conduct the proper rituals, a fact
readily admitted by informants. In practice, however, people seem
in general quite satisfied with *acting* the rituals from memory, casting
exile friends in ceremonial functions.

There are at least two possible interpretations of this situation, both
of which I believe to contain some truth. One is that some, influenced
by revolutionary political ideals, believe the hierarchical ordering of
people according to seniority and caste to be morally wrong. That is,
while retaining a sentimental relationship to traditions, the implications
of these traditions in terms of social inequality are not accepted. This
is true for individuals belonging to all parts of the age and caste
spectrum, including the upper ones. The other interpretation is that
many prefer to partake in family/caste competition through the
medium of 'Western' status criteria like cars, houses and conspicuous
consumption. There are stories told about people who have served

their time in Finnmark coming to Oslo and buying houses for the equivalent of 100–150,000 US$ in cash. Moreover, among those who can afford it, ritual events, especially puberty rites and marriages, are about to become occasions for the lavish display of economic means. One person proudly explained how, not being able to find a suitable *thali* for his wife, he had personally gone to Singapore to have it hand made about twice the normal size. About 500 people were invited, all accommodated and treated with food and drink to a puberty ceremony, which in Tamil Sri Lanka normally is a rather low-key celebration. While wealth does not, or precisely *because* it does not, constitute a separate social field in the sense of structuring interaction according to a class model, it is a means of conferring prestige within the other fields, especially within the field of traditional loyalties. This kind of competition would be difficult within what I have termed a recreated society because economic criteria could here never be anything but secondary.

What I suggest here, is that the bond to tradition is primarily a personal bond between the individual migrant and Sri Lanka. The daily or weekly religious service, as the case may be, is normally performed at home, in prayer before the small puja tray (*archchanai thaddu*) where representations of deities and pictures of close family members are placed side by side. Where there is a lack of socially situated religious centres, astrology tends to gain in importance. Astrology, of course, is closely connected to Hinduism as such and in Sri Lanka representations of the planets are found in most major temples. There, however, the *ritual* aspect of astrology is dominant, the dogma constituting a language in which solutions to mundane problems may be worked out between the client, the client's family and the specialist in dialogic fashion. Perinbanayagam (1982) argues that a major function of astrology in Jaffna is a 'cooling of the Self', the role of the ritual expert to intervene in life crisis situations to soothe and heal the wounded ego. Astrology may also have this effect with regard to exile migrants, but here the aspect of predetermination becomes dominant, tying the individual's destiny directly to his or her origin in Sri Lanka. The crucial difference between home and exile contexts is the lack of local specialists, and charts are therefore sent to India or Sri Lanka for 'reading'.

To the individual, astrology is important mainly in two respects. While the cosmic and karmic causal explanations of *why* things are the way they are are given little attention, astrology, for one, does provide a time frame for problems and difficulties experienced by a person. Whether this is incidental or not I cannot say, but many migrants I have met seem to have charts saying they will suffer five to eight difficult years after leaving Sri Lanka before the tide will begin to turn. To the extent that this is true, these charts help to locate the initial difficulties of exile in a familiar context and to make the loneliness and suffering more bearable. Secondly, astrology is of unrivalled significance in the contraction of marriages. The comparing of the couple's astrological charts is a compulsory part of initial marriage proceedings and if a no match is found the project is invariably given up. That the competence of judgement in this matter lies out of reach adds to the difficulty and ambivalence inherent in the circumstances of establishing a family discussed above. We must remember here that most Tamil refugees in the West do not have documents that enable them to go to Sri Lanka even to visit. For his own marriage a male migrant will normally have to rely for suggestions of candidates on his family at home and is effectively shut out of the process of negotiation and decision-making taking place there. For candidates he must, in effect, trust his family to adhere to the alphabetical rule: *A* for age, *B* for beauty, *C* for caste and *D* for dowry. Thereafter his future lies with the planets, fixing the married couple's destiny according to the parameters of Jaffna time-space. We should not be blind to the fact that this situation opens up the possibility for parents to secure their own investments in migrating children. One need not spend much time with young Tamil migrants before feelings of resentment towards the older generations at home occasionally show through. Often this resentment is caused by a feeling that parents are not taking any decisive action to help establish their marriages and may in fact be delaying them deliberately – 'her family background turned out to be the wrong one', 'her horoscope did not fit', 'the girl should finish school first'. Whatever the realities, such arguments may easily be interpreted as ways of stretching indefinitely their sons' obligation to support them economically. 'We do low-caste work in Europe so that our parents can have *parayars* sweeping their courtyards at home', one of my informants complained. There seems to be an understanding among many migrants that while the danger and insecurity is there, many of the 3–400,000 Tamils from the war zone living in Colombo do have a relatively good material standard of living. This underlying tension is elaborated in the short story, 'Chekku Madu' which was introduced

in the last chapter. What the author brings out in a masterly way is
the painful duality inherent in Kumaran's situation. On the one hand
he is not able to marry his beloved because of his father's demands
upon him:

While Kumaran arrived in Norway and degenerated as a refugee, his family
in Jaffna raised themselves socially and economically. Nagalingam [Kumaran's
father] who earlier had not been able to find a husband for his daughter among
schoolteachers, exalted himself among the rich and started looking among
doctors, engineers and university teachers ...

On the other hand, what is revealed through the story is that the reason
why the *pey* attacks Kumaran is that he himself has prevented his sister
from marrying the man she loves and has pressured her into having
an abortion when she was pregnant by this man. In spite of Kumaran's
socialist convictions, the reason for his action is the inferior status of
his sister's lover. In his new position as a breadwinner Kumaran takes
the responsibility for upholding the traditions and ideals of social
mobility which effectively hinder both his sister's and his own happiness.
The story thus brings out the moral complexity which I see as
characteristic of the young Tamils in exile. As so well put by the writer,
this ambivalent relationship to their own cultural standards also has
bearings on the way they see Norwegians and Norwegian society:

Even now, in the middle of the night, the streets were filled with women.
This was the beauty of Oslo ... Four girls and three boys walked passed him
carrying beer bottles. Kumaran suddenly became annoyed when he saw that
one of the girls had dark skin like himself. He mumbled 'whore!' but consoled
himself she was probably not Tamil ...

7   THE ETHNIC INTERFACE

In this chapter I will consider the question of an interconnection between the Tamils' legal status in Norway and the way they come to see themselves. Most Tamil refugees consider themselves unwanted by Norwegian society. This understanding is not so much a consequence of everyday discrimination, but results from the media focus on questions related to immigration and their 'interaction' with the officials who represent their main contact to Norwegian society – social workers, police officers and immigration personnel. Their understanding of Norwegians in general is coloured by the fact that these so easily seem to accept what is perceived as blatant government racism. They are seen as withdrawn, non-committing and governed by a rule-oriented morality. Consequently, in particular by those who have arrived in later years, Norwegians are left outside the sphere of emotional interaction and living in Norway is seen primarily as a set of conditions structuring the possibilities of taking care of their own affairs.

In this respect, however, the Norwegian presence is strongly felt. The commotion surrounding asylum matters leaves the individual exposed, standing out against the background. For Tamils the media interest has run in waves – 1987, 1990, 1992, 1995 – relative to the increased efforts to tighten up immigration policy. During the periods of high intensity, facing Norwegian colleagues at work or school becomes a trial in itself. 'People are trying to be friendly,' Nandan said during a period of media publicity, 'when I come to work they laugh and say things like, "Oh, they didn't catch you yet?" or "Please tell me if you need a place to hide!" To me it is a terrible strain.'

Nandan is a man in his early thirties. He came to Norway in 1984 from Palaly, the coastal area north of Jaffna now occupied by government forces. After the Colombo riots in 1983 he managed to obtain school admission through a relative in Norway and later continued as a technical student at the university. Time and again I

117

told him that he should apply for asylum while such applications were being granted, that the tide might turn and that sooner or later he would have to face the issue. Every time he evaded the question, made excuses and said that if the situation improved he would like to go back and do something for his country. Without saying it in so many words it was clear that he did not *want* to be an 'asylum seeker', that in his own eyes the legitimacy of his stay depended on the prospect of going back, of not becoming a permanent member of Norwegian society. Only after finishing his university education, finding it impossible, as I had in fact predicted, to have his student visa renewed, he applied for asylum in 1993 and received his first rejection the following year.

I know I should have applied for asylum long ago. After what happened in 1983 I just couldn't bring myself to face the police, being interrogated, having to tell the whole story, facing the distrust. For ten years I have been able to convince myself my difficulties were over. Now, waiting for the deportation order, I realise I have been living in a dream world. I feel I am now where I was ten years ago. Every morning I follow the same routine: first I check my mailbox for letters from the police, then I open the papers to see if there are any new stories about us. Only if there is nothing can I go out and face another day.

The police interrogation opening the legal procedure of asylum application is the focal point of contact with official Norway. One of the reasons why it is dreaded so much, I think, is due to the injustice which it is felt to do to the applicant's own biography. In the judicial procedure is contained a process of what Wood (1985) and Zetter (1988, 1991) have termed 'labelling'. The concept of 'asylum seeker' should not be seen as a clear-cut legal category but should be regarded as a bureaucratically formed identity label. Far from clarifying identity criteria the label conveys an extremely complex set of values and judgements which are more than just definitional. 'Labelling' denotes the process of arranging this complexity, the way in which people, conceived as objects of policy, are defined in convenient images (Wood 1985). Labelling, therefore, implies a process of stereotyping, of formulating a bureaucratically manageable category through dis-aggregation and standardisation. Through the judicial process a distinction is created between 'story' and 'case' in which the individual's legally evaluated protection needs are separated from their social context and transformed into compliance or non-compliance with a programmatic identity. By having their social background and reasons for flight reworked and framed in specific ways by police officers and immigration personnel many refugees come to feel that they exit from the process a different person than they entered.

Moreover, although the interrogation is part of the standard procedure for applying for asylum, it is perceived by most applicants as a criminal investigation. Police officers are described as hostile and menacing, and the possibility of indefinite detention is often being threatened if the truth about routes and agents is not forthcoming. Two dimensions of the stories about these meetings with the police are very striking, both illustrated by Nandan's statement above. The first is the feeling of being taken back to a situation which existed before fleeing, where the threat to one's integrity was experienced as acute. Most often the situation in Norway is compared to the period in Colombo before leaving, where the understanding of being unwanted as a Tamil was combined with a feeling of unprotectedness, of always being within the reach of representatives of the authorities. The second is a 'revelatory' dimension, the realisation that the police hostility and the situation of interrogation represents the 'true' Norway. Even for people who have lived for years without any major problems in the country before applying, facing this situation tends to give the image of democracy and legal security projected by Norwegians and Norwegian authorities the status of an illusion.

Neither does this understanding normally change when and if the application is granted. To an asylum seeker the official presence represents a constant intrusion beyond media attention and the asylum procedure itself. The nature of this situation is indicated by one man who was trying to bring his fiancée to Norway. He showed me a letter from immigration stating he was required to forward 23 documents, most of which had to be issued in Jaffna where he himself was not allowed to travel on his 'foreigner's passport'. Refugees are seriously affected by the fact that taking care of family responsibilities requires a mobility which is severely restricted through economic and bureaucratic impediments. A fundamental gap exists between the needs of refugees in their international existence and the 'needs' of nation states as articulated in legislation and procedure. Masila was going to marry a man in France, the marriage having been already arranged by her parents. Having lived in Norway for more than eight years and knowing she would lose her permanent visa if she stayed away for too long, she stubbornly refused to go without first having tried to obtain citizenship. She applied through the police in the proper way but they took one year to forward her application to the immigration service. When it reached the handling officer a copy of her ID document was missing in the file. Instead of giving her a call so that she could provide the copy herself, the officer sent the file back to the police and instructed them to ask her for it, which they did after another year had passed. Masila did in fact obtain her citizenship which, strictly speaking, she was not entitled to. By then, however, the marriage had long since been cancelled by the groom and Masila's relationship to her parents was no longer what it had been. To a refugee even the simplest aspects of life – residence, housing, work, travel, marriage – seem to depend on the will of administrators. There are always forms to be filled in, time spent waiting for answers, and as Silverman (1992: 132) says about the situation in France, this permanent contact with the administration 'is inevitably interiorised and contradicts the distinction between public and private life'.

DISCREPANT STORIES

Speaking as I did in Chapter 5 of 'fragmentation' and a lack of leadership in dealing with the official Norwegian presence may seem like adopting a rhetorical position, taking for granted assumptions which are highly questionable. It presupposes that there exists, or *should* exist, such a thing as a 'Tamil community', a bounded whole defined by internal structures and common values which now refuses to hold together. As I have tried to show, this should not be taken for granted when speaking of a society like the Tamil one. However, in self-perception as well as in the labelling by others, there is an ambiguity and oscillation between part and whole, between element and category. In facing Norwegian society there is a felt need, especially among long stayers, to do something about common problems, particularly those related to questions of immigration and harassment by the police. So far joint action has largely been impossible, partly because official taxonomy renders internal agreement on their own position difficult. Self-ascription and judgement by others engage in a very complicated dynamics, establishing identity in alternative gestalt-like configurations. Let me try to illustrate this.

In a meeting between immigration and one of the Tamil Oslo groups held in 1992, representatives of the immigration service suggested that if the other party were to take responsibility for visitors not to stay longer than their visas allowed, the policy on family visits from abroad could be relaxed. Representatives of the Tamil organisation admitted frankly that they were not in a position either to issue such guarantees or to exercise the degree of control that such a policy would imply. What this small example indicates is that whereas, to the government, the asylum seeker is and should be an individual, his social identity remains the ethnic outsider. While their legal status is individually determined, moral responsibility is conferred on the basis of group identity. To the refugee, on the other hand, the label of 'asylum seeker', and the individual assessment that it implies, is seen to undermine the collective identity which is embedded in family networks.

In the meeting mentioned above, the Tamil representatives put forward the proposal that Norwegian authorities, instead of dealing with asylum applicants individually, should take a quota of Tamil refugees and then close the border. Tamils' main wish is a recognition from the Norwegian authorities that they are all – whatever their age, sex and legal status – refugees fleeing from an objectively difficult situation; not in the sense that they should be granted specific privileges but in the sense that they should be granted the *same* privileges, that they are all here because they cannot be at home. The main complaint put forward by the Tamil side was that most Tamil asylum seekers arriving in the early 1980s had been granted recognition as refugees while those arriving after 1986 had not. In their understanding this was related to the fact that most of these early applicants had been active LTTE-members, in other words that Norwegian authorities intervene and take sides in internal conflicts, caring less about the killed than about the killers. Tamils in general find it very difficult to comprehend how a country like Norway, with a relatively recent refugee history of its own, may remain insensitive to the suffering of people in their own situation of civil war. Like the Norwegians after the Second World War, they argue, they will go back when the war is over and try to resolve the differences and heal the wounds. That their understanding of the Norwegian situation may not be entirely correct is of little relevance here. A recognition by Norwegian authorities that they are *all*, including members of conflicting guerrilla groups, in a sense victims of a common disaster would, in their opinion, help such a process.

What we have here is a somewhat inverted relationship between individual and group. The deciding of individual asylum applications is seen as an assessment of destitution, referring the person to a common category of the needy. Collective acceptance, on the other hand, would be a recognition of their industrious quality and of their willingness to work in Norway since the late 1960s. According to their implicit understanding, a collective basis for their presence must be found for them to be accepted as individuals. For this reason, great pains are taken not to make public internal controversies which would endanger the reputation of the community as a whole. This goes for political conflicts but also for aspects of traditional culture which is seen as contradicting core values in Norwegian society. A personal experience may illustrate this point.

In 1988 I was asked to visit a town in the northern part of the country to give a talk to a group of people who, through their work, were in daily contact with refugees from Sri Lanka. The subject of my speech was 'Tamil culture' in general, and as part of this I gave a standard presentation of caste and caste conflicts in Sri Lanka. On this occasion there were in the audience two Tamil men working as interpreters in a township in the region. At the end of my speech, one of them in particular protested loudly, arguing that caste in Tamil Sri Lanka was a thing of the past and that my presentation had portrayed his countrymen as 'uncivilised and barbaric'. As it turned out, no doubt partly because of our discussion after the meeting, this man became well known to me. Several years later he told me that the reason why he had moved to this northern town in the first place was that while living in the south he had married a girl of another, somewhat higher, caste in a 'love marriage'. Her family, which supported and had the support of the local LTTE people, did not accept the marriage and not only made the girl break with him but also threatened that if he did not leave the town he would face an early death.

The way the authorities frame the phenomenon of migration crystallises into public images. These images shape the stories migrants tell about themselves. In the old narrative the migrant was a noble character. He was a man wanted for his skill and his labour, a person whose honour depended on his loyalty to his employer and his benefit to his people. There is a sense in which the Tamil migrant, in order to keep his self-respect, needs to be *better* than those among whom he lives, to incorporate difference from a position of moral superiority. This understanding, still found among the early migrant workers, has in their own eyes been undermined by asylum migration. Many early settlers express harsher views on the young asylum seekers than any immigration official or right-wing politician does. In the early 1970s the number of Tamil migrants in Norway was no more than 50. Despite the fact that most saw themselves as having to leave their country they had no wish to seek asylum. On the contrary, having struggled to clear their own path in unknown territory, often investing in the lengthy acquisition of language and professional skills, some of them calling their children by Norwegian names, many deplore the coming of the asylum seekers, their lack of education and their disrespect towards Norwegian society. The experiences that migrant workers relate about their early years in Norway differ radically from the ones told by later refugees. In those days you were accepted if you worked hard and behaved decently. People would invite you home and enquire about the land and culture. If you were lost in a city anyone would show you the way, take you in their car or pay for your bus ticket. By demonstrating a willingness to work it was also possible to find a job for your brother, cousin or nephew. This has changed now, they say, but the worst part is that we helped to change it. Our own morale has degenerated. The people we brought here do not respect us. Our own relatives, whose tickets we paid for, have become strangers to us. The war and chaos have made them a different kind of people. The blame that the Norwegian authorities have to accept is that they have let the degeneration continue by letting material benefits come so easily to individuals being offered protection. 'The tragedy of our people is the indifference of our young', one early migrant, the leader of one of the caste communities on the west coast, explained to me:

The asylum seekers will never learn the real value of things. Education and learning used to be our trade mark. We studied because our success brought glory to our family and our people. Today they can go to the West and get everything for free. An asylum seeker being settled today will be given for free what I struggled for twenty years to achieve. They have become corrupt. They have become like Norwegians.

To become 'like Norwegians' is the condensed expression of what being Tamil is not about: individualism, self-interest, materialism, moral laxity, disrespect of elders.

Perhaps ironically, this view is shared by many asylum seekers themselves. With the possible exception of the few who were granted refugee status in the early 1980s, asylum seeker identity carries no social or political worth. When the early settlers' claim for leadership is sometimes refuted by the asylum seekers, this is with reference to the seniors' lack of knowledge about contemporary Jaffna, never on the basis of their own legal status in Norway. Seeking asylum is something you do when no other option is available; it means relinquishing your dignity for handouts and leftovers, entering a relationship of individual submission to authority. This is where the asylum seeker identity connects to the cultural logic of pollution discussed at the end of Chapter 5. To give and receive are not neutral concepts in Hindu thought. Being a benefactor to someone is a way of exerting dominance while accepting gifts is a sign of accepted inferiority (Appadurai 1985). As observed by Marriot (1968), there is a sense in which this acceptance also implies a state of pollution:

Gaining dominance over others through feeding them or securing dependence on others through being fed by them appear to be comprehensive goals of actors in the system of transactions. Purity and pollution, among other values, are used as expressions of achievements towards these goals. (p. 169)

While former work migration provided a possibility of re-establishing personal autonomy by paying back the debts to society through individual excellence, this is much more difficult for an asylum seeker who, by public discourse, is left to the existence of a welfare client.

Among asylum seekers the feeling that Tamils in exile only care about themselves is prevalent. 'You know, we are really not one people', is a comment one will hear as an explanation of why mobilising people for common interests never works. 'Tamils in exile only think about money', is another phrase often heard. Views like these are always expressed in confidence, however, told as secrets bordering on indecency. The gaze of the other makes it imperative to maintain a unity which was not originally there. Behind this facade you can trust no one except your own kin; not for help, not with money, not with information, not with anything that really matters. In fact, in exile even the support and loyalty of your own family may fail. Classificatory relationships, which at home would be reinforced by ritual transactions, are perceived as crumbling at the edges when in exile. Help with food and shelter when you arrive, yes, and occasionally a sum of money, but as a long-term thing there are limits to what they can carry. Karunan accepted responsibility for his distant, under-age cross-cousin, Kavitha, when her father sent her to Norway. He did his best, bought her clothes, sent her to school and chased the boys away in the evening. After two years, however, she would not take his orders any longer: 'You are not my brother', she told him. When he slapped her like a brother should do she disappeared and moved in with two single girls, he learned later.

This understanding of the present state of affairs may seem inconsistent with the existence of dyadic relationships as discussed in Chapter 5. I do not think it is for two reasons. In this chapter I remarked that 'vintage' relationships tend to replace family for friendship and daily company. Furthermore, the family network relationships which *are* reproduced in exile represent in most cases only part of a person's actual network connections. In other words, persons often have classificatory relatives and may even have relatively close blood-relatives in the same town or country without these being part of his or her *active* network. I have already observed that brothers and relations like nephews and paternal uncles (who are classificatory fathers) seldom seem to reside together in exile. The experience of refugee counsellors is that placing unaccompanied minor refugees in foster homes with distant relatives is often not very successful. Relatives have an obligation to assist in times of need but whether they do so or not, and whether they become part of a person's 'cluster', is an empirical question. A person may therefore experience both assistance and fragmentation at the same time.

The other reason is of a different character and is related to the concept of self-understanding as such. People's constant measuring of actions against cultural values, I suggest, reflects the mutual dependence between part and whole. Symbolic elements cannot be given meaning piecemeal, the presupposition of a whole will always be implied in the recognition of parts. Moreover, this whole must be *construed*, because it is something more than the sequence of components, it is what Ricoeur calls a 'cumulative, holistic process' (1981a: 211). The whole can only be construed through its details, however, and people's actions, like the honouring and non-honouring of obligations carry the nature of society within them. Before continuing this discussion, let me offer some observations on a family in Norway which I have come to know quite well, put together by pieces of information provided mainly by two of its members:

I have known Kuganathan for more than ten years. I met him at a seminar in 1985 while writing my MA on Sri Lankan politics and we stayed in touch on an occasional basis.

Having arrived in Norway in 1981, Kuganathan belongs to the group of early settlers. While the immigration ban had long since been implemented, he came to Norway on a tourist visa and stayed on after finding a job in a restaurant. 'There were no controls at that time,' Kuganathan told me, visibly amused, 'I just went to the Norwegian consulate in Colombo and they stamped a visa in my passport. When I landed in Norway the immigration officers at the airport did not even ask me where I came from, they just waved me through.' Three years later his wife and children, a boy and a girl, followed him and they all settled in a town on the west coast. Through Kuganathan's Norwegian contacts his wife had no difficulties finding work. 'She came on a Friday and started to work on the Monday', Kuganathan explained. The children, ten and fourteen at the time of arrival, became the first Tamil children to go to school in the town were they lived.

Kuganathan's case history is typical in its idiosyncrasy. Although we then met more rarely, it became clear to me around 1989 or 1990 that Kuganathan had increasing difficulties organising his family life in Norway. One problem was that a slump in the housing market had caused him some economic problems in relation to a house he had bought a few years earlier. His daughter, the younger of the two children, was about to finish school and Kuganathan had begun to plan for her marriage. These two worries were in fact related as the main reason why Kuganathan had invested his meagre savings in the house was that he had hoped for a rise in house prices which would help him raise a proper dowry for his daughter.

In a way characteristic of Tamils in Norway, Kuganathan's personal difficulties were aggravated by his complicated relationship to Norwegian immigration authorities. The basic problem was that to obtain a reunion with his family, something which is possible for students, two years after his arrival Kuganathan had embarked on a course to become a hospital nurse. When he graduated his student visa was not renewed and the legal basis of his and his family's residence in Norway disappeared. Eventually, around 1988, this made him apply for asylum, the only option available. As an asylum seeker he lost his work permit and, as his wife's income was insufficient to service their debts, they finally had to sell the house with a loss.

In 1992 Kuganathan was finally granted a valid resident's permit and the family could go on with their existence. However, his economic problems seemed to have changed Kuganathan's relationship to Norwegian society. During the first years of our acquaintance Kuganathan had taken a rather condescending attitude toward Tamil asylum seekers coming in large numbers in 1986–87. To me this was surprising, as he himself was very concerned about the situation in Sri Lanka. His main complaint seemed to be that by seeking asylum the refugees were giving up on their country, aiming for permanent settlement abroad. This patriotism was mixed with a resentment as to their taking advantage of the hospitality from which he himself had benefited. Now, in his own words, the encounters with banks and bureaucracy had given him a totally new understanding of Norwegian society and of himself. 'I had to come to Norway to understand what it means to be an "outcast"', he commented.

The frustration with Norwegian ways was not entirely related to his own situation, however. For example, having found work at a home for elderly people Kuganathan was appalled by the way patients were treated at his working place. 'It gives me comfort to see that there are people in Norway who are treated even worse than foreigners', he once remarked, claiming that no Tamil would accept seeing their parents growing old without the care of their children. His own implementation of Tamil family harmony was, however, not without its problems.

With the daughter's marriage becoming an increasingly important issue to the family, Kuganathan's son, Mahesh, found what he himself thought was a suitable boy for his sister, a boy the sister knew and wished to marry. He was a student of proper caste, with the added advantage that he agreed to marry her without any dowry whatsoever. When Mahesh proposed the solution to his parents, however, they refused after making enquiries in Sri Lanka, arguing that the boy was not of 'good family'. Instead Kuganathan insisted on giving the girl in marriage to his wife's brother's son who was living in Canada. He was willing to pay a dowry of about 200,000 Norwegian kroners, half of which Mahesh was told to raise. Mahesh and his sister both accepted the decision but Mahesh, whom I had come to know quite well after he moved to Oslo, cursed his parents, accusing them of destroying both their children's life. Pledging his student loan to the cause for

the next two years, he had to give up his studies in order to find a job
to support himself. According to his own explanation, his relocation
to Oslo was partly to get away from his father.

What intrigued me was that during the years when he was struggling
with these difficulties Kuganathan himself clearly became increasingly
attuned to the radical, nationalist politics represented by the LTTE.
He went to meetings, contributed financially, bought their music
cassettes, and when I visited his house in 1992 he strongly defended
the deportation of Muslims from Jaffna. LTTE's politics strongly
condemns dowry practices, but, paradoxically, it was as if their violent
rhetoric and a distant involvement in their bloody ventures in Sri Lanka
filled a personal need stemming from Kuganathan's growing frustration
with Western society and his inability to structure his own and his
family's life according to traditional Tamil values.

His children, on the other hand, were not particularly interested in
Tamil politics. At twenty Mahesh spoke Norwegian better than Tamil
and had never visited Sri Lanka as an adult. He did retain an emotional
relationship to the country, however, which grew stronger as he
himself grew older. When I asked him about it he claimed he was not
able to remember any discrimination against him as a boy in school.
As many children of the early migrants he did not feel at home among
the asylum seekers and preferred to be among Norwegian friends. 'If
I could choose I would become Norwegian', he said. The problem
was that as he reached adulthood he came to understand that he was
not able to choose, that becoming Norwegian in the sense he wished
was not possible. In particular, his loyalty to his sister in terms of financial
help, and through her to his parents, set him apart from his Norwegian
friends. When, after his sister had left for Canada, his parents urged
him to marry a woman from his father's village in Sri Lanka, he
gradually seemed to resign himself to a situation that he was not able
to control. When the young woman arrived, they married through
the civil registration procedure and moved into the one-room apartment
he was renting. When I asked him if he was not going to have a ritual
marriage, Mahesh said he would rather buy a car for himself than a
thali for his wife. 'I cannot deal with all this religious nonsense,' he
said, 'it's about time someone brings a little rational thinking into the
picture!' Six months later, however, he and his wife were on their
way to Singapore where his parents had arranged full marriage
proceedings in a Hindu temple. Singapore is one of the few places

where Tamils may go without a visa and the two families were assembling there. When I commented on what he had stated earlier, Mahesh said that he had acceded to the wish of his father. 'When he said he would pay for it all I really had no choice,' he said, 'although I know that in a few weeks he will send me the bills and inform me about a son's duties.'

One need not look hard to see that there are apparent moral inconsistencies contained in this story. While undermining social forms formerly taken for granted, exile reinforces the felt need for a cultural basis of identity. The question is where to find this basis, in tradition or in the revolutionary politics of national liberation.

DIASPORA, MODERNITY AND CULTURAL CODES

What has made me repeatedly return to the refugees' relationship with immigration is that this is the institutional fact around which exile life revolves, the dimension of Norwegianness which may not be avoided. What we see at work among exiles in facing this fact is a process where one cultural narrative is found to crumble and a new being constructed in opposition to the host society. The internal crumbling and the external distancing work together in defining a space for modified identities. On the one hand, exile existence breaks up families, modifies old distinctions and creates new divides. On the other hand, the process of migration does put people in a situation which is recognisably common to all. Sooner or later people will meet problems which others in different positions have. Migrant workers, who have often assisted relatives' asylum journey, will be granted responsibility for their future in Norway. Former guerrillas with refugee status have brothers and sisters without comparable backgrounds who also need security. In this situation rules and regulations appear as a jungle where *all* are lost. Before your sister arrives to claim the school admittance that you have secured, rules are changed and a student visa is no longer obtainable. If your fiancée arrives through Germany all is well, if she arrives through Sweden she will be sent back and you will have paid a year's salary for no purpose. Immigrants in general seem to have a profound lack of knowledge about the legal basis of their stay in Norway. Most Tamils do not know if unemployment will affect their resident's permits or if their 'foreigner's passports' will prevent them from being sent home if the fighting stops for a month or two in Sri Lanka. And if they are told by officials they will not trust what they hear. Immigration officials, according to them, are people who lie on principle. Mr J, my assistant, called one day about his work permit and was told that, sorry, he had to wait for three more months. The next day the answer was in his mailbox.

What most people perceive, therefore, is that to the authorities their presence constitutes a problem. They are unable to follow the twists and turns in the authorities' legal reasoning. Stories of individual experiences with particular officers are recounted and exchanged, the immigration service's quality of imperviousness to reason made worse by the knowledge that there are, in fact, people on the inside. During fieldwork I met Tamils who had lived in the country for ten years or more, thinking that they had nothing to worry about, until suddenly they received a notification by mail saying that they should be out of the country within three weeks. Such stories, and there are many, work as a kind of 'proto-ideology' in terms of which people's position *vis-à-vis* Norwegian society is framed. As for the Saami discussed by Henriksen (1991), the repertoire of stories depicting individual encounters and confrontations with the authorities functions as an interpretative framework providing a shared understanding of what it means to be a Tamil in Norway today. This understanding has provided some tangible consequences. At the end of 1994 a joint Tamil 'action committee' was established in Oslo in order to assist asylum applicants who have had their applications rejected. This committee included representatives of all major factions present in the capital. While the effectiveness of their work may be a matter for discussion, the experiment of working together was seen as a radical development by the participants themselves. A consequence of a different sort is the numerous indications that migrants who have lived in Norway for 15 years or more, are increasingly turning their backs on Norwegian society in order to search for a sense of belonging in the exclusive company of fellow Tamils.

I should clarify the point that I am trying to make here. I do not claim that this shared framework structures the nature of Tamil identity as such, only the nature of Tamil identity in exile. This statement is not as subtle as it may seem. Saussure has remarked somewhere (1960) that the same phoneme pronounced by two different people is not identical with itself. The task which social complexity presents is to find ways to describe and analyse how identity may simultaneously be 'same' and 'not same'. The best I can do at this stage is to point out that while interaction between the authorities and the exile population seems to further a delimitation of ethnic consciousness it seems to do so mainly in a negative way by providing a sense of what they are *not*. In other words, repetitive interaction does not seem, at least so far, to generate the integration or 'ethnic incorporation' expected from some of our traditional models (Bart 1969, Eidheim 1971). Instead of what Eidheim, with reference to the Saami minority situation, has termed 'dichotomisation' (1971: 79), that is, the making of ethnic designata into objects of incorporative transactions, we find a patterned reproduction of conflicts not only between traditional identities like village, family, etc., but also between a traditional model of society implying internal difference on the one hand and a revolutionary model imposing unity on the other. This may, of course, be depicted as a dichotomisation not yet concluded, but in fact I think the situation is more complicated.

I find this reproduction of conflicts to be related to Epstein's discussion of 'negative identity' (1978: 101 ff.). Epstein's point is that since ethnic identity is always a product of the interaction between inner perception and outer response, such identity should be envisaged as lying on a continuum marked by positive and negative poles. While at the positive pole ethnic identity depends upon shared inner concepts of exclusiveness, 'at the other extreme the identity may rest on no, or only minimal, inner definition, and is essentially imposed from without' (p. 102). I also find it related to Clifford's (1994) discussion of diasporic consciousness as breaking 'the binary relation of *minority* communities with *majority* societies' (p. 311). While conceptualisations of immigrant societies describe them as inherently temporary units, as sites from where narratives of assimilation or ethnic integration may be organised, diasporic discourses 'reflect the sense of being part of an ongoing transnational network that includes the homeland, not as something left behind, but as a place of attachment in a contrapuntal modernity' (Clifford 1994).

One way of reframing the difference from what Eidheim discusses would be to say that his 'dichotomisation' amounts to the establishment of a conventional relationship between signifier and signified. It does not really matter *which* designata take the positions of ethnic signifiers as long as an agreement can be reached on this question. Such agreement is possible, one must presume, because these designata refer to a *presence* engaging in the signifying activity. The conventional relationship is established through an interaction which is seen to conform to a dialogic model. In the Tamil case, on the other hand, ethnic designata are perceived as metonymically referring to an *absence*. What establishes the signifying difference from Norwegian society is that language, colour, morality and so on are seen as part of a 'totality' which is somewhere else. In this situation, agreement on referential meaning is more difficult because the signified is always also a signifier. While Tamil life in Norway is given meaning by its reference to Eelam, Eelam itself carries the referential burden of unifying the Sri Lanka-Tamil diaspora. This provides the signifying function with a fundamental instability but also with a certain amount of freedom. Two readings of the same book, Derrida observes, show an identity which can only be defined as difference:

From the moment that the circle turns, that the book is wound back upon itself, that the book repeats itself, its self-identity receives an imperceptible difference which allows us to step effectively, rigorously, and thus discreetly, out of the closure. Redoubling the closure, one splits it ... This departure outside of the identical within the same remains very slight, it weighs nothing, it thinks and weighs the book *as such*. The return to the book is also the abandoning of the book. (1976: xii)

This perspective allows us to see that while imposing an extra dimension on social organisation, the framework of inter-ethnic interaction does not, in itself, necessarily *determine* the individual's conceptualisation of himself and his situation. In relation to the Saami situation, Henriksen, in the article referred to above, notes that: 'While people in one context may forcibly argue in line with one shared interpretative framework, they may in another context adhere to, and even act according to an interpretative framework which implies contrary political strategies and even loyalties' (1991: 421). This matches perfectly my own observations among the people in question. In my material such contradictions range from people expressing their admiration for the thorough Norwegian bureaucracy but condemning the investigations which reveal their own concealment of information to stating their wish to go back to Sri Lanka but worrying about peace talks which might make this possible. While agreeing with Henriksen that such inconsistencies may reasonably be depicted as a consequence of actors' participation in different social fields, I would add that for the Tamils they also reflect a double vision inherent in transnationality. The Tamil setting clearly contains a very strong diasporic potential. Among the circle of my ten to fifteen closest informants, *all* have relatively close family members living in at least two Western countries outside Norway. Mr J, for example, has his father in Sri Lanka, his mother and one sister in India, one sister and one brother in Germany, one sister in France and one in England while the extended family is further dispersed. Nandan, whom we met above, has two sisters in England, one brother in Canada and one in the USA. In spatial terms Karunan's immediate family would appear as illustrated in the diagram.

These people's family situations are quite ordinary. Such networks and the information they contain provide a 'subsidiary sociality', an outside context of interaction breaking their 'binary relation' to Norwegian society. It is interesting to note that in the maintenance of these family networks an aspect of 'simultaneity' also makes itself present (see Chapter 5). When Karunan's grandmother died in Jaffna, funeral rites were performed at the same time in Sri Lanka, France,

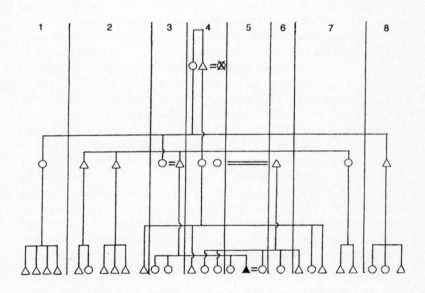

Karunan's immediate family. 1. Switzerland, 2. England, 3. France, 4. Sri Lanka, 5. Norway, 6. Germany, 7. Canada, 8. USA.

England and Canada. After the cremation in Jaffna, video copies of the events were circulated among members of the family. If there is a common, positive exile identity related to traditional family-based social structure, it consists in the claim of an ability to survive. 'We will manage,' people say, 'if not here, somewhere else.' In my understanding, Tamil refugees are true cosmopolitans, but *subaltern* cosmopolitans, able to intervene in the fields which try to regulate their presence, creating for themselves a space where the constraining order may be used for their own ends. Their problem as refugees is not their dispersal but the barriers restricting spatial mobility, in particular the restricted travel documents issued to *de facto* refugees. This, however, is after all a problem limited in time, at least it is so in Norway, and most Tamils aim for citizenship. Not because they have any illusion that this will make them more Norwegian or more accepted, but because the passport brings freedom from geographical boundaries. As against the *strategy* of nation states, which assumes a place that can be circumscribed and serve as the basis for generating relationships of power (de Certeau 1984), their operations rest on a concept of *tactic*, that is, insinuating themselves into the place of the other, constantly turning events into opportunities.

Nevertheless, the exact relationship between the contextual meanings and the larger cultural constructs needs to be considered. In other words, *the way* by which people come to share, or not share, a common understanding of their situation needs to be elucidated. One clue to this question, I believe, lies in the concept of 'contrapuntal modernity' found in the above quote from Clifford. This concept, borrowed from Said (1984: 172) who uses it to describe the exile's vision of 'the entire world as a foreign land', points to the fact that for individuals raised in a non-modern setting migration to the West may be said to entail a kind of 'imposed modernity'. The three sets of elements used by Giddens (1991: 16–21) to explain the dynamic character of modern social life – the separation of time and space, the disembedding of social relationships and the institutionalisation of reflexivity – are all present and dominant in exile existence. However, while to people in the West they are predominantly conceptual of character, for Tamil migrants they result from the physical movement in space:

- In Jaffna, as in other pre-modern settings, time and space remain connected through the situatedness of place. This goes for the continued ritual timing related to temples and village goddesses, but also for the new revolutionary calendar. No one visiting Jaffna will remain insensitive to the fact that the whole area stands forth in public consciousness as a representation of time: cyclical time through the annual celebrations of the leader in his native village and commemorations of the deaths of Black July at the actual spot where things happened, but also linear time: '*This* is where the ten people died during the first Tamil conference', '*these* are the ruins of our library which the Sinhala mob burned', '*here* the first Indian soldiers landed in 1987 and were shot by our boys'. Unlike in modern societies where the separation of time and space makes time an 'empty' dimension, however, migration – watching Eelam from the outside – tends to make space empty while the fullness of Jaffna time continues its course.

- In modern societies social relations are 'lifted out' of local contexts and are re-articulated across indefinite tracts of time-space. The parallel to this process in migration is obvious. It should be noted, however, that to Giddens this disembedding depends in an essential way on trust, 'a quality of "faith" which is irreducible' (p. 19). To migrants, on the other hand, this involuntary 'lifting out' promotes the opposite: a general attitude of *dis*-trust underlying day-to-day decisions. This is because both main disembedding mechanisms, money and expert systems, affect them negatively: as a lack or as knowledge and technology representing a potential danger to their position.

- In spite of the predominantly negative character of the disembedding process, this process does infuse social life with an unprecedented reflexivity. Even if mediated by a continued adherence to tradition, the migrant's life project, in a different way than before, becomes his own responsibility. By the very fact of having left, and therefore having a choice of going back which was not there before, the individual is forced to think and plan in the terms of option and risk so characteristic of modern life. This openness makes possible the 'composing' of a self-identity based on *selective* commitment to social relations and the incorporation of cultural elements from different settings.

A second clue to explain the inherent contradictions in exile social life is to observe that these contradictions are not necessarily unsystematic, not coming to life in and through the situation alone. The fundamental contradiction pertaining to Tamil refugees lies in the

fact that many, like Kuganathan above, come to look upon the LTTE
as a source of regeneration in their exile existence. In spite of the limited
number of their active members, the fact is that the LTTE, not only
in Norway but in most Western countries, draws support, and seems
to do so increasingly, from people who have fled to get away from
their dictatorship in Sri Lanka and have relatives still suffering under
their rule there. It is here, at this precise point, that the spirit of self-
sacrifice of the LTTE soldiers becomes important. The actual materiality
of death makes it difficult not to believe the LTTE when they say that
their fighters die on behalf of the Tamil nation. Even people who in
public take upon themselves the burden of speaking against the LTTE
may sometimes admit in private conversations that, emotionally, they
are not able to free themselves from sympathy for the organisation and
its cause.

In this situation, describing the relationship between the LTTE and
the non-LTTE positions as a conflict between groups is not satisfactory.
In the next chapters I will argue that there are at present two cultural
'models' or 'plots' existing side by side in the Jaffna-Tamil universe,
and that many contradictions in the lives of Tamil exiles go back to
the relationship between these two which I term the 'traditional' and
the 'revolutionary'.[1] The traditional model is founded on a hierarchy
which is open, in the sense of having the capacity to incorporate and
adjust to difference. In the same way that it pays no heed to the difference
between Sinhalese and Tamil but sees 'Ceylon' as a permeable
framework for the ordering of substance and quality (see Chapter 2),
it tends to integrate, and let itself be integrated into, representations
of the 'West'. The revolutionary model, on the other hand, is based
in a concept of bounded equality comprising, and being restricted to,
carriers of a Tamil national identity. In exile it involves the 'closing',
through new symbolic means, of the social body being exposed
through migration (see Chapter 5).

These two models, while both originating in South-Asian traditions
and political dynamism, lay down different premises for exile life.
Disregarding for a moment the external restrictions on doing so, the
traditional model would permit living a full Tamil life outside the home
country while the revolutionary one would not. While the traditional
model seeks to recreate in a local context the hierarchy of identities
in which it originates, the rituals of exile revolutionary life are
exclusively dedicated to the time-space of Eelam. In cultural meetings

organised by the LTTE, the emphasis is mainly on two themes. One is the construction of a common nationality, for example, combining Jaffna classical art with local folk dances from Batticaloa into a composite heritage to be preserved and defended. The other is a focus on the common destiny of the Eelam-Tamil people as linked to Eelam itself, and the temporary character of outside existence. In one speech from an LTTE meeting in 1993, given by a boy of about twelve years old with a great deal of pathos, this view was summarised in the following way:

How many days will this refugee life last? When the atrocities of the Sinhalese terrorists increased, to protect our lives we fled. But we never had a good life in these countries. The iron fist of our enemy is crushing our language, our culture. Like ourselves our children will become people who have lost both [*irandum illathavarkal*]. Wherever we live we are only temporarily separated from our home. Wherever we live our thoughts should go to our country. We are not a society of gypsies. We are cuckoo birds who do not know how to build nests in these borrowed motherlands [*iraval thai nadu*]. We will construct a country for ourselves. We cannot forget our homeland. From here we give our strength to the task of constructing our Motherland!

My view on the existence of 'cultural models' implies taking a theoretical position on the question of culture and agency. Barth (1993), in his recent book dealing specifically with this question, holds on to a generative model where social meaning, or 'knowledge' in his own terms, is seen to be an aggregated result of actors' individual instrumental intentions. His project is '... to show how the interpretations of events made by people from their diverse vantage points are aggregated so they converge on shared meanings – i.e., an ethnographically ascertained degree of common reality' (p. 96). Henriksen (1991), on the other hand, stresses the 'process of justification' as a crucial mechanism in linking choice and action to existing interpretative frameworks (p. 421). This is closer to my own view because it permits seeing cultural constructs as, in a phenomenological sense, always already constituted.

8   THE NATURE OF TRADITION

At a distance from the source of cultural values migrants are forced to reconstruct imaginatively their cultural identity, often from childhood memories. In the situation dealt with here, the lack of elders in the exile population implies a break in the transmission of cultural knowledge. For example, obtaining information in Norway on questions like the observance of death pollution or the precise nature of caste rules was close to impossible. Invariantly this was referred to as 'something our parents know'. This lack of knowledge provides a certain latitude with respect to undesired practices. At the same time it makes the performance of roles with which persons wish to identify difficult. In Chapter 7 I mentioned Karunan who fell out with his cross-cousin because, as she said, he behaved like the brother he was not. Karunan wanted to take responsibility, to live up to what he saw as the standard of Tamil family solidarity. What it meant to be a 'cross-cousin', however, was not at all clear to him. After living his adult life in Norway it was a role he had to construct for himself from whatever material was available.

In the legal discourse persons become refugees when entering a foreign territory. To refugees themselves, however, flight and exile are inherently associated with a specific relationship to their native place, with the rift forced between the self and its true home (Said 1984). My argument in this and the next two chapters is that to most Tamil migrants the conditions of exile are important, but important in the specific way of influencing their relationship to home. Their self-identity is constructed from the adoption of one or the other, or in most cases of elements from both, of two different conceptions of Tamil society in time. The first centres on the invariant nature of kinship obligations, the second on the progress of the Tamil nation in history. In other words, while the situation of exile influences the choices they make and the importance they place on each of the two conceptions, the raw material of Tamils' identity construction is invariantly brought from Sri Lanka. This makes it necessary to focus not only on what Sri Lanka means to the migrant, but also on how migrants are contextually defined in Sri Lanka.

From the viewpoint of their original social surroundings migrants' most conspicuous characteristic is their absence. By this fact alone their act of migration is open to interpretation by others. In the following I will argue that migration, to Jaffna society, has a 'specific plurivocity' (Ricoeur 1981a): as a social practice upholding hierarchy and, alternatively, as a decision not to take part in the struggle for liberation. What makes the plurivocity *specific* is that caste hierarchy and national liberation are embedded in different narratives centring on the same cluster of symbols.

Different aspects of the first narrative have already been touched upon in Chapter 2. What I call here the traditional reading of history is based upon what used to be the textbook version of culture, propagating the Tamil elite's unquestioned right to political power and social dominance. This elite saw its own position as a consequence and continuation of 2000 years of South-Asian history and religion. What is worth observing is that the traditional model or reading of culture contains many elements which we, from a different perspective, might wish to call 'modern'. In particular, when faced with the colonial situation this elite showed a large degree of openness to outside impulses; a willingness to adapt and change, but also a determination to use this new situation to preserve central elements of their own tradition. 'Tradition', as this term is used here, should therefore not be conceived as an absolute quality contrasted to the character of modern society. I use this term because what I refer to by it is *perceived* as tradition, in the sense of constituting a moral order which should remain unchanged, the explication of 'how things are' being handed down from one generation to the next.

What I will do in the following is to relate migration to the organisational elements of kinship and marriage in the make-up of Jaffna society. This discussion must include considerations of class and caste. In Jaffna, among the class of people struggling to preserve a bourgeois standard of life in the midst of war, one often hears the opinion voiced that those who join the LTTE are people who for social or economic reasons 'have no choice'. While I do not believe this to be entirely true, partly because I personally know people from well-off families who have joined the movement for purely ideological reasons, these statements reflect a social conceptualisation of the situation as in some way related to the class (and caste) character of society. Among people who used to be leading, migration stands forth as an explicit alternative to fighting. Youngsters *should* go in order not to be devoured by the militant movement. If children become involved, parents may go to any length in order to remove them from the clutches of the liberation fighters. Their immediate security is, of course, one reason for such action. There is, however, much more involved in their decision.

In a letter addressed to the first Norwegian administrator of the Cey-Nor project (see Chapter 4) from the residents of Thoppukadu, the site of the project, the signatories ask 'that a few of our young men are given the opportunity of being trained in some trade in your country'. What the letter says, in effect, is that development assistance is all very well, but the real wish of the people of Thoppukadu is to leave Sri Lanka altogether. This is one small example which shows that well before the war there existed in Tamil Sri Lanka what Caplan (1995), with reference to India, has termed a 'culture of emigration', that is, an understanding that 'life is only abroad, not here'. Jaffna today is a place where the older generation speaks better English than the younger one. Based on their experiences under British administration the traditional elite had an open mind towards the outside world. After 1948 this outside connection became the only guarantee against a hostile Sinhala nationalism and many from this older generation today deeply regret that they did not leave, or did not stay where they had already gone, before the tightening of immigration regulations in English-speaking countries made relocation more difficult. In a situation where language policy and rules for admission to higher education are understood to favour the ethnic majority, migration is not perceived as disowning one's origin but protecting what is truly Tamil. Today, seeing in the militant movement not only a vehicle of physical destruction but a socially inferior organisation totally unacceptable to the Tamil tradition of non-violent politics, their efforts concentrate on assisting their children to find a future abroad. This often means favouring *one* child with money for an agent, with a dowry or with an education which may qualify them for the high level of entry under the emigration point schemes operated by countries like Canada and Australia. Any of these ways requires large expenses, imposing hardship on the family as a whole, investments which can only be justified by the understanding that the one who leaves will bring something back. The migrant is expected to 'sponsor' siblings and cousins and to help provide for the older generation normally left behind. Consider the following illustration. In *Tamil Times*, the independent Tamil magazine issued in London, obituaries are published every month. The following is one example from the May 1993 issue:

Mr. Elangaiyar Gurusamy (86), Retired Ceylon Government Railway and former Chairman, Town Council, Kankesanthurai, beloved father of Dr. Langainarayanan (Trichy), Navukarasi Ponnampalam (U.K.), late Shanmugavadivu Panchadcharam (Inuvil, Sri Lanka) Parimalakanthy Pandithavarathan, Vijayaluxmy Paramasivam (both of Colombo), Kanchanamala Puvanenthiran (Switzerland), Thangaluxmy Tharmapalasingam, Yogambihai Gajendra (both of U.K.) and Gnanambihai Shanmugaraja (Canada) passed away in Inuvil, Sri Lanka 17th February 1993. We thank for all messages of sympathy and support during the period of grief ...

Families like the one of this elderly gentleman are what exile communities are made of. As we see, among his ten children one is in India, three in the UK, one in Switzerland and one in Canada. His position is not unique. Going through the obituaries for people who died in 1993, we find that the 16 people who died in Sri Lanka (exile deaths excluded) had 80 children altogether. Among these only 30 were still living in Sri Lanka, 23 were living in Great Britain, 11 in Canada, 9 in Australia, 2 in the USA, 2 in Germany, 1 in Switzerland, 1 in Oman and 1 in India.

While this statistical material is, of course, too limited to draw any firm conclusions, there is something to be learned from this. First, the obituaries strongly indicate that migration is not a random fact; that the decision to leave is taken more often in some families than in others. The total number of advertisements testifies to the fact that most Tamil migrants do come from families comparable to that of the deceased above: railway officials, postmasters, teachers, landowners – in short, the economic middle class. Second, it is worth noting the fact that the children's residence, when outside the Tamil homeland, is always given in obituaries. Where this is recommendable the relative's profession or actual working place is always included in the text: 'XX, Doctor of Medicine (Geneva)', 'NN, National Development Bank (Toronto)'. A migrating member of the family is clearly something which brings renown to the dead.

There is another side to this, however. While the majority of migration histories may adhere to the ideal pattern of relatives helping each other along, many do not, for the simple reason that to 'sponsor' relations may not be possible or that work on which to support family members may not be available. In Sri Lanka such failure to fulfil obligations is often a cause of bitterness within the family, a situation only worsened by migrants' inclination not to tell the real story of their social devaluation in the West. I will return to this later.

While they are important to the individual migrant, personal obligations do not provide a satisfactory understanding of the kinship-migration nexus. In discussing migration as a class-based phenomenon we must consider the ideological importance of kinship. Migration as a *controversial* fact can only be appreciated through its relationship to marriage, the core symbol around which the two dominant interpretations of Jaffna society revolve. That the Indian movies banned by LTTE censorship in guerrilla-controlled areas since the early 1990s are the ones portraying traditional gender roles and the sensuous pleasures of married life is no accident. It is because marriage, and the transfer of property with which it is connected, is the main mechanism through which traditional society as a social formation was, and to some extent still is, reproduced. To catch a first glimpse of the guerrilla's counter-hegemonic project, we may note as a preliminary observation that the two hallmarks of a common LTTE soldier are, one, that he or she is unmarried and, two, that the cyanide capsule is worn like a *thali*, the women's marriage necklace, around the neck. In Jaffna, 'wearing the cyanide' has the implication of being wedded to the cause and therefore that considerations of family and domestic life are relinquished for Eelam. That the replacement of the *thali* by the capsule is an image not confined to the anthropologist's mind is made clear by the young soldier-poet Vanati, a former captain of the LTTE, later killed in the battle of Elephant Pass at the age of 27. In one of her poems, which appears in a collection approved by her organisation, she addresses the role of women under present conditions:

Her forehead shall be adorned not with kunkumam[1]
but with red blood
What is seen in her eyes is not the sweetness of youth
but the graves of the dead
Her lips shall utter not useless sentences
but the firm declarations of those who have fallen

On her neck will hang no *thali*
but a cyanide capsule!
She has embraced not men
but weapons!
Her legs are going not to search companionship with family
but towards the liberation of Tamil Eelam's soil
Her gun will fire shots
Correct action will cause the enemy to fall!
It will break the fetters of Tamil Eelam!!
Then from our people's lips a national anthem will sound!!!

That marriage and marriage payment has come into focus is because in Jaffna, as Comaroff argues is the case in general, marriage prestations represent 'a point of articulation between the organisational principles which underlie and constitute a socio-cultural system and the surface forms and processes which together comprise the lived-in universe' (1980: 33). This view implies seeing social reality as analytically distinguishable into separate orders: on the one hand the everyday context of prohibitions and preferences, of association and conflict; on the other the constitutive set of principles which lie behind these everyday realities, what Ricoeur would call a 'depth semantics' (1981a: 218). As elaborated by the Comaroffs in a later work (Comaroff and Comaroff 1991), this latter order may itself be depicted on a continuum from 'hegemony' to 'ideology', from the mute acceptance of power in its naturalised, non-recognised form to the formulation of argument and counter-argument, often backed by non-verbal means of enforcement. What revolutionary politics has done is to bring into awareness what was earlier below the level of discourse, only to enforce, or try to enforce, a new hegemonic order.

THE AMBIVALENCE OF KINSHIP

The arena of South Indian kinship studies is full of technical details and dogmatic theoretical positions which I see no reason to discuss in detail. In the present context the most important aspect of Dravidian kinship semantics is that it strongly indicates an ideal of bilateral cross-cousin marriage (Trautman 1981), an ideal actually found in Jaffna. In theory one can imagine two men exchanging sisters in marriage and their sons again exchanging sisters down through generations, so that mother's brother's daughter and father's sister's daughter will be the same person. In real life, of course, this structural ideal will never be sustained over generations. In Jaffna at the level of marriage, the level which Banks (1960) termed *sondakara* caste – *sondakara* literally meaning 'relations' – each caste is divided into unnamed units composed of local residence groups which are scattered in different villages and which are viewed by its members as mutually stratified.[2] These units are conceptualised as endogamous or, perhaps more correctly, as partners in exclusive inter-generational marriage alliances.

Common to several of the more well-known approaches to Dravidian kinship is that the wish for comparison in terms of systematic typification leads to a de-contextualisation of features from the social arrangements which give them meaning to the people involved (Comaroff 1980). One example of this is the tendency to make a functional distinction between marriage and marriage prestations, and to treat the latter primarily as a means of facilitating the former. This view is particularly evident in structural approaches where marriage is seen as the exchange of women between groups or persons in structurally determined positions (see Dumont 1983). A second example of social de-contextualisation is the tendency to assume *a priori* that marriage is the concern of groups, regulated by group boundaries, instead of allowing for the opposite possibility: that group boundaries may be regulated by marriage. Jaffna kinship has been depicted by different writers as both matrilineal (Coomeraswamy 1933) and bilateral (Banks 1957, Pfaffenberger 1982), while David (1973b) presents a picture which lends itself to a patrilineal interpretation (see Kapadia 1994).

It seems to me that we need a different starting point than unilineal exogamy for enquiries into kinship and marriage, a starting point which sees people's own experiences as the articulation of ideological structures. This means, first of all, regarding kinship not as an abstract system working on its own but as a field of conflicting interests and ambiguous feelings moulded and transformed by real people. It also means not regarding marriage as an isolated or structurally prior phenomenon but establishing relations between different organisational elements within more encompassing structures. In our context it seems particularly important to observe the complementary relationship between marriage and dowry. Dowry among Jaffna Tamils should not be regarded as a symbolic mediation of the flow of women between groups but as the element with reference to which mating and cohabitation are transformed into a recognised social fact. In the traditional conception of society it also constitutes a 'grammar', underlying the ordering of familial and affinal bonds in hierarchical patterns.

By considering the structure of the Dravidian sibling group to be the key to cross-cousin marriage, in my opinion Yalman (1967, also 1962) provides a fruitful starting point for the understanding of Tamil kinship. By seeing brothers' and sisters' mutual rights in their parents' estate as setting up claims between them on the children of the other as spouses for their own children, Yalman emphasises not diachronic alliances but the lateral spread of kin in marriageable and non-marriageable categories. As he says about the Sinhalese, it is women's rights in land which:

... makes their connections of great interest to the men who control them. Hence the fathers, mother's brothers, and the actual brothers of the women are vitally interested in their marriages. This forms the backbone of the dowry system. (1962: 552)[3]

While regarding this statement as being also true in the Jaffna-Tamil situation, I must add two comments. One is that we should not forget that there are strong emotions connected with kinship and marriage and that these emotions are not of secondary importance. Cross-cousin marriage is not only preferred by the older generation but remains a romantic ideal. My second comment is that, by focusing the *ideal* of marriage between the children of brother and sister, Yalman by implication also points to the fact that this is an ideal not necessarily fulfilled in real life. This may be because no cousin of the right age is available, but just as often it is because other priorities are made. Women are carriers not only of rights in land but also of kinship connections as such and represent the possibility of incorporating new members into the kindred whenever this is found to be opportune. As an historically founded ideological structure the traditional conceptualisation of kinship is, therefore, characterised by ambivalence. This ambivalence may be described as a contradiction between unity and expansion, between solidarity and social mobility or, in terms of structural positions, between the brother–sister and the wife–husband relationships.

To me Trawick's comment (1990) that the French psychoanalytic semiotician Jacques Lacan has hit upon some truths that Tamils have also discovered (p. 143) makes sense, at least in a metaphorical way. To Lacan the point of departure in analysis is not a process of 'integration' through exchange or communication; the self is born as part of the larger social whole. Being defined in and through this larger pattern, the individual as a subject is constituted not through communication but through fragmentation, through a rupture of the primordial wholeness; of the original mirror stage where the self sees itself in the mother. This rupture is effected by the outside, by the Father, by Culture; and through this rupture the self becomes a subject in a double sense: through fragmentation the Subject now belongs to the world of the Father; it gets a name, becomes a symbol, it is defined negatively and relationally, and by being constituted through absence it acts out of desire for a unity which is lost. But Language, the wholeness for which the Subject strives, cannot be appropriated through action; it belongs to the Father, to the will of collective social authority. The Subject therefore also becomes a subject, a subject to the father's authority. Driven by a desire for wholeness the Subject acts, but the culture as a whole cannot be possessed. The *quelque chose d'un*, the Father's promise of redemption, is a fraud. 'Meaning', the referentiality of the symbol, has no permanence. It, too, is contingent and arbitrary, a matter of shifting relations. What is behind appearances, the other of the other which is oneself, can never be captured, only searched for.

What makes Lacan's theory relevant to the understanding of kinship is that the principle of exchange has a personal side to it that is rarely considered. The fact that transactions outside the market are never completed, the norm that you must seek wholeness outside what is already part of you, points to the fact that the integration of society may be felt to happen at the cost of a fundamental incompleteness of the individual. To most Jaffna-Tamils, at home or in exile, the distinction between kin and non-kin, *sondakarar* and *sondakarar illai*, is the single most important distinction in the social universe. Again and again I have heard Tamils in exile say, 'You know, we are really not like you ...', wishing to express some variant of the understanding that the unit of agency which I should look for is not the single person. Kartigesu Sivathamby, professor in Tamil at the University of Jaffna, says that '... if an "in-dividual" is what the original meaning of the word says it is, something which cannot be divided into smaller parts, then among ilankai-Tamils the "individual" is identical to the *kutumpam* and not to the single person' (1989). *Kutumpam* is the Tamil term for 'family' but it is neither the nuclear family nor an extended family in the sense of people living together; it is the bilateral, self-reproductive set-up from which all other kinship relations may be seen as extensions; parents, these parents' siblings and their children. According to tradition the ideal marriage is with the closest possible kin and, since marriages are established in both directions between units of the *sondakara* caste, the important distinction in this respect is not between 'consanguines' and 'affines' but between those one is more or less close to within the totality of the bilateral *sondam* ('kin'). Rather than the establishment of 'alliances' between patrilineages, marriage is seen as reproducing the already existing kindred. That is the explicit reason why cross-cousin marriage is valued, as expressed in the saying *sondam viddup pokhamal* ('the *sondam* should not be lost'). It is the existing bond rather than the 'exchange' which is focused on.

While, unlike in many parts of South India, sister's daughter–mother's brother marriage is not acceptable in Jaffna, there is a definite sense in which many, both men and women, feel more closely related to their mother's brother than to their father's brother. This is a consequence of the normally close and protective brother–sister and mother–children relationships as opposed to the hierarchic husband–wife and father–children relationships, a situation having its material correlate in the obligation of a brother to help raise the dowry for his sister and sister's daughter which in theory should come from the maternal line. In fact, according to my male Vellala informants MBD (Mother's Brother's Daughter) marriage should not be seen as a 'marrying out' of the woman (see Trautman 1981, also Kapadia 1993) but as the man returning to his mother's kin. One reason given for this preference is connected to the practice of uxorilocal residence where a married couple's first quarters will normally be in a house provided by the bride's parents as dowry, situated in her native ward. This practice is formalised in the '*Alaippu*', the third-day marriage ceremony, where after spending the two first days with his parents the groom is formally invited by the bride's family to come and live with them together with his wife. Because a son retains his claims and obligations towards the parental estate located in the ward where his sister lives as a married woman, this normative settlement pattern tends to make the wife's parents' ward or village a centre of social gravity. While it is stressed by informants that both mother's brother's daughter–father's sister's son and father's sister's daughter–mother's brother's son are possible spouses, and already before marrying are seen as having potentially sexual relationships, a preference for MBD is considered natural because, it is argued, children on the mother's side will often be 'closer'; it will therefore be easier for their families to judge their future compatibility in marriage.

From an anthropological point of view this conception of family is not a natural fact; it is an ideological configuration, a self-representation perpetuated through the fiction of kinship semantics. The closed nature of the Dravidian system construes change in terms of invariability, expansion in terms of unity. A man *becomes* your cross-cousin (*maccan*) when he marries your sister, your sister's son (*marumakan*) when he marries your daughter. A significant aspect of a woman's power, a power which may be used but must also be controlled, is her ability to transform difference into identity. A reasonable interpretation of the social importance of dowry in Jaffna is that this is neither a consequence of 'patrilineal predominance' (Kapadia 1993) nor of any systematic distinction between wife-takers and wife-givers. Rather, it is a result of male bias, institutionalised in a tradition administered by the parental generation, combined with changes under the impact of a colonial administration which made possible a certain degree social mobility. As Banks (1957) perceptively observed:

Marriage in Jaffna is essentially a matching of status and wealth ... the status of the parties depends on the sex of their child who is being married; it is not a matter of long-continuing relations between groups of different rank. (p. 191)

As almost any contemporary Jaffna-Tamil will agree, the understanding that the dowry is a kind of 'compensation' for the husband's higher rank is clear in this area. In fact, a viewpoint that I have heard Tamil men half – but only *half* – jokingly adopt is that they are goods on offer, available for the highest bidder. One informant, explaining to me the practice of uxorilocality, expressed himself like this: 'You know, in marriage we are sold to our wife's family.' In pre-capitalist society a man of good origin would be an attractive groom, but whether he was within the reach of your daughter's dowry would by and large already be decided by your landed assets. The educational facilities and the input of capital under the colonial administration changed this. It brought with it the possibility of an unprecedented build-up of wealth which could be invested in the dowry of daughters *or* in the education of sons – with the profit either way to be harvested by the grandchildren. Monetary income invested in children's marriages could and would be used to raise the sub-caste, or even caste status of one's family. There is a saying in Jaffna: '*Kallar Maravar konatta Agampadir mella mella vandu Vellala akimame*', meaning that Kallars become Maravars who in turn become Agampadirs, who 'slowly, slowly' become Vellalas. The families identified as belonging to the Madapalli caste, the Thanakarar caste and the Parathesy caste in the 1824 census were to become incorporated as Vellala sub-castes during the next hundred years. In Jaffna this development is well known among elderly people and is attributed to the tradition of hypergamous marriages.

One should note, however, that the input of money did not break the structure of society. The process of assimilation into the Vellala caste, and the internal mobility within this caste, represents an incorporation of capitalist principles into the mechanics of culture through the lifting of internal 'trade barriers' between families of corresponding ritual purity. Individually negotiated marriages created a basis for the culturally specific caste-class formation to be found in Jaffna. Through family connections a consolidated economic middle class was created within the upper-middle range of the traditional caste structure. At the same time the possibility of gaining social mobility through marriage raised the level of dowries needed to attract a groom suited to the new horizon of expectation. It is here that the migrant finds his place as a living reality in Jaffna-Tamil society. The historical importance of migration in the Tamil areas stems from it being one of the few, and therefore one of the major, vehicles of capitalisation in the area. It was the export of manpower under the protection of the British Empire which injected large amounts of capital into the economic system of Jaffna. With the British development of the Malay States and the Straits settlements (Singapore, Penang and Malacca) in the latter half of the nineteenth century, possibilities of employment were opened. The mining industry, and the programmes for road construction, railway building and telegraph communications created a demand for imported labour. The Ceylon-Tamil community seized this opportunity. While accurate figures for the early years are not available, in 1911 there were a little more than 7000 Ceylon-Tamils in Malaya alone, increasing steadily to about 25,000 in 1957 (Ramasamy 1988).

If the numbers do not seem overwhelming, it should be noted that the migration profile of this community was different from most other groups trying their luck in the same areas. The Ceylon-Tamil migrants were able to gain admission into the lower strata of the administrative sector, avoiding unskilled work. Within some sectors, like the railways, they constituted the dominant workforce. In 1903, for example, there were 2021 Jaffna-Tamils employed as functionaries in the federated Malay States Railways compared to 84 Sinhalese, 278 Malays and 1084 Chinese (Ramasamy 1988). One reason for this situation was that British colonial officers having served in Ceylon were important in the opening up of the new territories. The administrative transference of the Straits Settlement from the Indian Government to the Colonial Office in 1867 resulted in the leaving of many former government employees. As a result the Straits Settlements Government turned to Ceylon for the recruitment of experienced British officers to fill up the vacancies, a process which continued in Malaya when the Federated Malay States were formed in 1896. In fact it seems that most of the British officers who served in Malaya prior to 1900 were not directly recruited from England but had earlier worked in Ceylon (*Sunday Times*, 17 February 1934). These officers brought with them Tamil technical staff, clerks, accountants and overseers, and this laid the foundation for a subsequent process of chain migration.

The main reasons why Ceylon Tamils were favoured by the British administrators were their recognised industriousness and their fluency in English. As noted in Chapter 2, at the turn of the century the Tamil community already had a long-standing relationship with English-speaking missionaries. The acquiring of language proficiency was, however, not a passive process. Education was an asset seized upon by the ambitious, something that aspiring Jaffna families put their minds to without regard for the costs. As it says in one of the reports from the director of education, the Jaffna parent

... realises that an English education is a valuable asset, and is readily convertible to cash ... Hence it is that hundreds of parents of the farming and labouring classes, who have themselves received no English education, insist on an English education for their sons. This education is often acquired in a spirit of self sacrifice; parents, brothers and sisters undergoing hardships at their homes in order that at least one member of the family may receive an English education. (Ceylon Administrative Report A-6, 1921)

Migration to areas like British Malaya was clearly one way of 'converting English education into cash'. The Money Order remittances returned to Ceylon in a good year like 1918 totalled 736,652 Ceylon rupees from the Federated Malay States and 289,651 rupees from the Straits Settlements, quite substantial amounts at that time. The importance of these remittances was such that on two occasions, with a twenty-seven years' interval, the government agent in the Northern Province found it necessary to point out that it was the money coming from Malaya which accounted for the relative prosperity of Jaffna (Ceylon Administrative Report 1903 and 1930). Although to my knowledge any accurate statistics on the caste composition of migrants to Malaya do not exist, there is reason to believe that the group benefiting most from this early migration was the middle section of society. In his study Ramasamy (1988) points out that one reason why most migrants preferred to leave Jaffna on the ferries run by the Ceylon Steamship Company was that these provided special arrangements for high-caste passengers. At the same time migrants had the incentive for migration which the lack of agricultural land gave them. Seen against the relative growth of the Vellala caste, the assumption that the majority of migrants were members of landless but ritually clean castes is reasonable.

It seems clear, however, that at the centre of migration was not only cash, but the value of cosmopolitanism as such. Michael Banks's observations during fieldwork in Jaffna in the 1950s provide a valuable record of attitudes towards migration from an important intermediary period in Sri Lankan (Ceylonese) history, between the colonial era and the present times of refugee migration. Discussing rank between wards in relation to marriage, Banks notes that, 'It is well known that wards with many Malayan "pensioneers" are high-ranking wards by definition' (Banks 1957: 205). In another passage Banks briefly outlines the ethos of the colonial migrant:

This emigrant surge of the educated altered not so much the ultimate definition of 'the good life' as the means to be followed to obtain it ... They see themselves as faithful and reliable servants spread all over the East under the protection of the Raj, finally rewarded with ample pensions. This relationship is sometimes expressed in kinship terms: 'the government is a father to me.' Queen Victoria's reign is thought of as the golden age, and even today Victoria sovereigns command a premium over all others for melting down to make into *thalis* – the symbol of marriage worn around the

neck – because it is said that her reign was the most auspicious for the
Jaffnanese. (1957: 26, 27)

In this last sentence we see how migration translates directly into the
reproduction of kinship connections within the overall hierarchy.
What we need to establish is that the prestige coming to the colonial
migrant was not a result of the single adventurous act but come from
engaging oneself in a personal transaction with the outside. Sri Lankan
Tamils count among those groups where a large part had truly accepted
British standards of civilisation and saw themselves as engaged in a
relationship of complementary equality to the Western world. Rather
than the embracing of an ideology based in universal values, however,
this acceptance took the form of an incorporation of Western imagery
into the existing social structure. That is to say, while the loosening
of caste hierarchy was deeply resented among the conservative elite,
this elite itself was partly defined by the adoption of a European
lifestyle and an internal competition in terms of wealth and Western
ornamentary. As examples of applicable resources in pursuit of rank,
Banks mentions (a) English education, (b) employment as a clerk or
similar capacity in which an English education is needed, (c) wealth
resulting from (b), and (d) adoption of or use of certain European habits,
such as use of Western clothing – trousers, shoes etc. – and Western
foods and manners, like shaking hands (1957: 202, 203). The main
arena for this competition was, and is, marriage.

The ideology of kinship and the historical dimension of migration
provide a necessary backdrop for understanding the dilemmas of
present-day refugees. Among the older generation migrant 'role
models' are in ample supply. Contemporary migrants find themselves
in a situation which, seen from Jaffna, is a prestigious one and which
carry high expectations on behalf of the family as a whole. Forty years
after Banks's fieldwork wards and families with migrating members
are still pointed at with respect and envy. This is one curious
consequence of the increasingly strict immigration regulations in the
West: because of the extremely high costs of circumventing them,
migration has retained its aura of social mobility into the era of fully
fledged civil war. To the individual migrant the situation is different
however. Not only may the expectations of his (or her) family be
impossible to fulfil under present refugee conditions, but also because
of the social devaluation which the migrant encounters abroad – a
devaluation which is normally permanent because it is defined in

terms of colour and race – investment in family prestige deposited at home, e.g. in sisters' weddings, becomes one of the few ways of clinging on to a position of self-respect as defined by traditional values. In fact, many refugee migrants consciously seem to sacrifice their own material satisfaction and success in terms of these values in order to obey the commands of kinship ideology.

To the young migrants' kinship ties, reproduced through the ideals and obligations of arranged marriage, represent the embodiment of 'authentic culture'. In their economic aspects, however, they also represent a tremendous problem and a constant worry, emphasising the attraction of the revolutionary paradigm. To the older generation staying behind in Jaffna these ties are a way of securing the future of family members through marriage to émigrés. But they also mean the possibility of continuing a way of life reflecting the cosmopolitan values of the colonial era. One factor contributing to the present disjunctured character of discourses on identity is that contemporary migration not only has a political aspect but, like revolutionary politics itself, is also infused with generational tensions: opposition, guilt and feelings of insufficiency. They both represent the young against the old. As Mr J pointed out to me, the LTTE's killing of the TULF leader, Amirthalingam, in 1989 is well suited to an interpretation along oedipal lines. 'It is Prabhakaran killing his father', he said at the time. 'He wants Mother Eelam for himself.' Refugee migration is not simply a continuation of the earlier work migration, but it is when seen against this proud history of former generations that the altered circumstances of the refugee often become particularly problematic. And while many refugees have fled the LTTE, the organisation may still represent to them a secret wish to take possession of the future, of throwing off the burden of tradition.

9 FROM THE TRADITIONAL TO THE REVOLUTIONARY

In this chapter I will take a closer look at the LTTE. The reason for embarking upon a review of this organisation is their manifest presence in countries where Tamil refugees live. In a study like this their ideology and political activity cannot be dealt with under a heading of 'Refugee Background', because when the refugee migrants arrive the LTTE are already there, claiming to represent their interests. In a world which from a Tamil point of view is characterised not by transnationality alone but by a combination of transnational worries and national boundaries, LTTE is the only institution which has the skills, manpower and financial resources to act with determination, autonomy and confidence. In Norway their Tamil phone service is the most important source of information on the situation in the different parts of Eelam. Their video news bulletins from Jaffna, irregular but appreciated, are to most the only possibility of actually *seeing* pictures of places where their family members live. Representatives occasionally flying in from London and Paris to give speeches provide an understanding that their own problems in Norway are part of a bigger cause. Political messages, normally 'softened' by artistic performances, are taped and distributed by video and music cassettes. Such messages may be questioned if intellectually scrutinised but undoubtedly carry an emotional appeal of recognition, a sense of high and low sharing a common destiny. The particular individuals in charge of LTTE activity outside Jaffna are of little importance. Unlike other positions, being an official representative of the LTTE is a non-negotiated status. When they speak, they do so with the undoubted authority of an organisation which shares the responsibility for 60,000 lives having ended violently in the last 15 years. The appeal of the LTTE in exile lies in their capacity to appropriate people's suffering; to take it, transform it and to stand forth as its only representative. It is the fact that they are there *and* here, at both ends of the road – whether this road leads to London, Toronto or Oslo – which makes it necessary to discuss further their activity in Sri Lanka.

While the traditional model of society is closely connected to the colonial period, what I have termed the 'revolutionary' model is based on a deliberate linking up to conceptualisations of pre-colonial ideals and moral standards. In public symbolism the effort to establish a connection between the present fight for national liberation and the image of past imperial glory is distinctive. In this project the Tamil kingdom which existed in northern Sri Lanka prior to the arrival of the Portuguese, and the three empires Chola, Pandiya and Chera of South India in what is called the Sangam period (300 BC to AD 300), serve as sources of legendary material. The Chola empire is where the LTTE has taken its Tiger emblem and Prabhakaran's *nom de guerre*, Karakalan, which was the name of the first Chola king, has the rhetorical effect of making a homology between then and now explicit. In an article in the LTTE organ, *Viduthalai Pulihal*, from February 1991 on the making of the Tiger insignia into the 'national flag' of Tamil Eelam, we can read:

The Tiger insignia is an image rooted in Dravidian civilisation. It is a symbol that illustrates the martial history and national upheaval of the Tamils. Our national flag is the symbol of the independent state of Tamil Eelam to be created, rooted in the martial traditions of the Tamils. (p. 3)

In an LTTE cassette with songs dedicated to six well-known Sea Tigers fallen in battle, we find the following opening speech:

In those days all the deep seas were ruled by the Chola kings. The ships flying the Tiger flags spread the news of Tamil heroism to the world. All these things were washed away by the flood of time, and the Tamils became slaves and refugees [*akathi*]. Now the Sangam period has come back. The Liberation Tigers make the world focus on Tamil Eelam. The boats of Sea Tigers flying Tiger flags are anew roaming in the seas ... [*Neithal*]

In one of the songs from the same cassette it says:

Then the great Chola kings ruled the deep seas
Now our Karikalan is climbing over our Eelam ocean
Dance as the day is breaking
Dance as the Sangam period is coming back ...
This is the sea of our ancestors
this coast is the lap from which we were born ...

Who come to drink our sea?
Who come to burn our land?
No country can touch our soil,
No hand can touch the flag raised by the Tiger
We never hesitate to face the wind and rain
We are not afraid to face the battalions coming across the sea
We sing our praise to our able leader
When the time of Tambi's rule comes we will dance[1]

As indicated by these texts the process of cultural redefinition, based on a selection and recontextualising of historical bits and pieces, is planned and led by the LTTE. Somewhat amused informants in Norway say that they have problems reading LTTE material because in their project of restoring Tamil culture to its former status of glory, archaic language and idioms are used which are not understandable to ordinary people. In one sense, therefore, this process of redefinition is an elitist project organised by university professors and cultural experts under the leadership of the LTTE. To say that it is *only* this would, however, be an oversimplification. Not only are the authorised statements of the LTTE accompanied by a plethora of non-authorised cultural expressions supporting them, but there is little doubt either that the metaphors and images used by the official propaganda apparatus find resonance far outside their own ranks. Successful rhetoric always relies on a mutual relationship between speaker and audience, and the position of the Liberation Tigers becomes impossible to understand if one does not appreciate their genius in giving expression to feelings and values which are deeply rooted in the Tamil population. These feelings, nurtured by post-independence politics and more than a decade of civil war, centre on a need for national sovereignty and a growing acceptance of the principle of equal rights between members of the Tamil community. To sections of the exile community the LTTE's linking of the need for self-determination to a rejection of ethnic pluralism and Western cosmopolitanism has a particular appeal under present conditions of living. Such a rejection is clear in the organisation's propaganda, as the following example may show:

If a national race loves its history filled with greatness and its language and culture, its tradition and ancient customs, that we call patriotism. One who discards this progressive patriotism, this love of the nation and calls for cosmopolitanism, is not a true socialist. People like these are bourgeois cosmopolitans.[2]

By revolutionary politics these feelings are given an historical interpretation and put to use for specific purposes.

PEASANTS AND WARRIORS

One of the most consistent efforts to give the struggle led by the LTTE a proper place in Tamil history has been made by an intellectual who is not part of the organisation. In 1992 the writer D.P. Sivaram published in the well-esteemed Colombo magazine, *Lanka Guardian*, a series of articles on Tamil militarism (Sivaram 1992). The series is particularly interesting because to news readers in Sri Lanka D.P. Sivaram is better known by his alias *Taraki*, under which name he writes as a military analyst in the Anglo-Sinhala papers, often criticising both parties to the war (see, for instance, Taraki 1991). It is also a well-known fact that Sivaram, at least until the late 1980s, was connected to one of the Tamil militant groups in conflict with the LTTE and it may therefore be presumed that his views reflect a somewhat broader range of radical thinking than the inner circles of the LTTE.

The reason for looking at Sivaram's study is neither the historical facts he presents nor the truth or falsity of these facts. What is interesting is his interpretation of Tamil history as a struggle between two opposing forces, one associated with the Vellala landowners and their claim for high-caste status, the other associated with the fishing communities and their presumed *kshatryia* ancestry (see Chapter 2). While presented as a historical analysis pure and simple, Sivaram's work, like so much writing of history in Sri Lanka, is a contribution to an ongoing ideological discussion on national identity.

Sivaram's point of departure is the South-Indian Dravidian movement which has dominated Tamil politics for the larger part of this century. He points out that this movement primarily has been studied in terms of the Brahmin–non-Brahmin contradiction, reflecting a conflict between the traditional authority of the Brahmins and a non-Brahmin Tamil elite propagating a linguistic 'Pure Tamil' nationalism. This, according to Sivaram, is not the full story:

... the other important component of Tamil nationalism – its militarism – has not figured in studies of the Dravidian movement. This is partly attributable to the influence of a historiographic tradition that has shaped concepts of Tamil culture and society in Dravidian studies. It arose from a strong political compulsion in the nascent and early phases of the Dravidian ideology to portray the Tamil people as peaceful and unwarlike. (1: 7)

This historiographic tradition has overlooked, or rather *suppressed*, the role of the military castes in Tamil society, in particular the castes referred to as Maravars.

Traditional Tamil militarism in the Tamil region as elsewhere in India was confined to a group of castes which considered 'the use of arms as a matter of birth and right'. The Maravar were, according to the Madras Presidency census report for 1891, 'a fierce and turbulent race, famous for their military prowess' ... They were a people whom the British attempted to totally demilitarize by depriving them of their traditional status in Tamil society through social, economic and penal measures ... They were not only disfranchised but were turned into and classified as a delinquent mass – the subject of a disciplinary and penal discourse – relegated to the fringes of the new social order which was being established in the Tamil South of the Madras Presidency. (2: 17)

In Sivaram's view, therefore, the caste structure of the colonial period, and in effect the model of society which I have termed traditional, is a result of Western influence and power:

The gains of ... demartialization were consolidated by favouring and encouraging non-military castes in Tamil society which 'contrasted favourably with the Maravar'. (2: 18)

The caste which took this position as a servant to colonial interests was the Vellala caste, the dominant caste of the last centuries:

The culture and values of the 'peace loving' (Madras census 1871) Vellalas who had 'no other calling than the cultivation of the soil' eminently suited the aims of demartialization and suppression of the traditional military castes. (2: 17)

In its relationship to the colonial powers lies the answer to the Vellalas' prominent position and the reason for their high regard for education:

In 1627 Lancarote de Seixas, the Portuguese Captain Major of Jaffna, put forward the idea that the peninsula's security lay in having none there but cultivators. Thus began the rise of the Vellalas in Jaffna ... (3: 90)
    Successive colonial powers found Vellala scribal groups useful where Brahmins were not forthcoming ... (3: 90)

In this way two forces, or 'narratives', came to be posed against each other.

... in the early decades of the twentieth century we find two contending
narratives of Tamil National identity – the ideology and caste culture of the
anti-British and 'turbulent' military castes, and the ideology and caste culture
of the pro-British and 'peace loving' Vellala elite – claiming authentic readings
of the Tamilian past and present. The one claiming that the 'pure Tamils'
were Vellalas. The other claiming that all Tamils were Maravar and that the
Tamil nation was distinguished by its ancient martial heritage. (2: 18)

These narratives were not continued as equal and contending, however,
because 'under active British patronage the Vellala caste established
its dominance and its culture became representative and hegemonic
in Tamil society' (2: 18).

The dominance of the Vellala caste, and by implication the society
based on landownership and 'bound mode' relations (Chapter 2),
would not, therefore, have been possible without the influence and
intervention of outside forces. It represents the twin interests of
Western imperialism and Vellala caste interest. In Dravidian
historiography, according to Sivaram, the imperialist interests are
represented by the Christian missionaries, first among them Bishop
Robert Caldwell of Tinnevely (1819–91). Through his *Comparative
Grammar of the Dravidian Languages*, published in 1856, Caldwell laid
the theoretical foundation for the Dravidian movement. While thus,
in a sense, serving Tamil interests, at the same time he distorted the
image of Tamil society by serving Vellala interests against securing their
loyalty to the colonial administration:

The views of Bishop Caldwell were found to be extremely useful by the newly
arisen Vellala elite which was contending for higher status in the varna
hierarchy of caste. (4: 10)

In our context it is interesting to note that Sivaram, by letting Caldwell
credit their enterprise, also criticises the migrants involving themselves
in the outside world:

It was to these 'loyal' classes of Tamils that Caldwell referred when he wrote
in the introduction to his *Grammar* that ... 'The majority of the Klings or
Hindus, who are found in Pegu, Penang, Singapore and other places in further
east, are Tamilians: a large portion of the Coolies who have emigrated in such
numbers to the Mauritius and to the West Indian colonies are Tamilians; in
short wherever money is to be made, wherever a more apathetic or a more
aristocratic people is waiting to be pushed aside, tither swarm the Tamilians,

the Greeks or Scotch of the east, the least superstitious and the most enterprising and persevering race of the Hindus. (Caldwell, *Corporate Grammar*, p. 7)' (7: 12)

Against this background must be understood the historical role of the fishing castes of Jaffna, the Karaiyars in particular, in preserving and protecting the true essence of Tamil culture all through the colonial period. The Karaiyars are the offspring of and heirs to the Maravars:

A narrative related to the founding of Valvettithurai,[3] based on folk etymology states that the village arose on land given to a Marava chieftain called Valliathevan by the founder of the Tamil kingdom of Jaffna. ... such connections between the coastal military castes of south Tamilnadu and the Karaiyar of Jaffna were cemented through marriage. (5: 10)

It is as protectors of independence and defenders against foreign influence that Karaiyar warriors today take command of the Tamil nation:

... a strong tradition was prevalent among the Karaiyar of Valvettithurai that they had fought the Portuguese as the soldiers of the last king of Jaffna *Sankili* ... Although Jaffna-Tamil society was the earliest to have been demartialized ... it has become the ground in which the most fierce manifestation of Tamil militarism has taken root in modern times. (5: 10)

INDIAN NATIONALISM AND THE FEMALE IMAGE

To readers familiar with recent Indian history this tendency to look back in order to find the key to unlock the future will present no surprise. In a broad perspective the Sri Lanka-Tamil liberation struggle may be said to take place within the larger arena of a pan-Tamil ethnic *cum* nationalist movement, something attested to by the popular support for this struggle in Tamil Nadu until recently. In the Indian Tamil nationalism of the first part of this century, by which Prabhakaran himself has admitted being inspired,[4] the revivalist element was very strong. Both the fervour and the symbolic structure of this revivalism is of interest to my analysis. Nationalism in the Tamil areas of South-Asia did and do contain a number of overlapping discourses. It is remarkable how many of these contain a dimension of gender, making woman as a multilayered symbol the foundation of identity (e.g. Pandian 1982, Lakshmi 1990, Ramaswamy 1993). Of particular importance is *Tamilttay*, the Tamil language perceived and portrayed as a goddess.

The declaration of Tamil as the official language of Tamil Nadu in 1956 was publicly submitted as a ritual prestation to this goddess, schoolchildren sing a daily morning prayer to her glory, the successes of the pro-Tamil party, the DMK, in the elections of 1967 and 1971 were presented as her victories in the Tamil press. In one of the Indian poet Bharati's texts, of whom a battered statue still stands in Jaffna town after more than a decade of war, it says:

There is gold and greenery everywhere;
The smile of our illustrious Queen who reigns over the cool Tamil grove
is like the glow of the morning light that destroys darkness ...
The land flourishes again ...
Holding the auspicious sceptre in her fine hands, our Mother reclines on
her fine throne, decked in priceless knowledge!
(S. Bharati in Ramaswamy 1993)

This queen who will make 'the land flourish again' is the Tamil language. This discourse on language concerns the establishment of boundaries against the outer world through according the female body with sacred values.

The goddess as female appears in two different images which later reappear in contemporary political symbolism in Tamil Sri Lanka. The most dominant image is that of the mother. As declared by Tamilttay herself in a text from the 1960s,

Do not forget that you are all children who emerged from my womb. I am your mother. The learned call me Tamilttay. You are all called Tamilians [*tamilar*]. You and I are inextricably bound together for ever and ever through language ... (Panchanathan n.d.)

This view, of course, implies an ethnicist argument, regarding common language as overriding dividing identities like caste, village or region.

We also find, however, the image of language as a young virginal woman, dwelling on her 'glorious golden body', her 'lustrous lips', her 'abundant breasts' etc. For example,

Whenever I think of the virginal Tamil [*kannittamil*] ... of her dark beautiful eyes, flower-like ears, glowing face, and the grace of a plumed peahen ... my heart surges with the nectar of pleasure.
(Velayutam Pillai 1971)

This comparison between language and the young woman is not exceptional or idiosyncratic. It is a comparison which rests on two key polysemic words which are recurrent in praising both the qualities of the Tamil language and, at least among Tamil men in Norway, the qualities of young Tamil women. These words are *kannimai* which means young, youthful, but also virginal, pure, chaste, and *inimai* which means sweet, delightful, but also sensual, erotic. Thus the purity of the Tamil language comes to be seen in terms of the sexual purity and faithfulness of women (Lakshmi 1990).

It is notable that the statue of Barathi was raised in Jaffna long before the war started, indicating a long-term influence from South-Indian linguistic nationalism on Jaffna society. In Jaffna reverence of language is learned from an early age and throughout childhood is deferred to as a holy subject. For example, children should not be allowed to read or write in the morning before brushing their teeth and washing their face. Until recently the 'biography' of Tamilttay as born in the Potikai mountains was taught as a fact in Jaffna schools (Suseendirarajah 1980). Children are never made to write letters in the Tamil alphabet until the auspicious ceremony known as *eetu tuvakkiratu*, 'initiation to the alphabet', has been performed. Being a solemn occasion to the child and family, this ceremony should ideally be performed in the temple, preferably on the most auspicious day of *vijayadasami* in September. Here the priest, after performing the *puja*, holds the child's second finger on the right hand and makes him or her write the symbol of Ganesh so that he may clear all obstacles on the long road of learning. The child then recites the twelve vowels with the priest and writes them on white rice spread out on a tray.

Among the several nationalist discourses in India the religious discourse of Shaiva Siddhanta, which called for a return to the worship of Shiva through the medium of Tamil as a 'pure' and divine language (Ramaswamy 1993, Sivathamby 1984, Pfaffenberger 1994) became of particular importance in Jaffna. Suseendirarajah (1980) has observed that when she asked villagers in Jaffna what their religion was, they answered 'Tamil'. To them their religion could not be conceptually separated from their language – 'Tamil language and Saivism are ... for them two sides of the same coin' (p. 347). In South India the propagation of Shaiva Siddhanta philosophy around the turn of the century was part of a struggle against the power of Aryan Brahmins and entailed a campaign of social reform, part of which was the fight against caste hierarchy. In Tamil Ceylon, where Brahmins had little or no power this philosophy came to serve as a legitimation of the power of the non–Brahmin elite. Nevertheless, the influence from South Indian political currents on the development in Sri Lanka should be recognised. In Sri Lanka LTTE, as a revolutionary movement, shares with the previous generation of Tamil political leaders a focus on tradition and history. What separates LTTE from the previous generation is the understanding that there is a need for a true revival, constituting a break with history, and that a main element of this revival must be the militarism described by Sivaram above.

SYMBOLIC REINTERPRETATION

I said in Chapter 6 that the three main principles of hierarchy in traditional Jaffna society were caste, seniority and gender, coming together in the institution of arranged marriage. In Jaffna today the way these principles are publicly negated is striking. The parts of Sri Lanka controlled by the LTTE for all practical purposes constitute a separate state, an authoritarian military state where only a handful of people in power are above 20 years of age and the veterans in the small circle of leadership positions are all around 40. In spite of the relatively limited number of uniformed soldiers, probably not more than 15,000, the military order serves as a model of society opposed to the one based on caste and seniority. It is not simply that the older generation has no official function in society, the LTTE's scepticism towards the ideology of caste and kinship shows in a number of ways. On every corner in Jaffna during the LTTE's years in power, there were memorials of young soldiers, celebrating their death for the freedom of the Tamil nation. LTTE soldiers are buried at military burial grounds, side by side, according to their time of death. The fact alone that they are remembered not as coming from a particular segment of the population but for their individual achievements, represents a radical break with the epistemology of caste. Caste practices as such were banned by the LTTE's own Penal Code of 1994 and offences are judged by the court system instituted that year. These courts are administered by 'judges' drawn from the ranks of military, still wearing the cyanide, most of them seasoned combat soldiers around 20 years of age.

In March 1995 I interviewed the female leader of 'Chencholai', LTTE's orphanage in Jaffna, who was a soldier only temporarily released from active duty. In describing their policy, she emphasised the effort to 'protect' the children from the influence of their extended families. This was not, she argued, in order to facilitate a subsequent recruitment into the organisation but to allow the children to grow up 'as free and independent individuals'. Whether they would later join the organisation as soldiers would be their own personal choice.

While I do not wish to venture any comment on the truth or falsity of this claim, the presentation fits the narrative structure in which LTTE presents itself. In their recruitment movies, widely spread also to the exile communities, the audience is typically made to follow a person's way from everyday, taken for granted village life, to a realisation of the imperative importance of the liberation struggle. The decision to join the organisation is presented as the main character's individual decision, normally following death in his or her family. Through this (symbolic) death the loyalty to family is transferred to the country and to the military leader (*talaivar*). One such film, interestingly named *Mother of War*, shown to the exile audience in Norway in 1994, portrays a mother with three children as the Sri Lankan army attacks their village. One of the children is disabled and, as the family tries to run away, the mother and the disabled daughter are caught while the two others, one girl and a boy, manage to run and hide under some bushes. From there they watch as their mother and handicapped sister are killed in cold blood. Constantly reliving the terrible experience, the two drift through life in shock and confusion until they are taken care of by a friendly person in uniform. He convinces them that fighting for country and people is the only way to go forward in life. As they decide to follow him and undergo training the audience can see how life and energy return to their limbs, their eyes fixed on the horizon with visionary determination.

One of the most interesting questions regarding a break with the traditional concept of society pertains to the position of women. The LTTE has a separate section for women, 'Women's Front of the Liberation Tigers', which was established as early as 1983. Their goals as formulated in 1991 are:

1. To secure the right of self-determination of the people of Tamil Eelam and establish an independent democratic state of Tamil Eelam
2. To abolish oppressive caste discrimination and semi-feudal customs such as the dowry system

3. To eliminate all discrimination against Tamil women, and secure social, political and economic equality
4. To ensure that Tamil women control their own lives
5. To secure legal protection of women against sexual harassment, rape and domestic violence[5]

The implementation of points 2–5 would entail not only a change in the situation of women as such, but a change in the entire fabric of Jaffna society. The view of the Women's Front is that Tamil women must fight a dual oppression by male chauvinism and the Sinhala state and, as an expression of the former, dowry is singled out for special attention. Their views have been summarised by Adele Ann, the wife of LTTE's ideologue, Anton Balasingham, and herself a leading figure within the Women's Front:

In the past two decades in particular, the dowry system has emerged as an acute social problem. It has created an irreconcilable contradiction between social expectations and material reality. It has polluted and corrupted the social sanctity of marriage. It has reduced the human relationship between woman and man into a calculated financial contract. The practice of dowry has plunged a vast number of families onto the brink of poverty and despair. Most importantly, this practice has deprived inestimable numbers of women of their right to marriage and family life. (1994: 30)

In the views of these women we find a different reading of the migration-dowry nexus from the one outlined in the previous chapter:

The employment of Tamil youth in foreign countries has had wide scale repercussions on the society. The steady flow of foreign currency with high exchange rate to a large community of families created a reliable income and the so-called 'postal order economy' came into existence. One of the consequences of the flow of funds from abroad was a rise in social expectations and aspirations ... Men, as a way out of their economic and social impotence, seek dowry as a quick way to financial gain. (1994: 31, 32)

The ingrained character of dowry may be indicated by a conversation I had with one of LTTE's (male) legal advisers in Jaffna. While supporting his organisation's goal of abolishing the practice, he admitted seeing this as impossible to implement. Concerning his own daughter he somewhat laconically estimated that by the time she was ready to marry he would need to raise a dowry of about 2,500,000 rupees, close to 55,000 US$, to find her a husband. The dedication of the LTTE women themselves to change is, however, proven in their contribution to bringing about the goal of national self-determination (point 1). There is in LTTE's writings no indication that women may contribute in a gender-specific way to the question of independence. Women within the movement are not referred to 'feminine' roles like nursing, cooking or secretarial functions. Liberation is a question where men and women should contribute in the same way: in the taking up of arms. This emphasis on equality was underlined when in 1992 LTTE women started cutting their hair short, thus removing the external symbol of their traditional gender role. Indeed, in Sri Lanka female LTTE soldiers have earned a reputation for being particularly determined and merciless. The LTTE itself in 1991 released the number of female fighters as being 3000,[6] but by the mid-1990s the number may well be higher. In 1992 Peter Schalk (Schalk 1992) noted that the number of young women killed in battle had increased rapidly since 1990, a development which seems to have accelerated since. After a battle in the Welioya region in July 1995, for example, the LTTE radio informed that 128 out of 180 soldiers they had lost were female.[7] This indicates an increased relative importance of women in the fighting force.

The controversial nature of the female fighters' position with regard to society in general was brought home to me during one of my visits to Jaffna. Local NGO people pointed out what a formidable task it would be to 'rehabilitate' these young women, not because of their psychological traumas but because of the difficulties they would face in being accepted back into society after breaking so radically with traditional gender roles and expectations. Nevertheless, revolutionary ideology retains a relationship of dependence with gender, transforming the familial, the traditional and the everyday into a holy cause for which to die. It is worth observing the continued segregation of sexes among LTTE soldiers. Sexual relationships between soldiers are strictly forbidden and severely punished. In fact, portrayals of what may be termed the 'armed virgin' have recently become frequent in the political art of the organisation (Schalk 1992). These expressions, particularly in pictures and drawings, consciously combine the *naïveté* and innocence of the traditional conception of virginal femininity with the determination of professional soldiers. Against this background it is interesting that neither in Adele Ann's writings, which condemn male chauvinism, nor in the material published by the Women's Front, is there anything said about the concept of *karpu* (chastity). This may be because an attack on this core value of Tamil culture would prove counterproductive to the organisation. I think there is also another reason, which is that holding on to this value allows it to be projected on to the country as such. The suppression of the female soldiers' own femininity through uniforms and short hair assists this move of symbolic displacement. In an LTTE song, written against the Indian military occupation in 1987, we can see how female sexual purity remains a sub-text within the struggle for liberty:

The soldiers stamping over our virgin flowers;
plundering their *karpu*[8]
The younger ones hit by bullets

The virtue of the land and the virtue of the women of the land are merged here, to be both protected from outside aggression. Correspondingly, in a popular drawing appearing on walls around Jaffna, Eelam is portrayed as a young woman breaking free from the chains tying her to the southern part of the country. With her face in the Jaffna peninsula, the Tamil areas on the western and eastern coasts appear as her long, free-flowing hair.

As in the linguistic nationalism discussed above, it is probably correct to say that the mother is the more dominant of the female images figuring in revolutionary nationalist symbolism. This conceptualisation of the Tamil territory appears, for example, in the expression *Tayakam* – 'Motherland' – as in the all-present LTTE slogan *pulikalin takam tamililat tayakam*, 'The thirst of the Tigers is the Motherland Tamil Eelam.' Tayakam, in other words, is the liberated geographical space of the Tamil nation – the 'nation' being conceived as *inam* or the extended kin group where internal contradictions are dissolved. In the interview by *Velicham* referred to above, Prabhakaran is asked about his care for the children whose parents have been killed in the war. His answer follows:

We have taken the small boys and girls who have been affected by the war into our fond embrace and are nurturing them. I do not consider them orphans or children bereft of kit and kin. They are the children of our motherland and they are the flowers which have blossomed on our soil. Just as we envisage our language and our soil as our Mother, I consider these as the children of the nation which is the Mother of us all.[9]

We are here a long way away from Pfaffenberger's labourers who did not consider themselves to be Tamil. In fact, we are much closer to a European understanding of what constitutes a national group – a connection between people, language and territory disappearing into mythical history:

The soil where we were born, the soil where our ancestors were born, the soil where we have lived through generations from ancient times, our own soil; how can we tolerate the robbing of this soil from us, doing nothing? Ours is a language of antiquity and magnificence, ours is a superior culture and a true and good tradition. We are a people excelling in education, excelling in the arts, and who have seen hard work and hardship. A true national race like ours, who have a firm historical existence should live in submission to another national race? Why?[10]

The conceptualisation of territory-as-mother underlies all the subtle references to the nurturing, comforting, etc. qualities of the country – see 'this coast is the lap from which we were born ...' (above). It serves to naturalise the relationship between people and land by couching this relationship in terms of the selfless devotion which Tamil children are expected to feel, and most often *do* feel, towards their mothers. It also de-historises this bond by presenting it as essential and timeless and depoliticises it by allowing the imagining of the nation as members of a family born from the same mother. This conceptualisation is given explicit ritual expressions. For example, the central commemorative ritual during the annual Great Heroes' Day (see next chapter), celebrated simultaneously in all Tamil communities in all parts of the world, is the celebration of martyrs' mothers while they garland pictures of their dead children. This ritual must be read as part of the effort to homologise the pre- and post-colonial situation, alluding to the portrayal of mothers in the Sangam poetry which is widely known among Tamils. In keeping with the military needs of the time, in these texts Tamil mothers are endowed with mystical qualities producing what is termed 'milk of valour' for their sons, turning them into courageous warriors. Correspondingly, a son's cowardice reflect a mother's imperfection:

When people said
her son had taken fright,
had turned his back on battle
and died,
she raged and shouted,
'If he really broke down
in the thick of battle,
I'll slash these breasts

that gave him suck'
and went there,
sword in hand
Turning over body after fallen body,
she rummaged through the blood-red field
till she found her son,
quarted in pieces,
and she rejoiced
more than on the day
she gave him birth
(in Ramanujan 1985)

Sometimes this comparison of previous and present mothers is made explicit. In a commentary of a BBC documentary on Jaffna, where mothers are shown praising the death of their sons on the battlefield, the newspaper *Tamil Nation* claims: 'Such was the hallmark of Tamil Womanhood two thousand years ago. Once again that ideal womanhood has been born in the North and East of Sri Lanka.'[11]

The revived imagery of motherhood within revolutionary rhetoric has two main overlapping aspects. One is the establishing of an equivalence between the biological mother and the territory of the motherland. While it is the quality of the Tamil mother which provides valour to sons (or today: children), the death of these children is part of what provides the land with its specific quality. While the mother's body is made a metaphor for what is sacred, by being taken out of its traditional context of family and caste to be celebrated in its specific role as mother of dead soldiers, this sacredness of the mother is projected onto the land for which the children have died. The other aspect of mother imagery is the establishing of a continuity of the fight through the reproduction of soldiers. For example, on a poster widely spread by the LTTE, we see a drawing of a mother with her young son. The mother gives her dead husband's AK 47 (an assault rifle) to the boy. On the stone of the husband's grave there is the following text:

For the dawn of our soil the fighting Great Heroes are those who have been sown here
For the birth of our Motherland the deaths of the Tigers succeed each other.
The thirst of the Tigers is the Motherland Tamil Eelam

In relation to continuity, we also see here a two-way referential movement. At the same time as mothers secure the (biological and social) reproduction of soldiers, by being born of Tamil mothers these soldiers come to embody the Tamil motherland. The military ideology of the LTTE centres on the concept of *tiyakam*. Tiyakam, which lexically means 'abandonment', can be more conveniently translated into English as 'martyrdom'. It is important to note that this understanding of martyrdom is different from the Christian one. The Tamil martyr is not a martyr for whom the qualifying trait is the endurance of suffering as such – a suffering in which civilians and refugees might take part. The concept of *tiyakam* specifically implies the taking up of armed struggle. A *tiyaki* is someone who has given his or her life for Eelam, who has made the choice of abandoning life in the very act of taking life, *of dying while killing*. The LTTE martyrs are officially recorded in a book called *Mavirar Kurippetu*, 'Diary of Heroes', which briefly provides name, rank and date of death of the person. Sometimes the entry is accompanied by a short comment on the person or the event of his or her dying. The book is a diary in the sense that it is arranged according to the time of death, starting with Lieutenant Cankar who is recorded as dying on 27 November 1982 (Schalk 1992).

The salient point here is that it is through willingness to die, and through actual dying in battle, that you become connected to the unfolding of history and become part of Tamil destiny. As it happens, the Tamil term for 'independence' – *cutantiram* – also conveys the meaning of 'heritage'. Independence, in other words, is part of the Tamil inheritance, a part of what constitutes their community as a nation. One may argue, however, that in LTTE's thinking present-day autonomy is not mainly a question of arguing for historically established rights. Rather, 'history' – *carittiram* – here operates as a depersonalised subject, realising itself in a Hegelian sense through the representatives of the Tamil nation. We find this expressed, for instance, in Prabhakaran's, the leader of LTTE's, introduction to the 'Diary' when he says to the parents of the dead fighters: 'Your children shall not die; they left having become history.' In another message, widely spread by video cassettes, the *talaivar* ('leader') states:

The deaths of these fighters is a force which is driving and moving our history ...

The heroic *maravars* ['warriors'] have sown in our soil the seed for a unique liberation ...

The death of a liberation fighter is not a normal event of death. This death is an event of history, a lofty ideal, a miraculous event which bestows life. The truth is that a liberation fighter dies not. Indeed, what is called the 'flame of his aim' which has shone for his life, will not be extinguished. This aim is like a fire, like a force in history, and it takes hold of the others. The national soul of the people has been touched and wakened up ...

We must achieve our motherland's liberation. Slavery's fetters which have bound us, we must break. Our people must live with independence, dignity and security. In order to achieve this aim we must fight indeed. We must indeed shed blood. We must indeed live in the shadow of death ...

10   BETWEEN NATION AND STATE

When I landed in Colombo in August 1993, Ravi met me at the airport. He had finally become a Norwegian citizen and after ten years he was able to go back in order to look for a wife. When I arrived Ravi had just come back from Jaffna where his grandparents in their eighties were now his only relatives. In Colombo Ravi was sleeping on the floor in the living room of a family known to his uncle.

The visit to Jaffna seemed to have made a strong impression on Ravi. The trip north took him close to three weeks, including ten days waiting in Kilinochchi for transport across the lagoon. While waiting he was visited by LTTE intelligence, three young boys who checked his papers and asked him questions about his family background and his time in Norway. They returned after two days telling him he was cleared and free to continue. Having feared harassment and extortion as a 'Westerner', Ravi was visibly impressed by the discipline shown by these and other LTTE soldiers he later met in Jaffna. We were spending the evenings in Colombo discussing politics and the military situation. When I voiced my usual reservations against an independent Eelam, questioning why the development of a common Sri Lankan identity should not be possible, he said history had proven this to be impossible and that secession was already a fact. 'If you had been there with me you would understand', he kept telling me. According to him life in Jaffna was now smooth sailing. Schools were open and there was food on the tables. In particular he was impressed during his visit by the law and order aspect of the situation, claiming that for the first time in years people could now walk about safely. 'Even young girls are paid respect now', he said, referring to the female LTTE soldiers. When I asked him if the 'law and order' also applied to the 4000 prisoners allegedly held by the LTTE, he just told me one cannot have it both ways. 'My whole understanding of things has changed', he said. 'I thought I was lucky going to Norway. Now I realise that it is we in the West who are suffering. In Jaffna there is a full life, and when you die, you die. We, on the other hand, spend our lives in shadowland.'

A few days after my arrival Ravi and I went up to Trincomalee together where Ravi wanted to see again some tourist attractions he had visited as a schoolboy. Just after Haberane, where the last tourist hotels are located and the paved roads end, the first military checkpost appeared. There were five posts on this last stretch into Trinco. We had been told the express bus was normally let through without being stopped, and had therefore paid the extra price, but it turned out to be in vain. All checks proceeded in the same way. With the other Tamil civilians Ravi had to step out in the scorching sun while I was left in the bus with the few Sinhalese, most of them soldiers on their way back to barracks from leave in the south. The bus would then drive about 200 metres and stop, waiting for the passengers who had to walk through the armed check post where papers, pockets and bags were controlled. Ravi had feared these controls before leaving, expecting trouble because his old identity card was issued in Jaffna. He was worried he would be suspected of being a Tiger trying to sneak into Trincomalee under the cover of a visiting refugee. Hoping to pass off as a Sinhalese he had put on a cap showing the Sinhalese lion but the officers entering the bus were not fooled. His alternative strategy of getting by showing only his Norwegian passport was gruffly waved off – it was local identity or nothing. While the soldiers did accept his story of wishing to take a foreign friend to see the beauty of Trincomalee, he still had to go through the rigorous controls. Climbing off the bus for the fifth time, cap and all, to face the heat while the Sinhalese and I remained seated, he asked me laconically in Norwegian: 'Common identity? Do you see any common identity around here ...?'

Having reached the last chapter, the discussion of individual bonds to Tamil Sri Lanka and a shared distance from Norwegian society should be concluded. What I will do in this chapter is to incorporate these issues in a brief description of exile identity.

If an identity specifically connected with life in exile exists, concluding this work by returning to Sri Lanka as I did in the last two chapters may seem an awkward editorial choice. This objection, I believe, arises from our misguided anthropological conception of society as a place where migrants necessarily partake in a project of 'integration'. Our anthropological concepts are so tuned to localised contexts of interaction that we have difficulties adjusting our own perception of space to that of the migrant's. The fact is, while the refugee may stay, the movement of signification does not end in exile. My choice of returning to Sri Lanka was linked to what I see as the main concern of Tamil refugees in Norway: retrieving a sense of who they are by overcoming their separation from home. In trying to capture this 'movement of return', the emphasis on history in the last two chapters was deliberate. The way I see it, their road to retrieval is the construction of a (hi)story in which they themselves take part.

Before I elaborate on this point, it should be noted that many refugees find it difficult to let go of Sri Lanka physically. Several migrants to Norway, who have Norwegian citizenship, have stories to tell of unsuccessful efforts to re-establish themselves in Sri Lanka, often losing years' of financial savings in the process. Not everyone has reason to share Ravi's (above) high regard for the forces of liberation. In several instances such returnees or their family members have been taken hostage for ransom by local guerrillas, their Western connection seemingly making them legitimate prey. In the era of nationalist struggle a history of absence implies exclusion, if not from the nation at least from the *soul* of the nation, its inner core constituted by the ones who stay, fight and die. On the other hand, many Tamils in Norway have been back to help their remaining family, to attend funerals, to look for a spouse or to see if it is safe to relocate. These visits have put many of them in a very difficult position in Norway as the immigration authorities argue that their continued contact with Sri Lanka prove that they have no need for protection. To Norwegian authorities as well as to local Tamil authorities membership in the political body is dependent on permanent physical presence, and refugees are asked by both to choose where they want to spend their future.

NARRATIVE SELVES

This is the dilemma, then, to which refugee migrants need to find a solution; how to use the in between as a space within which to reconstitute themselves. Reframed in terms of self-identity the dilemma consists in making sense of the practical choices one has already made, of justifying one's actions in terms of constructs of meaning larger than one's own. Even more than for John Berger's migrant worker (1975), who might go back and harvest his investment in wealth and glory, to the refugee migration is like 'an event in a dream dreamt by another', because the intentionality of his action is permeated by historical necessities of which he is not aware. Narrative theory may help us gain a better understanding of this situation.

Before looking more closely at this, it is worth looking briefly at Ewing's (1990) discussion of 'self'. Ewing points out that in academic discourse the concept of 'self' is applied in at least two different ways. The concept is used by some authors to designate a primary psychic constellation, a person's main motivating agency and centre of initiative and experience. This is an understanding of self which often reflects a Western individualistic bias. What anthropologists within the relativist tradition have tended do, on the other hand, is to retain the concept of self as a pre-reflexive structure of agency but argue that both the constitution of this structure and the fact of human experience itself is radically variable (e.g. Geertz 1983, Marriott 1976, Rosaldo 1980).

As Ewing points out there is, however, another sense in which the concept of self may be used. This is self as self-representation, as the result of a semiotic process organising experiential fragments into illusory wholes. In this perspective the person is one of the 'things' about which we speak rather than itself a speaking subject (Ricoeur 1992), and mental events (like intentions or motivations) among the predicates attributed to the person by the self or by others.[1] The important point is the understanding of self as a result of constant adjustment to changing circumstances where the striving for wholeness requires a reworking of memory.

This process, which philosophers have termed 'repetition' (Heidegger 1972, Ricoeur 1981b), rests upon the plot as an act of configuration; the reading of the end into the beginning, the recapitulation of initial conditions of action in its projected final consequences. Memory *repeats* the course of events according to an order where the backward move towards the past is retrieved in anticipation and the openness of history is grafted on the finite structure of a lifetime. This repetition is not a private undertaking pure and simple, however. As the young Eelam martyrs illustrate in a clear if extreme manner, the 'being-toward-death', to use Heidegger's expression, always unfolds in a dialectic between personal fate and common destiny. And 'fate' is always articulated in narrative form, because it is read as the result of events in time which are internally connected. By being so articulated the priority of common destiny is imposed upon it. Not only does narrative take place in public time, in the *before* and *after*, the *too soon* or *too late*, but no narrative is possible without co-actors. What the personal narrative does is to portray an actor – a hero – struggling in circumstances he or she has not created, producing consequences he or she has not intended. As Ricoeur puts it, the time of the narrative is the time of the '*now that* ...' (1981b: 172) wherein a person is both abandoned and responsible at the same time.

Where, then, do the two readings of history outlined in the two previous chapters belong in this discussion? I argue that the answer to this question depends on the perspective chosen. In a discussion of meaning, temporal repetition stands as an alternative to the dechronologised model of a structuralist perspective. Regarded as a structural opposition the two would represent alternative destinies imposing themselves on personal fate and alternative ways for a person of connecting to a larger social whole. Seen in a perspective of narrative unfolding, however, they may come to represent a process of development, the transition from one stage to another. The fact that they rest upon a common dominant symbol – *karpu* – makes it possible to establish a relationship of continuity between them. In one of them this quality is related to women, family and hierarchy, and in the other it is projected on to territory and nation.

To see how individuals deal with the contradictory implications of the two cultural models, how they are able to tolerate inconsistencies and strive to create a sense of wholeness in their 'being-toward-death', it is important to observe that the two narratives are different not only in content but also in character. While both are communal narratives and establish temporal continuity in terms of origin and common destiny, they do so in different ways. The 'traditional' is of a kind which Crites (1971) has termed 'sacred stories', stories which cannot be fully and directly told because to most people they lie too deep in consciousness to be formulated in words. The main characteristic of these narratives is not that they are religious as such, but that they are *anonymous* and, at the community level, are most clearly expressed in ritual. As Crites puts it, the symbolic worlds which sacred stories project 'are not like monuments that men behold, but like dwelling places. People live in them' (Crites 1971: 295). With respect to historicity the traditional narrative suspends history. Its relationship to the colonial situation is a conclusion drawn by the observer. To the people who actually 'live in them' the narrative of tradition, intertwined as it is with the religious legitimation of hierarchy, locates origin outside history, in the eternal repetition of ritual cycles. The 'revolutionary' one, on the other hand, is what Crites would call a 'mundane story', a fully articulated story placed within a world which it reveals and clarifies. This world is a universe of discourse, correlative to a specific form of historical consciousness which perceives the world in terms of history.

In other words, my argument is that to the individual the incorporation of revolutionary elements means a stepping out into chronological time, locating the self in a world of temporal development. To the refugee migration itself is part of this world. As indicated by Ravi's comments above, the personal narrative of migration adheres in its form to the epic structure of the quest where a process of enchantment leads the main character astray. The ensuing state of confusion serves to disrupt the taken-for-grantedness of the initial state (home/self) and projects the main character forward on a search for what has been lost.

As a social fact this narrative form seems to exist in a number of cultural traditions and certainly does in the Hindu Tamil one. Among Tamils religion is epic. The tiresome pilgrimage, so central to religious experience, is a form of asceticism, *tapas*, preparing the individual for the journey into the self, backwards in time (Shulman 1980, also Daniel 1984). The epics are also religion, worshipping the individual struggling with forces he cannot control.[2] What is important in this narrative form is that the travel in space, or the battle to be won, is *duplicated* by a struggle against adverse forces assuming the shape of a return to the origin. Individual repetition thus incorporates communal destiny by *generating* the quest as a condition for personal development. This form is illustrated in Augustine's *Confessions*, where the travel is interiorised to the extent that there is no longer any privileged place to which to return. Augustine's story of how he became a Christian – like, I argue, Kuganathan's and Ravi's stories of how they became nationalists – is a travel *ab exterioribus ad interiora, ab interioribus ad superiora* – 'from the exterior to the interior, from the interior to the superior'. As Ricoeur says about Augustine:

The quest has been absorbed into the movement by which the hero – if we can still call him by that name – becomes who he is. Memory, therefore, is no longer the narrative of external adventures stretching along episodic time. It is itself the spiral movement that, through anecdotes and episodes, brings us back to the almost motionless constellation of potentialities that the narrative retrieves. The end of the story is what equates the present with the past, the actual with the potential. (1981b: 182)

It is in this in this perspective that we should understand what has been called the 'mysteries of exile' (Knudsen 1994), or even the 'poetics of exile' (Longva n.d.). Exile is not primarily a geographical location, it is a state of mind through which one becomes what one has left behind. In the Tamil case many actually become what they have fled from. Between the extremes of the warrior and the victim the refugee must carry out his 'bricolage', assemble the pieces and carry on. For many this life project takes the form of internalised martyrdom, the fight for Eelam being replaced by a *longing* for Eelam which grows into a constant part of the personality and becomes a counterweight, *the* counterweight, to the vicissitudes of exile. What is characteristic of the Tamil exile situation, therefore, is a blurring of 'here' and 'there'; the dis-membering of social networks, the re-membering of an imaginary homeland, the attachment of an imagined community to an imagined place. It is that from which they are excluded which makes them not only 'refugees' but '*Tamil* refugees'.

In this description is implied the understanding that being a Tamil nationalist in exile is somehow different from being an LTTE member in Sri Lanka. Outside the small inner circle of the exile LTTE administration most migrants, as well as quite a few on the inside of this circle, have never been politically active at home. What revolutionary nationalism does in exile is to provide a name for individual nostalgia and shared exclusion from the host society. To refugees the development of national consciousness is, at least in part, a transformation created by the conditions of exile. Incorporating exile into the narrative of the nation is a way of giving meaning to this existence in terms of 'thereness' (Said 1986: 28), as a liminal condition preceding the return of the nation – a *new* nation – to the traditional homeland.

This process of repetition is assisted by aspects of LTTE's activity abroad. In Norway the LTTE – under a more neutral name – organise the two most important annual functions, the *Suthanthira Takam* ('Thirst for Freedom') in August and the *Mavirar Nal* ('Heroes' Day') in November, both open to all members of the Tamil community and celebrated in all parts of the world. As one may guess from the names, they are both dedicated to the freedom struggle; *Mavirar Nal* specifically celebrating the dead martyrs and being staged on the birthday of Prabhakaran, the LTTE's leader. In Oslo, where the majority of Tamils live in Norway, the annual March celebration of the LTTE-organised *Annai Poopathi* school for children is the third annual function. Annai Poopathi was a Tamil woman living in eastern Sri Lanka who, during the IPKF-period, fasted to death as a protest against the army's presence and who is now honoured as a martyr by the organisation. The school itself provides teaching in Tamil language and lessons in dance and song within the framework of LTTE's political ideology. On the day of the celebration the children give speeches and perform cultural activities containing powerful nationalist messages for a larger Tamil audience.

Within the Tamil exile community itself the different approaches to the Sri Lankan crises may be illustrated by two episodes. In the latter part of 1993 I attended a conference organised by one of the Tamil non-LTTE groups in Oslo. The subject of the meeting was 'Human Rights in Sri Lanka'; five or six members of the group, who had all been living in Norway for a long time, attended the meeting and had invited representatives of Norwegian humanitarian organisations, human rights groups, ministries, etc. who were offered copious amounts of food and drink. The situation in Sri Lanka was presented in an academic way with equal emphasis on human rights violations by the two sides involved in the conflict, the individual's right to life and freedom of speech being at the centre of the discussions. Only a few days later the *Mavirar Nal* was celebrated, bringing together about 700 Tamils in a noisy crowd and without a single European in the audience. Here no mention was made of individual rights but instead there were music, dramatic performances and speeches on oppression, freedom struggle, martyrdom and collective destiny.

The point I wish to emphasise is that the majority of people present at this latter festival are normally not what I would call 'LTTE-people' but people by whom the historical consciousness of this organisation is sought in order to provide meaning to their own marginal existence in Norway. The grand narrative of revolutionary nationalism is adapted, by refugees who accept it, to provide a genesis of the diaspora, as illustrated by the example provided in Chapter 7: 'When the atrocities of the Sinhalese terrorists increased, to protect our lives we fled ...' This explanation goes beyond scientific history and represents a 'mythico-history'. Not because it is untrue but because the Tamils *as a people* are here heroised and placed within a more encompassing moral ordering of the world (Malkki 1990) where relationships and processes are reinterpreted within a dichotomy of good and evil.

It is with reference to this binary moral framework that the significance of different levels of communication must be sought. While internally there is a continuous ordering and reordering of events and actors, externally most people will project an image of the world in categorical terms where Tamils are locked in an oppositional relationship with their surroundings. Many, in fact, express the opinion that Tamils are a 'cursed people', abandoned by gods and men alike. When asked about their background, Tamil refugees tend to slip from the story of their own lives into the field of collective history. The individual and the collective fuse into one standardised discourse explaining *'why I am here now'*. Broadly speaking, this mythico-history focuses on three themes. The first concerns the ancient origin of Tamils in Sri Lanka, their separateness as a people and their tradition of political independence as expressed, for instance, in the kingdom of Jaffna. The second theme is the betrayal of the Tamil people by the British in handing power over to the Sinhalese at the time of independence, the inherent evil of Sinhalese politicians and their determination in destroying the Tamil community. The third theme is the betrayal of the Western world in providing economic assistance to Sri Lanka, in failing to intervene to stop the genocidal politics of the Sri Lankan government and in failing to recognise Tamil civilians as legitimate refugees from ethnic oppression. This narrative is open in the specific sense that new misfortunes may be incorporated and given a political interpretation within its binary structure. For example, when, during the intense offensive against Jaffna in the fall of 1995, the LTTE in Norway managed to organise a well-attended demonstration against the Sri Lankan regime and this demonstration did not receive any attention from the Norwegian media, this was construed by some of the organisers as part of a 'conspiracy' on the part of the Norwegian government.

What is worth observing is that this moral ordering of the universe implies, and to some extent rests upon, an 'emic' – in the sense of non-legal – conceptualisation of what it means to be a 'refugee'. Among Tamils, 'refugee' as a collective social category stands opposed to the 'migrant worker' and the 'asylum seeker' who, in accordance with official ideology, are seen as individually incorporated into the host society. A refugee is someone who does not put down roots in exile and who remains categorically 'pure' in maintaining boundaries between self and other (see Malkki 1990). In this respect early migrants who exhibit their acquired 'Norwegianness', and the handful of individuals who are recruited into positions in Norwegian public administration, come to represent potential internal enemies.

CONCLUSION: NAMING – AND BEYOND?

Does this mean that what I earlier termed two models are, after all, only one, reunited as development in the life course of the individual? My argument has been that at present which one of the two sets of ethical prescriptions takes precedence varies according to the field of interaction in which the actor takes part. Something has changed from a previous state of affairs, however. Today, in exile, the obligations of tradition are still imperative, but their fulfilment increasingly seems to be the result of conscious decision; the ideal no longer has the doxic quality where things 'go without saying because they come without saying' and tradition is silent about itself as tradition (Bourdieu 1977). In bound mode social interaction is largely confined to two separate domains: to the household sphere and to the 'worldwide web' of family networks. Outside these domains friendship groups, the fellowship of the unmarried workers and the communality of exile nationalism are all based upon varieties of 'revolutionary' interaction where participation is not restricted by birth or background.

It is worth reflecting for a moment on the social development which this situation mirrors. The way I see it, the importance of narrative selves and the partial breakdown of hierarchy are intimately related, to each other and to nationalist politics as such. They all reflect 'dislocations', individual and collective, resulting from the dissolution of taken for granted social categories and fuelling what Charles Taylor (1994) has termed a 'politics of recognition'. In exile consciousness nationalism represents a strand of modernity and at the heart of this modernity lies the need, and demand, for recognition.

Of course, on the individual level the need for recognition is not something new. In pre-modern societies, however, this recognition does not arise as a problem because it is firmly built into socially derived identities. What is new, and what defines modernity as a social condition, is the situation in which an attempt to achieve recognition may fail.

This development is related to *dignity* taking the place of *honour*. The concept of honour, seen here to include the value around which transactions are structured in traditional bound mode interaction, is inherently linked to inequality. Honour in this sense is by definition a scarce good. For someone to have honour it is essential that not everyone has it, at least not to the same degree. As opposed to this understanding of honour stands the modern notion of dignity as something which everyone shares, the 'dignity of human beings' expressing universalist and egalitarian values.

What is of particular interest in the present context is the importance of this transition for self-identity and for nationalism. With the breakdown of hierarchically ordered social categories emerges a self conceptualised as an inner depth and where identity – my absolute sameness with myself – presupposes the discovery of my self, the reaching into this depth in order to get in touch with my true being. With dignity, in other words, comes the ideal of authenticity, and nationalism may be regarded as a natural consequence of this conception. My language is part of what I truly am, and so is the history of my forefathers and the land on which they were raised. These things are part of me and if I am not emotionally in touch with them I am not identical with myself.

Readers may wish to know *to what extent* dignity is replacing honour as a transactional value in Tamil society. This question, to be answered on a general basis, undoubtedly needs further investigation. However, exile nationalism has a strong organisational potential and, in Norway, is in the process of constructing a new refugee identity. This process of construction has followed a predictable course: being made a victim of representation by the authority of government the ethnic self has realised it has a name by having one forced upon it. Seeking to avoid marginalisation, the ethnic self strives to dismantle discrimination through a process of 'inverse displacement' (Radhakrishnan 1987), giving *itself* a name, representing itself from within its own point of view.

On the other hand, I have already indicated that in my opinion nationalism in exile is, in terms of political consciousness, not coterminous with the LTTE's political motives in Sri Lanka. As implied by my discussion of 'imposed modernity' in Chapter 7, I argue that the migratory experience itself creates the basis, in terms of individualised identity, for nationalism considered as a politics of recognition. The present situation in Tamil Sri Lanka has not been the main focus of my fieldwork. For what it is worth, however, I offer the opinion that the LTTE in Sri Lanka still operates within a social landscape which they define in pre-modern terms. Their repressive manner and internal killings testify to this fact. The present tragedy of the Tamil people is the situation where in Sri Lanka a rhetoric of ethnicity is (still) being employed to further sectional interests, but where this dynamics is now fuelled and financed by the externally displaced who, in general, are sincerely searching for a common future.

In which direction this future will take Tamil exile identity depends upon a number of factors. So far their diasporic tendency, their 'transnational networks built from multiple attachments' (Clifford 1994) have provided them with a cultural openness, a capacity to adapt and make use of what serves their interests. The entrenchment as a minority within the framework of the nation state would probably strengthen the tendency towards closure. There are strong indications that Tamils, as part of the larger refugee population, are in danger of becoming permanently excluded from mainstream Norwegian society. The statistical report on the situation of refugees in Oslo referred to in Chapter 6 (Djuve and Hagen 1995) shows that in terms of poverty the difference between refugees in general and Norwegian citizens is now much greater than the corresponding difference between the black and white population in the USA. In Oslo 44 per cent of refugee children grow up in households which are totally or partly dependent on welfare. Fifty per cent of refugee children grow up in families where parents neither work nor go to school. While the Tamil population, as discussed in Chapter 6, has an exceptionally high rate of employment in terms of refugees, statistics confirm that their contact with Norwegians is very limited. For the next generation, which presumably will have less economic responsibilities towards relations in Sri Lanka, the combination of their parents' isolation from Norwegian society and of their growing up in immigrant neighbourhoods where many live on welfare may present a challenge in terms of staking out their own future.

Within the next generation also lies the answer as to whether kinship obligations, and kinship itself in its present classificatory form, will be sustained across national borders, keeping the diasporic connections alive. As noted by Longva (1996), what Appadurai has termed 'transnational cultural flows' (1991) take place in a world of bounded states, where space is more ordered and regulated than ever

before. The conclusion that Longva draws from this fact is that it is
'in human subjectivities that deterritorialisation causes "all that is
solid (to) melt into air"'. There is reason to point out that there exists
another distinct possibility, which is a 're-territorialised' subjectivity,
defined in terms of ethnic binarity and infused by a desire for an absolute
and irrefragable self (Radhakrishnan 1987). Judging by their reception
upon arrival and their present conditions of exile in the West, one
should recognise the need for refugees to search for a common
ground in their shared geographical origin. However this process poses
questions. If empowered by the present concept of nationalism, it is
legitimate to ask *in whose name* this new name of ethnicity is authorised.
It is not the case that the discourse of a majority may be oppressive
while that of a minority may not. The construction of a discourse
which leaves the self only one possible position always implies the
silencing of a non-self, even when this construction takes place *within*
the minority.

NOTES

CHAPTER 1

1. See Special Report, *Hinduism Today*, April 1997.
2. 'Eelam' is the name given by Tamil militants to the liberated nation which they are fighting for. I have chosen this transcription rather than the more correct 'Ilam', because this is how the term normally appears in their own English writings.
3. 'Asylum-seekers in Western Europe (EC and EFTA) in 1992. Preliminary statistical survey prepared by the Secretariat of the Inter-governmental Consultations on Asylum, Refugee and Migration Policies in Europe, North America and Australia'. Unpublished.
4. *The World Almanac and Book of Facts 1992* (New York: Pharos, 1992).
5. Or 'l'essence d'une nation est que tous les individus aient beaucoup de choses en commun, et aussi que tous aient oublié bien des choses ... tout citoyen français doit avoir oublié la Saint-Barthélemy, les massacres du Midi au XIIIe siècle' (Ernest Renan: *Qu'est-ce qu'une nation?*, Oeuvres Complètes, 1, p. 892).
6. Cf. e.g. Daniel (1990: 235): 'In 1983, many a chocolate-coloured Sinhala apprehended a chocolate-coloured fellow Sinhala, and, denying the victim's claim to his "race" on the grounds that his skin was not of the shade that a Sinhala skin ought to be ... nor his face-shape that of an Aryan's ... beat him up and, in one instance known to me, even killed him for being a "Tamil trying to pass as Sinhala".'

CHAPTER 2

1. This 'deviant' caste ranking is not confined to Tamil Sri Lanka but seems to be part of a characteristic South Indian (Dravidian) pattern where the two middle *varnas* are generally not found, something which has been acknowledged by Dumont himself (1980: xxxvii). See also Srivinas (1959), Beteille (1969) and Pfaffenberger (1982).

2. The word 'choice' is here put in inverted commas because often members had in fact no choice and were conscripted by force.

3. For a description of the operation, see Hole *et al* (1990) and *Sri Lanka Monitor* (1987), the monthly information bulletin published by the British Refugee Council.

CHAPTER 3

1. To those not familiar with his works it must be emphasised that Daniel, in spite of his principled stand, is one of the few anthropologists to have shown a long-term interest in violence. He has delivered several valuable analyses based on a consistent use of Peircean semiotics, which is one of his trademarks. My objection to Daniel's approach has to do with the fact that he, regarding pain as a Peircean *sinsign* – a sign exhausting itself in its own singularity; '[i]ts outermost limit is the boundary of the victim's body' (1994: 223) – focuses exclusively on the *subjective* experience of violence. In my view, based on Scarry (1985), the individuating aspect of pain is precisely what makes it possible for the body where pain is located to re-enter the semiotic process as a *representamen* ('sign') for another interpretant.

2. AI Index: ASA 37/14/91: 17.

3. Cf. Inform, *Sri Lankan Information Monitor*, Colombo, 15 May 1992.

4. Readers are also referred to Somasundaram (1993a, 1993b, 1994).

5. EPRLF: 'Eelam People's Revolutionary Liberation Front', PLOTE: 'People's Liberation Organisation of Tamil Eelam', TELO: 'Tamil Eelam Liberation Organisation'.

6. See Amnesty International, AI Index: ASA 37/21/90.

7. See Amnesty International, ASA Index: 37/21/90: 43.

8. News report by DPA, 28 May 1994.

CHAPTER 4

1. See e.g. Reuters, 31 July 1995.

CHAPTER 5

1. *Sunday Times*, 29 January 1995.

2. Of 5666 Sri Lankan citizens registered as living in Norway as of 1 January 1992, only 82 persons were above 50 years of age.

3. See e.g. *Frontline*, 20 October 1995.

4. V.I.S. Jayapalan is a personal friend, and I base my presentation of his short story on my own translation from Tamil into Norwegian which was made with his co-operation. In Tamil the story has been published in Rajathuraj (1994).

5. What is at issue here is really what Banks (1957, 1960) has termed '*sondakara castes*', which are bilateral kindreds uniting caste members from different villages through marriage. These kindreds are normally conceptualised as 'castes' in their own right. See discussion in Chapter 8.

CHAPTER 6

1. News release by Associated Press, 29 April 1994 (0717).

2. I use this misspelled term here in Derrida's sense (e.g. 1976). In my opinion Derrida's insight that (cultural) signification proceeds through signs which are always different from themselves is particularly important to the questions of migration and diasporic consciousness: 'The "ance" ending is the mark of suspended status. Since the difference between "difference" and "differance" is inaudible, this "neographism" reminds us that ... even within the graphic structure, the perfectly spelled word is always absent, constituted through an endless series of spelling mistakes' (p. xliii).

CHAPTER 7

1. The difference between 'model' and 'plot' has to do with the two conceptions' relationship to time, a question I will discuss in Chapters 8 and 10.

CHAPTER 8

1. Kunkumam is saffron put on the forehead as part of the funeral ceremony.

2. '*Sondakara caste*' is not a term which Jaffna people would use and in this sense has the status of an analytical concept. I have kept it here to keep the continuity with Banks's works. By Jaffna people '*sondakara caste*' is conceptualised simply as 'caste' (*cadi*).

3. This comparison is not accidental. Except for the stronger Tamil formality in all aspects of marriage (and sexual relations in general), Jaffna–Tamil notions of kinship have much in common with the Kandyan Sinhalese as described by Yalman. Transferred to Jaffna, Yalman's perspective provides a different,

and in my view more correct, understanding of Tamil kinship and caste than that of David (1973b) (see in particular Yalman 1967: 138 ff.).

CHAPTER 9

1. *Tambi*, 'little brother', is a pet name for the LTTE's leader, Prabhakaran.
2. *Cociiyalicat Tamil Ilattai nokki* ('Towards a socialist Tamil Eelam'), LTTE publication 1980.
3. Valvettithurai, or VVT as it is normallly called in daily language, is the village of LTTE's leader, Prabhakaran, and in Tamil consciousness is forever associated with the position and destiny of this organisation.
4. See the interview with Prabhakaran in the Jaffna literary magazine, *Velicham*, reprinted in English in *Tamil Times*, 15 July 1994.
5. In Schalk (1992).
6. 'Tamil Women in the Struggle for a Free and Independent Tamil Eelam', LTTE, London, 1991.
7. IPS news, 9 August 1995.
8. This expression, *karpu alliththal*, could also be translated as 'raping' in English.
9. *Tamil Times*, 15 July 1995: 19.
10. *Cociyalicat Tamil Ilattai nokki* ('Towards a socialist Tamil Eelam'), LTTE publication 1980.
11. December 1992, p. 24.

CHAPTER 10

1. This, of course, does not mean that we (always) act without thinking but that we understand our own psychic landscape in terms of categories of meaning which are socially constituted and are embedded in language. In other words that we have no privileged access to ourselves. See also Taylor (1985).
2. For an example of the importance of the epic in Sri Lanka Tamil ritual, see Tanaka (1991).

BIBLIOGRAPHY

Abu-Lughod, L. 1990: 'Introduction: emotion, discourse, and the politics of everyday life' in Catherine A. Lutz and Lila Abu-Lughod (eds): *Language and the politics of emotion* Cambridge: Cambridge University Press

Anderson, B. 1983: *Imagined Communities* London: Verso

—— 1992: *Long-Distance Nationalism: World Capitalism and the Rise of Identity Politics* Amsterdam: Centre for Asian Studies Amsterdam (CASA)

Ann, A. 1994: *Unbroken Chains: Explorations into the Jaffna Dowry System* Jaffna: Malathi Press

Appadurai, A. 1985: 'Gratitude as a Social Mode in South India' *Ethos* Vol. 13 No. 3: 237–45

—— 1990: 'Disjuncture and Difference in the Global Cultural Economy' in Mike Featherstone (ed.): *Global Culture* London, Newbury Park, New Delhi: Sage Publications

—— 1991: 'Global Ethnoscapes: Notes and Queries for a Transnational Anthropology' in Richard G. Fox: *Recapturing Anthropology: Working in the Present* Santa Fe, New Mexico: School of American Research Press

Appadurai, A. and C. A. Breckenridge 1976: 'The South Indian Temple: Authority, Honour and Redistribution' *Contribution to Indian Sociology* 10: 187–211

Arasaratnam, S. 1994: 'Sri Lanka's Tamils: Under Colonial Rule' in C. Manogaran and B. Pfaffenberger: *The Sri Lankan Tamils: Ethnicity and Identity* Boulder, San Francisco and Oxford: Westview Press

Banks, M. Y. 1957: 'The Social Organization of the Jaffna Tamils of North Ceylon, with special reference to Kinship, Marriage, and Inheritance' Cambridge University: unpublished PhD dissertation

—— 1960: 'Caste in Jaffna' in E.R. Leach (ed.): *Aspects of Caste in South India, Ceylon, and North-West Pakistan* Cambridge: Cambridge University Press

Barnett, S. 1977: 'Identity Choice and Caste Ideology in Contemporary South India' in K. David (ed.): *The New Wind; Changing Identities in South Asia* The Hague and Paris: Mouton Publishers

Barth, F. 1969: 'Introduction' in Fredrik Barth (ed.): *Ethnic Groups and Boundaries* Bergen and Oslo: Universitetsforlaget

—— 1978: 'Introduction' in Fredrik Barth (ed.): *Scale and Social Organization* Oslo, Bergen and Tromsø: Universitetsforlaget

—— 1989: 'The analysis of culture in complex societies' *Ethnos* 54 (3–4): 120–42

—— 1993: *Balinese Worlds* Chicago and London: University of Chicago Press

Beiser, B. 1987: 'Changing time perspective and mental health among Southeast Asian refugees' *Culture, Medicine and Psychiatry* 28 (5): 457–64

Berger, J. and J. Mohr 1975: *A Seventh Man: The Story of a Migrant Worker in Europe* Harmondsworth: Penguin

Béteille, A. 1969: *Caste, Class and Power: Changing Patterns of Stratification in a Tanjore Village* Berkeley: University of California Press

Bettelheim, B. 1991: *The Informed Heart: A study of the psychosocial consequences of living under extreme fear and terror* Harmondsworth: Penguin

Bhabha, H. K. 1990: 'DissemiNation: time, narrative, and the margins of the modern nation' in H. K. Bhabha (ed.): *Nation and Narration* London and New York: Routledge

Bourdieu, P. 1977: *Outline of a Theory of Practice* Cambridge Studies in Social Anthropology: Cambridge University Press

Bruner, J. 1990: *Acts of Meaning* Harvard: Harvard University Press

Buck, H. M. and G. E. Yocum (eds) 1974: *Structural Approaches to South India Studies* Chambersburgh: Wilson Books

Caplan, L. 1995: ' 'Life is Only Abroad, Not Here'; The Culture of Emigration among Anglo-Indians in Madras' *Immigrants and Minorities* Vol. 14 No. 1: 26–46

Chan, K. and D. Loveridge 1987: 'Refugees in "transit": Vietnamese in a refugee camp in Hong Kong' *International Migration Review* 21 (3): 745–59

Clarke, C., C. Peach and S. Vertovec (eds) 1990: *South Asians Overseas: Migration and ethnicity* Cambridge, New York and Melbourne: Cambridge University Press

Clifford, J. 1988: *The Predicament of Culture: Twentieth-Century Ethnography, Literature, and Art.* Cambridge, Massachusetts and London: Harvard University Press

—— 1994: 'Diasporas' *Cultural Anthropology* 9 (3): 302–38

Comaroff, J. L. 1980: 'Introduction' in J. L. Comaroff (ed): *The Meaning of Marriage Payment* London: Academic Press

Comaroff, J. 1985: *Body of Power, Spirit of Resistance: The Culture and History of a South African People* Chicago: University of Chicago Press

Comaroff, J. L. and Comaroff, J. 1991: *Of Revelation and Revolution* Chicago: University of Chicago Press

Connerton, P. 1992: *How Societies Remember* Cambridge: Cambridge University Press

Coomeraswamy, B. A. 1933: ' "Thesawalame" or the Customary Law of Jaffna' *The Hindu Organ* 19 June, 6 July and 3 August

Crites, S. 1971: 'The Narrative Quality of Experience' *Journal of the American Academy of Religion* Vol. XXXIX: 286–311

Daniel, V. 1984: *Fluid Signs: Being a Person the Tamil Way* Berkeley: University of California Press

—— 1989: 'The Semiotics of Suicide in Sri Lanka' in B. Lee and G. Urban (eds): *Semiotics, Self and Society* Berlin: Mouton de Gruyter

—— 1990: 'Afterword: scared places, violent spaces' in J. Spencer (ed.): *Sri Lanka: History and the Roots of Conflictt* London and New York: Routledge

—— 1991: 'Is there a Counterpoint to Culture?' *The Wertheim Lecture 1991* Amsterdam: Centre for Asian Studies Amsterdam (CASA)

—— 1994: 'The individual in terror' in Thomas J. Csordas (ed.): *Embodiment and experience* Cambridge: Cambridge University Press

David, K. 1973a: 'Spatial Organization and Normative Schemes in Jaffna, Northern Sri Lanka' *Modern Ceylon Studies* Vol. 4 Nos. 1 and 2: 21–52

—— 1973b: 'Until Marriage Do Us Part: A Cultural Account of Jaffna Tamil Categories for Kinsmen' *Man* 8: 521–35

—— 1977: 'Hierarchy and Equivalence in Jaffna, North Sri Lanka: Normative Codes as Mediator' in K. David (ed.): *The New Wind: Changing Identities in South Asia* The Hague and Paris: Mouton Publishers

De Alwis, J. 1866: 'On the Origin of the Sinhalese Language' *Journal of the Ceylon Branch of the Royal Asiatic Society* Vol. XXIV: 241–8

de Certeau, M. 1984: *The Practice of Everyday Life* Berkeley, Los Angeles and London: University of California Press

Derrida, J. 1976: *Of Grammatology* Baltimore and London: Johns Hopkins University Press

Dissanayaka, T. D. S. A. 1983: *The Agony of Sri Lanka* Colombo: Swastika Press

Djuve, A. B. and K. Hagen 1995: *'Skaff meg en jobb'; Levekår blant flyktninger i Oslo ('Get Me a Job': Living Conditions Among Refugees in Oslo)* Oslo: Fafo

Dumont, L. 1980: *Homo Hierarchicus: The Caste System and its Implications* Complete Revised English Edition Chicago and London: University of Chicago Press

—— 1983: *Affinity as Value: Marriage Alliance in South India, with Comparative Essays on Australia* Chicago and London: University of Chicago Press

Eidheim, H. 1971: *Aspects of the Lappish Minority Situation* Oslo, Bergen and Tromsø: Universitetsforlaget

Epstein, A. 1978: *Ethos and Identity: Three Studies in Ethnicity* London: Tavistock

Ewing, K. P. 1990: 'The Illusion of Wholeness: Culture, Self, and the Experience of Inconsistency' *Ethos* Vol. 18 No. 3: 251–78

Farmanfarmaian, A. 1992: 'Subsystems, subjectivity and subversion: Iranian Refugees in Illegal Transit' *History and Anthropology* Vol. 6 No. 1: 87–102

Feldman, A. 1991: *Formations of Violence* Chicago and London: University of Chicago Press

Folkehøgskolerådet (FHSR) 1986: *Utlendingar i norsk folkehøgskole; ei utgreing frå Folkehøgskolerådet* (Foreigners in Norwegian Folk High Schools: A Review From the Board of the Folk High Schools) unpublished report

Foucault, M. 1972: *The Archeology of Knowledge* New York: Tavistock
—— 1986: 'Of Other Spaces' *Diacritics* Spring: 22–7
—— 1988: *Technologies of Self* London: Tavistock

Franco, J. 1985: 'Killing priests, nuns, women, children' in M. Blonsky (ed.): *On Signs* Baltimore: Blackwell

Friedman, J. 1994: *Cultural Identity and Global Process* London: Sage

Fuglerud, Ø. 1986: *I Løvens Tegn: Myteproduksjon, kommunalisme og politisk legitimitet i Ceylon. En historisk-antropologisk fortolkning* (*In the Sign of Leo: Myth Production, Communalism and Political Legitimacy in Ceylon. A Historico-anthropological Interpretation*) Oslo: International Peace Research Institute, Report No. 10/86
—— 1994: ' 'Working for My Sisters ...' – Tamil Life on the 71st Parallel' *Migration* Vol. 23–24: 87–103
—— 1997: 'Ambivalent Incorporation: Norwegian Policy towards Tamil Asylum-seekers from Sri Lanka' *Journal of Refugee Studies* Vol. 10 No. 4: 443–61

Gellner, E. 1983: *Nations and Nationalism* Oxford: Blackwell

Geertz, C. 1983: '"From the Native's Point of View": On the Nature of Anthropological Understanding' in C. Geertz: *Local Knowledge* New York: Basic

Giddens, A. 1991: *Modernity and Self-Identity: Self and Society in the Late Modern Age* Cambridge: Polity Press

Good, A. 1991: *The Female Bridegroom: A Comparative Study of Life-Crisis Rituals in South India and Sri Lanka* Oxford: Clarendon Press

Granovetter, M. S. 1973: 'The Strength of Weak Ties' *American Journal of Sociology* Vol. 78 No. 6: 1360–80

Graziano, F. 1992: *Divine Violence: Spectacle, Psychosexuality & Radical Christianity in the Argentine 'dirty war'* Boulder: Westview Press

Grønhaug, R. 1978: 'Scale as a Variable in Analysis: Fields in Social Organization in Herat, Northwest Afghanistan' in F. Barth (ed.): *Scale and Social Organization* Oslo, Bergen and Tromsø: Universitetsforlaget

Gunaratna, R. 1993: *Indian Intervention in Sri Lanka: The Role of India's Intelligence Agencies* Colombo: South Asian Network on Conflict Research

Gunasinghe, N. 1984: 'The open economy and its impact on ethnic relations in Sri Lanka' in Committee for Rational Development : *Sri Lanka: The Ethnic Conflict. Myths, realities and perspectives* New Delhi: Navrang

Gupta, A. and J. Ferguson 1992: 'Beyond "Culture": Space, Identity, and the Politics of Difference' *Cultural Anthropology* Vol. 7 No. 1 (February): 6–23

Hannerz, U. 1989: 'Culture Between Center and Periphery: Toward a Macro-anthropology' *Ethnos* Vol. 54 (3/4): 200–17

Heidegger, M. 1972: *Zein und Zeit* (*Being and Time*) Tybingen: Niemeyer

Hellmann-Rajanayagam, D. 1986: 'The Tamil "Tigers" in Northern Sri Lanka: Origins, Factions, Programmes' *Internationales Asienforum* Vol. 17 No. 1/2: 63–85

Henriksen, G. 1991: 'The experience of social worth as a force in inter-ethnic relations' in R. Grønhaug, G. Henriksen and A. Håland (eds): *The ecology of choice and symbol* Bergen: Alma Mater

Hocart, A. M. 1950: *Caste: A Comparative Study* New York: Russel & Russel

Hole, R., D. Somasundaran, K. Sritharan and R. Thiranagama 1990: *The Broken Palmyra; The Tamil Crisis in Sri Lanka – An Inside Account* Claremont: The Sri Lanka Studies Institute

Hollup, O. 1994: *Bonded Labour: Caste and cultural identity among Tamil plantation workers in Sri Lanka* New Delhi: Sterling Publishers

Jayapalan, V. I. S. 1991: 'The Socio-Economic and Cultural Background of Batticaloa District' *Economic Review* (Colombo) Vol. 17 No. 1: 29–31

——1991/92: 'Migrasjon fra Jaffna' in UDI: *Tamilene på Sri Lanka* Oslo: Grunninformasjon fra Utlendingsdirektoratet ('Migration from Jaffna' in UDI: *Tamils in Sri Lanka*)

KAD 1994: *Nyhetsbrev om norsk flyktningpolitikk 9.11.94 (Newsletter on Norwegian Refugee Policy 9.11.94)* Oslo: Kommunal og arbeidsdepartementet

Kakar, S. 1981: *The Inner World: A Psycho-analytic Study of Childhood and Society in India* Oxford, New York and New Delhi: Oxford University Press

Kaldor, M. 1993: 'Yugoslavia and the New Nationalism' *New Left Review* No. 197: 96–112

Kapadia, K. 1993: 'Marrying money: Changing preference and practice in Tamil marriage' *Contribution to Indian Sociology* 27 (1): 25–51

—— 1994: '"Kinship burns": kinship discourse and gender in Tamil South India' *Social Anthropology* Vol. 2 Part 3: 281–98

Kapferer, B. 1988: *Legends of People, Myths of State: Violence, Intolerance, and Political Culture in Sri Lanka and Australia* Washington and London: Smithsonian Institute Press

Knudsen, J. Chr. 1988: 'Vietnamese survivors: Processes involved in refugee coping and adaption' University of Bergen, unpublished PhD thesis

—— 1990: 'Cognitive Models in Life Histories' *Anthropological Quarterly* Vol. 63 No. 3: 122–32

—— 1994: 'Eksilets mysterier' in T. Evans, I. Frønes and L. Kjølsrød (eds): *Velferdssamfunnets barn* ('Mysteries of Exile' in *The Children of the Welfare Society*) Oslo: Ad Notam

Kunz, E. F. 1973: 'The Refugee in flight: Kinetic Models and Forms of Displacement' *International Migration* Vol. VII No. 2: 125–46

Lakshmi, C. S. 1990: 'Mother, Mother-Community, and Mother-Politics in Tamilnadu' *Economic and Political Weekly* 25: 42–3, 72–83

Longva, A. N. 1996: *Walls built on Sand. Migration, Exclusion, and Society in Kuwait* Boulder: Westview Press

—— n.d.: 'Beyond Empathy; Anthropologists and the Poetics of Exile' unpublished paper

Malkki, L. 1990: 'Context and Consciousness: Local Conditions for the Production of Historical and National Thought among Hutu Refugees in Tanzania' in R. G. Fox (ed.): *Nationalist Ideologies and the Production of Nationalist Cultures* Washington: American Ethnological Society Monograph Series No. 2

Manogaran, C. and B. Pfaffenberger 1994: *The Sri Lankan Tamils: Ethnicity and Identity* Boulder, San Francisco and Oxford: Westview Press

Marcus, G. E. and M. M. J. Fisher 1986: *Anthropology as Cultural Critique* Chicago and London: University of Chicago Press

Marglin, F. A. 1977: 'Power, purity, and pollution: aspects of the caste system reconsidered' *Contributions to Indian Sociology* Vol. 11 No. 2: 245–70

Marriot, M. 1968: 'Caste ranking and food transactions, a matrix analysis' in M. Singer and B. Cohn (eds): *Structure and change in Indian society* Chicago: Aldine

—— 1976: 'Hindu transactions: diversity without dualism' in B. Kapferer (ed.): *Transaction and meaning: directions in the anthropology of exchange and symbolic behaviour* Philadelphia: Institute for the Study of Human Issues

Martin, D. A. (ed.) 1988: *The New Asylum Seekers; Refugee Law in the 1980s* Dordrecht: Martinus Nijhoff Publishers

Massey, D. 1993: 'Power–geometry and a progressive sense of place' in J. Bird *et al* (eds): *Mapping the Futures: Local cultures, global change* London and New York: Routledge

Mauss, M. 1969: *The Gift: Forms and functions of exchange in archaic societies* London: Routledge & Kegan Paul

McGilvray, D. 1973: 'Caste and Matriclan Structure in Sri Lanka: A Preliminary Report on Fieldwork in Akkraipattu' *Modern Ceylon Studies* Vol. 4 Nos. 1 and 2: 5–20

Meyer, E. 1984: 'Seeking the Roots of the Tragedy' in J. Manor (ed.): *Sri Lanka in Change and Crisis* London: Croom Helm

Moore, H. L. 1994: *A Passion for Difference* Cambridge: Polity Press

Müller, M. 1888: *Biography of Words* London: Longmans, Green

Nordstrom, C. 1990: 'The Cultural "Front" of the Dirty War' Paper presented at the IPRA, ICON Conference, Groningen 3–7 July 1990

Obeyesekere, G. 1990: *The Works of Culture: Symbolic transformation in psychoanalysis and anthropology* Chicago and London: University of Chicago Press

Ohno, S., A. Sanmugadas and M. Sanmugadas 1985: *Worldview and Rituals among Japanese and Tamils* Gakushin: Gakushin University

Olwig, K. F. 1993: *Global Culture, Island Identity. Continuity and Change in the Afro-Caribbean Community of Nevis* Reading: Harwood Academic Publishers

—— 1997: 'Cultural sites: Sustaining a home in a deterritorialized world' in K. F. Olwig and K. Hastrup (eds): *Siting Culture: The shifting anthropological object* London and New York: Routledge

Panchanathan n.d.: *Tamil Annai Collukiral* Ponneri: Tamilccelvi Nilayam

Pandian, J. 1982: 'The Goddess Kannagi: A Dominant Symbol of South Indian Tamil Society' in: J. J. Preston (ed.): *Mother Worship* Chapel Hill: University of North Carolina Press

Perinbanayagam, R. S. 1982: *The Karmic Theater: Self, Society, and Astrology in Jaffna* Amherst: University of Massachusetts Press

Pfaffenberger, B. 1982: *Caste in Tamil Culture: The Religious Foundations of Sudra Domination in Tamil Sri Lanka* Syracuse, NY: Maxwell School of Citizenship and Public Affairs

—— 1994: 'The Political Construction of Defensive Nationalism: The 1968 Temple Entry Crisis in Sri Lanka' in C. Manogaran and B. Pfaffenberger (eds): *The Sri LankanTamils: Ethnicity and Identity* San Francisco and Oxford: Westview Press

Piyadasa, L. 1984: *Sri Lanka: The Holocaust and After* London: Marran

Radhakrishnan, R. 1987: 'Ethnic Identity and Post-Structural Difference' *Cultural Critique* Vol. 6: 199–220

Raheja, G. G. 1988: *The Poison in the Gift: Ritual, Prestation, and the Dominant Caste in a North Indian Village* Chicago and London: University of Chicago Press

Ramanujan, A. K. 1985: *Poems of Love and War* New York: Columbia University Press

Ramasamy, R. 1988: *Sojourners to Citizens: Sri Lankan Tamils in Malaysia 1885–1965* Kuala Lumpur: Sri Veera Trading

Ramaswamy, S. 1993: 'En/gendering Language: The Poetics of Tamil Identity' *Comparative Study of Society and History* Vol. 34: 683–725

Reppesgaard, H. O. 1993: 'Final Report: Studies on psychosocial problems among displaced people in Sri Lanka' FORUT, unpublished report

Ricoeur, P. 1981a: *Hermeneutics and the Human Sciences* Cambridge: Cambridge University Press

—— 1981b: 'Narrative Time' in W. J. T. Mitchell (ed.): *On Narrative* Chicago: University of Chicago Press

—— 1992: *Oneself as Another* Chicago: University of Chicago Press

Roberts, M. (ed.) 1977: *Documents of the Ceylon National Congress and nationalist politics in Ceylon, 1929–50* Colombo: Department of National Archives

Robertson, R. 1987: 'Globalisation theory and civilization analysis' *Comparative Civilization Review* 17 (Fall): 20–30

Rosaldo, M. 1980: *Knowledge and Passion: Ilongot Notions of Self & Social Life* Cambridge: Cambridge University Press

Rosaldo, R. 1989: *Culture and Truth: The Remaking of Social Analysis* Boston: Beacon Press

Rouse, R. 1992: 'Mexican Migration and the Social Space of Postmodernism' *Diaspora* 1 (1): 8–23

Russel, J. 1982: *Communal Politics under the Donoughmore Constitution 1931–1947* Dehiwala: Tisara Prakasakayo Ltd

Ryan, K. S. 1980: 'Pollution in Practice: Ritual, Structure and Change in Tamil Sri Lanka' Cornell University: unpublished PhD thesis

Safran, W. 1991: 'Diasporas in Modern Societies: Myths of Homeland and Return' *Diaspora* 1 (1): 83–99

Said, E. W. 1984: 'Reflections on Exile' *Granta* No. 13: 159–72

—— 1986: *After the Last Sky: Palestinian Lives* New York: Pantheon

Sardeshpande, S. C. Lt. Gen. 1992: *Assignment Jaffna* New Delhi: Lancer Publishers

Saussure, F. de. 1960: *Course in General Linguistics* London: Peter Owen

Scarry, E. 1985: *The Body in Pain: The making and unmaking of the world* New York and Oxford: Oxford University Press

Schalk, P. 1992: 'Birds of Independence: on the participation of Tamil women in armed struggle' *Lanka*, December

Scheper-Hughes, N. 1992: 'Hungry bodies, medicine, and the state: toward a critical psychological anthropology' in T. Schwartz, G. M. White and C. A. Lutz (eds): *New directions in psychological anthropology* Cambridge: Cambridge University Press

—— 1994: 'Embodied Knowledge: Thinking with the Body in Critical Medical Anthropology' in R. Borofsky (ed.): *Assessing Cultural Anthropology* New York: McGraw-Hill

Schutz, A. and T. Luckman 1973: *The Structures of the Life-World* Evanston: Northwestern University Press

Selvanayagam, S. 1966: 'Market Gardening in the Jaffna Region' *Ceylon Journal of History and Social Sciences* 9: 172–6

Shulman, D. D. 1980: *Tamil Temple Myths: Sacrifice and Divine Marriage in the South Indian Saiva Tradition* Princeton, NJ: Princeton University Press

Silverman, M. 1992: *Deconstructing the nation: immigration, racism and citizenship in modern France* London and New York: Routledge

Singer, M. R. 1964: *The emerging elite: A study of political leadership in Ceylon* Cambridge, MA: MIT Press

Sivaram, D. P. 1992: 'Tamil Militarism' *Lanka Guardian* 1 May–1 November

Sivathamby, K. 1984: 'Towards an understanding of the Culture and Ideology of the Tamils of Jaffna' Paper published in the Commemorative Souvenir of the Rebuilt Jaffna Library

—— 1989: 'Innledning till de lankesiska tamilernas etnografi' ('Introduction to the Ethnography of the Srilankan Tamils') *Lanka* (2).

Smith, A. D. 1991: *National Identity* Harmondsworth: Penguin

Somasundaram, D. 1993a: *Scarred Mind* New Delhi: Sage

—— 1993b: 'Psychiatric Morbidity Due to the War in Northern Sri Lanka' in J. Wilson and B. Raphael (eds): *Post Traumatic Stress Syndromes* New York: Plenum Press

—— 1994: 'Mental Health in Northern Sri Lanka – An Overview' in *Victims of War in Sri Lanka – Conference Proceedings* London: Medical Institute of Tamils

Spencer, J. 1990: 'Collective Violence and Everyday Practice in Sri Lanka' *Modern Asian Studies* Vol. 24: 603–23

Staub, E. 1994: *The Roots of Evil: The Origins of Genocide and Other Group Violence* Cambridge: Cambridge University Press

Steen, A. B. 1993: *Varieties of the Tamil Refugee Experience in Denmark and England* Copenhagen: University of Copenhagen and The Danish Centre for Human Rights

Suseendirarajah, S. 1980: 'Religion and Language in Jaffna Society' *Anthropological Linguistics* Vol. 22 No. 8: 345–62

Sørli, K. 1994: *Unge innvandreres flytting i Norge* (*The Pattern of Movement among Young Immigrants in Norway*) Oslo: NIBR-Rapport No. 5

Tambiah, S. J. 1986: *Sri Lanka: Ethnic Fratricide and the Dismantling of Democracy* Chicago: University of Chicago Press

Tanaka, M. 1991: *Patrons, devotees and Goddesses: Ritual and Power among the Tamil fishermen of Sri Lanka* Kyoto: Kyoto University, Institute for Research in Humanities

Taraki 1991: *The Eluding Peace: An inside political analysis of the ethnic conflict in Sri Lanka* Paris: ASSEAY

Taylor, C. 1985: 'The Person' in Michael Carrithers, Steven Collins and Steven Lukes (eds): *The Category of the person: Anthropology, philosophy, history*, Cambridge: Cambridge University Press

—— 1994: 'The Politics of Recognition' in David T. Goldberg (ed.): *Multiculturalism* Oxford UK and Cambridge USA: Blackwell

Taussig, M. 1984: 'Culture of Terror, Space of Death: Roger Casement's Putumayo Report and the Exploration of Torture' *Comparative Studies in Society and History* 26: 467–97

Trautman, T. 1981: *Dravidian Kinship* New Delhi: Vistar Publications

Trawick, M. 1990: *Notes on Love in a Tamil Family* Los Angeles and London: University of California Press

Turner, T. 1994: 'Anthropology and Multiculturalism: What is Anthropology that Multiculturalists Should be Mindful of It?' in D. T. Goldberg (ed.): *Multiculturalism: A Critical Reader* Oxford UK and Cambridge USA: Blackwell

Turner, V. 1974: *Dramas, Fields, and Metaphors* Ithaca and London: Cornell University Press

UDI 1992: *Årsmelding for Utlendingsdirektotatet 1992* (*Annual Report for the Directorate of Immigration 1992*) Oslo: Utlendingsdirektotatet

van der Veer, P. (ed.) 1995: *Nation and Migration. The Politics of Space in the South Asian Diaspora* Philadelphia: University of Pennsylvania Press

Velayutam, P. 1971: *Moliyaraci (Language Research)* Madras: Shaiva Siddhanta Kazhagam

Wadley, S. (ed.) 1980: *The Powers of Tamil Women* Syracuse University: South Asian Series No. 6

Wilson, J. 1988: *The Break-up of Sri Lanka: The Sinhalese–Tamil Conflict* Honolulu: University of Hawaii Press

—— 1994: 'The Colombo Man, the Jaffna Man, and the Batticaloa Man: Regional Identities and Rise of the Federal Party' in C. Manogaran and B. Pfaffenberger: *The Sri Lankan Tamils: Ethnicity and Identity* San Francisco and Oxford: Westview Press

Wiser, W. 1936: *The Hindu jajmani system* Lucknow: Lucknow Publishing House

Wood, G. (ed.) 1985: *Labelling in Development Policy* London: Sage

Yalman, N. 1962: 'The Structure of the Sinhalese Kindred: A Re-Examination of the Dravidian Terminology' *American Anthropologist* 64: 548–75

—— 1967: *Under the Bo tree: Studies in Caste, Kinship, and Marriage in the Interior of Ceylon* Berkeley and Los Angeles: University of California Press

Zetter, R. 1988: 'Refugees and Refugee Studies – A Label and an Agenda' *Journal of Refugee Studies* Vol. 1 No. 1: 1–8

—— 1991: 'Labelling Refugees: Forming and Transforming a Bureaucratic Identity' *Journal of Refugee Studies* Vol. 4 No. 1: 39–62

INDEX

199

JF

DEPAUL UNIVERSITY LIBRARY

3 0511 00781 8024